Marketing

First edition September 1993

ISBN 0 7517 2015 1

British Library Cataloguing-in-Publication Data

A catalogue record for this book
is available from the British Library

Printed in Great Britain by
Ashford Colour Press, Gosport, Hampshire

Published by

BPP Publishing Limited
Aldine House, Aldine Place
London W12 8AW

We would like to acknowledge the assistance given by Linda Phillips of Staffordshire University and Chris Fill of the University of Portsmouth in the preparation of this book.

CONTENTS

PREFACE

FIRST YEAR Study Guides are a new series targeted specifically at the needs of:

- first year students taking business studies degrees;
- students taking business-related modules of other degrees;
- HND students;
- others requiring business information at this level.

This *Marketing* Study Guide has been written with two key goals in mind.

- To present a substantial and useful body of knowledge on marketing at degree level. This is not just a set of revision notes - it explains the subject in detail and does not assume prior knowledge.

- To make learning and revision as easy as possible. Each chapter:

    - starts with clear objectives;
    - contains numerous exercises;
    - includes a chapter roundup summarising the points made; and
    - ends with a quick quiz.

The philosophy of the series is thus to combine techniques which actively promote learning with a no-nonsense, systematic approach to the necessary factual content of the course.

BPP Publishing have for many years been the leading providers of targeted texts for students of professional qualifications. We know that our customers need to study effectively in order to pass their exams, and that they cannot afford to waste time. They expect clear, concise and highly-focused study material. We expect first year degree and HND students to be equally demanding. And we have addressed the specific requirements of degree courses: each title has been developed in consultation with university lecturers.

We believe that the resulting material will prove to be the most helpful - and cost-effective - resource available to today's business students.

BPP Publishing
September 1993

If you would like to send in your comments on this Study Guide, please turn to the review form on page 251.

HOW TO USE THIS BOOK

This Study Guide can simply be read straight through from beginning to end, but you will get far more out of it if you keep a pen and paper to hand. The most effective form of learning is *active learning*, and we have therefore filled the text with exercises for you to try as you go along. We have also provided objectives, a chapter roundup and a quick quiz for each chapter. Here is a suggested approach to enable you to get the most out of this book.

(a) Select a chapter to study, and read the objectives in the box at the start of the chapter.

(b) Next read the chapter roundup at the end of the chapter (before the quick quiz and the solutions to exercises). Do not expect this brief summary to mean too much at this stage, but see whether you can relate some of the points made in it to some of the objectives.

(c) Next read the chapter itself. Do attempt each exercise as you come to it. You will derive the greatest benefit from the exercises if you write down your solutions before checking them against the solutions at the end of the chapter.

(d) As you read, make use of the 'notes' column to add your own comments, references to other material and so on. Do try to formulate your own views. In marketing, many things are matters of interpretation and there is often scope for alternative views. The more you engage in a dialogue with the book, the more you will get out of your study.

(e) When you reach the end of the chapter, read the chapter roundup again. Then go back to the objectives at the start of the chapter, and ask yourself whether you have achieved them.

(f) Finally, consolidate your knowledge by writing down your answers to the quick quiz. You can check your answers by going back to the text. The very act of going back and searching the text for relevant details will further improve your grasp of the subject.

Further reading

While we are confident that the FIRST YEAR Study Guides offer excellent range and depth of subject coverage, we are aware that you will be encouraged to follow up particular points in books other than your main textbook, in order to get alternative points of view and more detail on key topics. We recommend the following books as a starting point for your further reading on *Marketing*.

Baker, *The Marketing Book*, 2nd edition 1991, Butterworth-Heinemann

Kotler, *Marketing Management*, 1977, Prentice Hall

Lancaster and Massingham, *Marketing Management*, 1993 McGraw

Oliver, *Marketing Today*, 3rd edition 1990, Prentice Hall

1 AN OVERVIEW OF MARKETING

> *Your objectives*
>
> After completing this chapter you should:
>
> (a) be aware of what is meant by marketing and the marketing concept;
> (b) understand the elements that make up the 'marketing mix';
> (c) understand how marketing activities are organised within a marketing department.

1 The marketing concept

Exercise 1

To get started, write down what you consider to be the meaning of the term 'marketing'. Is it the same as selling? What issues does it embrace? As you read through this chapter, compare the points that are made with your answer.

The concept and practice of marketing is centred around putting the customer first. Marketing can be thought of as a philosophy that business organisations should adhere to. It can also be a functional area of management located within a departmental structure. This chapter aims to give an overview of the marketing concept including the various marketing environments and the scope of marketing. It will also investigate, in detail, the organisation of marketing within the company structure. To begin with, it is worthwhile to look at the historical development of marketing.

Before the industrial revolution, the manufacture of goods was usually local and small-scale. During the industrial revolution production became organised into larger units. Towns developed and trade increased as people became more dependent on buying goods for their consumption rather than on producing these goods themselves. There was much greater geographical divergence of buyers and sellers. Before the industrial revolution buyers had direct contact with sellers and so producers knew their customers' needs and wants. Later, when buyers lived some distance from producers, it became necessary for producers to find out what products buyers wanted and what product attributes were desired.

Mass production techniques, such as the division of labour, also meant that the number and types of goods increased dramatically. This industrialisation also increased productivity and so reduced unit costs. With new cheaper products on offer to the public, demand was high and until very recently many business problems centred on production and selling rather than marketing.

Notes

As production capacity increased, and competition became tougher, the focus changed. Production is no longer the main problem facing business concerns. Indeed, for many products and services, it is excess supply rather than excess demand which is the problem. In these circumstances, the focus of attention has switched from 'how to produce enough' (supply factor) to 'how to increase demand' (demand factor). Marketing techniques have been developed partly as a result of this switch in orientation.

Exercise 2

If you walk into your local chemist, or a supermarket, you will notice anything up to 20 different brands of toothpaste on sale. Why do you think there are so many?

Later in this chapter we will distinguish between production, sales and marketing orientations. To some extent, the distinction arises from the historical developments outlined above.

Initially marketing techniques were applied in the area of fast moving consumer goods such as washing powder, toothpaste and groceries because these types of good benefited earliest from the use of mass production techniques. Subsequently, marketing methods have been applied in addition to industrial goods and, more recently, to services (both public and private sector). It can be said, then, that marketing techniques have grown in importance as a response to competitive pressure. Marketing methods are seen as a means of competing with rivals.

Some services and industrial markets are only now becoming *marketing orientated*. What does this term mean?

Definitions of marketing

There are many definitions of marketing. Here we will consider two which each give a useful insight into how marketing can be used in practice.

Definition 1

'Marketing is the management of exchange relationships'.

This definition emphasises the role of marketing in relating to the world outside the organisation. All relationships which cross the boundary between the organisation and the outside world, especially when they relate to customers, need to be managed. Looked at from the outside, the organisation will be judged by customers, suppliers, competitors and others according to their personal experience in dealing with it.

Exercise 3

Think about some organisations with which you have come into contact. What was the nature of your first contact? Did it help to 'sell' the organisations' products/services to you, or did you find it off-putting?

Notes

Definition 2

'Marketing is concerned with meeting organisation objectives by providing customer satisfactions.'

This definition is important because it stresses the importance of the customer, and more particularly, customer satisfaction. When people buy products or services they do not simply want the products, they also want the benefits from using the products or services. Products and services help to solve a customer's problems. It is the solution to these problems that customers are buying.

Exercise 4

When people buy the products listed below, what problems or types of problems are they trying to solve?

(a) Lawn mowers
(b) Life insurance
(c) A particular model of car

Defintion 3

Another definition is that of the Chartered Institute of Marketing: 'marketing is the management process which identifies, anticipates and supplies customer requirements efficiently and profitably'.

This definition emphasises the wide scope of marketing, ranging from initial identification of customer needs by means of research, right through to eventual, profitable satisfaction of those needs.

Definition 4

Kotler, in *Marketing Management: Analysis, Planning and Control* provides one of the widest definitions of all.

'Marketing is human activity directed at satisfying needs and wants through exchange processes'.

A marketing orientated organisation will possess two key characteristics.

(a) Firstly, there will be a commitment to meeting the needs of customers more successfully than the competition.

(b) Secondly, the organisation will need to operate in a fashion that will achieve this aim. It is not sufficient that the company employs a marketing manager or has a market research department. It is necessary that all of the company's activities are co-ordinated to ensure that the needs of the customer are considered when making decisions about what to produce and subsequently how and where the product or service is to be made available.

Underlying all of this is the belief that adopting a marketing orientation will maximise the long-term profitability of the company.

Notes

The definitions and analysis above suggest that the marketing concept has three elements:

(a) customer orientation;
(b) a co-ordination of marketing led activities; and
(c) profit orientation (though it is worth noting that not-for-profit organisations, such as charities, also engage in marketing activities).

We will now contrast the activities and philosophy of marketing orientated companies with production orientated and sales orientated organisations.

Peter Doyle provides a useful distinction between these viewpoints:

'A *production orientation* may be defined as the management view that success is achieved through producing goods of optimum quality and cost, and that therefore, the major task of management is to pursue improved production and distribution efficiency. A *sales orientation* is the management view that effective selling and promotion are the keys to success.'

MARKETING ORIENTATION | SALES/PRODUCTION ORIENTATION

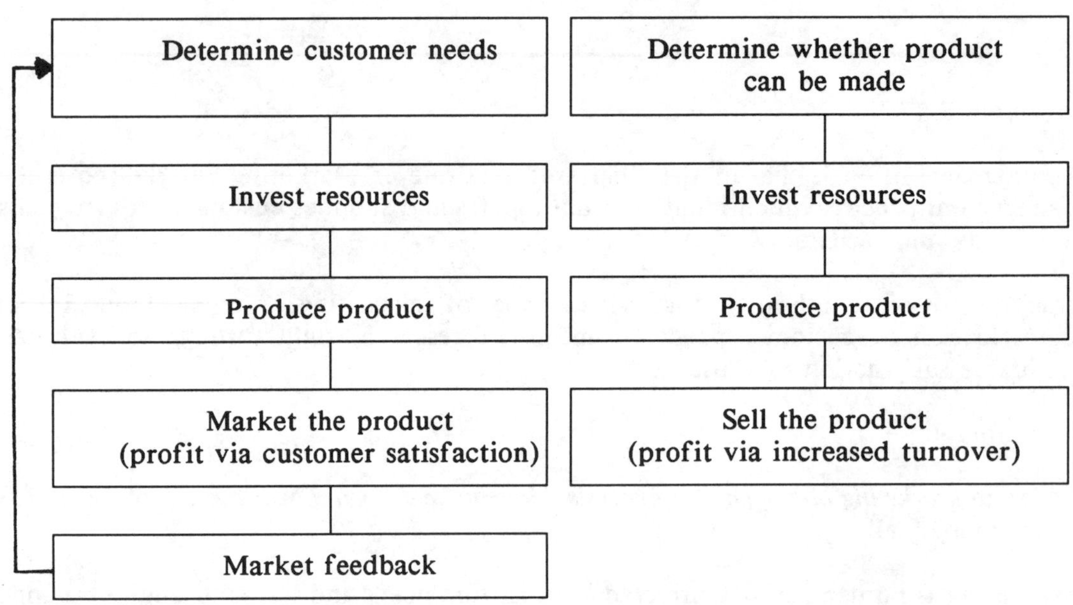

Customer orientation

It is an old truism that 'without customers, you don't have a business.' This, in essence, remains the logic for maintaining a customer orientation where satisfying customers' needs at a profit is the central drive of the company.

Notes

In contrast to following a marketing orientation many companies follow what can be described as a sales orientation. In such sales orientated companies the tendency is to make the product first and then to worry about whether it will sell. Underlying this philosophy is a belief that a good sales force can sell just about anything to anybody.

Professor Levitt distinguishes between sales and marketing orientations in terms of the place of the customer in the marketing process.

> 'Selling focuses on the needs of the seller; marketing on the needs of the buyer. Selling is preoccupied with the seller's need to convert his product into cash; marketing with the idea of satisfying the needs of the customer by means of the product and the whole cluster of things associated with creating, delivering and finally consuming it.'

The marketing concept suggests that companies should focus their operations on their customers' needs rather than be driven solely by the organisation's technical competence to produce a particular range of products or services.

A quotation attributed to Charles Revlon describes the customer orientation of a marketing led organisation:

> 'In the factory we make cosmetics. In the store we sell hope.'

Exercise 5

The Charles Revlon quote above is a neat statement of marketing orientation, but it also points to the possibility of internal conflict within organisations. Can you see how such conflict might arise?

If new products and services are developed with an inadequate regard for customer requirements, the result will be the need for an expensive selling effort to persuade customers that they should purchase something from the company that does not quite fit their purpose.

As the management theorist Peter Drucker says, 'The aim of marketing is to make selling superfluous.' Thus, if the organisation has got its marketing right, it will have produced products and services that meet customers' requirements. If these are readily available at a price that customers accept then relatively little or no selling effort will be needed.

Co-ordinating marketing activities

A true marketing orientation requires a co-ordinated marketing effort. This covers market research to identify customer needs, market-led product development, sales promotion and advertising to ensure that customers know of the existence of the product and its benefits, effective distribution and delivery to ensure availability, and market-based pricing.

It follows that marketing orientated companies will need to exhibit some key organisational characteristics if an integrated marketing effort is to be achieved.

Notes

The following two organisational features are present in marketing orientated companies.

(a) Marketing tasks are recognised and co-ordinated under a single executive (market research, product-market planning, advertising and promotion, sales and distribution).

(b) Clear formal communications are established between the chief marketing executive and executives responsible for development, design and manufacturing, and finance. This ensures that a linkage exists between market needs and production decisions.

If a company's marketing effort is directed at making long-run profits the whole organisation clearly benefits. However, at least in the short run, many companies will set sales maximising objectives to the sales force. High *sales* don't necessarily guarantee high profits.

Exercise 6

Before reading on, try to work out for yourself how a policy of maximising sales may have a detrimental effect on profits.

If the sales force is motivated solely to maximise revenue (sales), then it may wish to reduce prices or attempt to offer speedier delivery. There will be a greater incentive to reduce prices and disrupt planned production at the cost of overall profitability. Under these circumstances there is likely to be frequent and unhelpful conflict between production and sales departments with an inevitable loss of customer service. Profit margins will fall.

However, when the sales force is motivated to maximise profit rather than sales, it will only wish to make extra sales if this is profitable for the company. The impact on profits will be weighed before securing a sale by offering a price cut. Similarly, the costs of disrupting production will be born in mind when deciding whether or not to make a delivery promise that would involve rescheduling production of the next batch of the product.

Thus, marketing performance should be judged by profit and return on investment - not by volume of sales. This ensures that the wider implications of marketing decisions are recognised, avoiding the possible conflict with the production department if sales are an end in themselves.

There may be the need for clear administrative decrees to ensure that the marketing department and in particular the field sales force acts in a manner that increases corporate profits. As an example, the UK subsidiary of Landis and Gyr, the Swiss multi-national, has a rule whereby the sales department can make changes to the production plan without penalty for up to six weeks before manufacture but after this date the sales department's budget must carry all the costs of disrupting the line. The six week period was determined as being a reasonable lead time within which an efficient production system should be able to accommodate change without incurring significant extra costs. Naturally, the appropriate length of such a lead time will be determined by the particular technology being employed in the manufacturing process.

The marketing concept in practice

The term marketing has only become widely used since the 1960s in the United Kingdom. Before this time, most companies had a sales department but not a marketing department. However, it is by no means certain that the increasing use of marketing rather than sales in job titles necessarily means that all such companies are becoming more marketing orientated. A study by Professor Peter Doyle, funded by the Chartered Institute of Marketing in 1987, concluded that:

> 'British chief executives increasingly recognise the need to make their companies more marketing orientated. But boards of directors are still dominated by a financial outlook and most lack a professional approach to strategy and market innovation.'

Doyle's study went on to give a good indication of the degree of acceptance of the marketing concept within British industry. The survey was based on a detailed questionnaire mailed to the chief executives of all the Times 1,000 companies. 365 companies responded. Of these, 92 were in consumer manufacturing, 119 in industrial manufacturing, 54 in industrial services, 41 in consumer services and 59 in retailing.

CORPORATE PHILOSOPHIES

	%
Production orientated	10
Sales orientated	21
Marketing orientated	50

Doyle concluded that the remaining 19% of companies responding could best be classified as having a financial orientation, by which he meant:

> 'the management view that success is about using assets and resources to optimise profit and return on capital employed.'

However, in spite of the widespread acceptance of the need for a marketing orientation within companies that attempt to produce goods and services that match their customers' requirements, there will always be a need for a persuasive sales force. The need to convince the customer that they should buy the company's products arises because it is highly unlikely that their market needs can be exactly satisfied.

Exercise 7

Try to think of reasons why a sales force may still be needed, despite management's commitment to a marketing orientation.

Whilst it is accepted that there will always be the need for a sales force, sales effort will be more successful if products and services have been developed in response to market needs. Such a marketing led approach will reduce the time and expense involved in trying to make what is on sale more acceptable to customers by attempting to persuade potential buyers to change their perceptions of what they need. The sales force can then be employed on more productive activities such as developing leads and providing better customer service and identifying changes in customer requirements to which the organisation needs to respond. Such sales force activities constitute a key element of any company following a marketing orientation.

Notes

All good sales presentations follow the maxim of a customer orientation. Instead of merely cataloguing a series of product features, the intelligent sales force concentrates on promoting the benefits that will be derived by the customer using or consuming the company's product or service. The DIY enthusiast is not necessarily interested in the technical specification of a power drill's electric motor. Whilst this might be the pride and joy of the company's research and development team, the customer is only really interested in finding a solution to a particular range of DIY tasks. The customer may really be looking for a way of getting a series of 3/16 inch holes to fix some brackets. The good salesperson will ensure that the potential purchaser is assured that using the product will provide the particular benefits that the purchaser seeks. In industrial markets such benefits might include the cost reductions that can be achieved using the company's products, and the reliability of the supplier in terms of delivery and consistent quality.

So far the discussion of the applicability of the marketing concept has concentrated on tactical issues - the day to day operations of a company's marketing activities. At this level it is possible to argue that under certain circumstances a sales orientation might be preferred. After all, it is undoubtedly true that people do buy things that they have little need of after being at the receiving end of some persuasive selling. The argument might develop that a particular company has a charismatic sales force that is highly effective but lacks any skill to comprehend or respond explicitly to customer needs. Such a company may well be profitable operating its sales orientation and would find it difficult and costly to change its direction towards a market needs focus.

However, when the argument moves on to the longer-term consequences of ignoring market needs the case for adopting a marketing orientation appears to be overwhelming. Theodore Levitt published the seminal article *Marketing Myopia,* originally published in the Harvard Business Review in July-August 1960, on the imperative that a marketing orientation should provide the driving force that determines the longer-term strategic direction of companies. He warned of the perils of perceiving the company's business solely in technical and production terms. Managers will then view products according to their physical properties. The company will be seen as operating in an industry where competitors share similar technical competences allowing them to produce similar products.

Levitt started by making the bold statement that :

> 'Shortsighted managements often fail to recognise that in fact there is no such thing as a growth industry.'

Levitt's argument is that there are clearly large numbers of growth *markets* in terms of society's needs. However, the *industries* that serve these needs at a particular time may decline if another industry's new technology better matches the growing market's needs.

Levitt goes on to illustrate his argument with examples of blinkered thinking that focuses on the production concept of competing for business in a particular industry. The following question is posed.

Q : Why did the American Railways not respond to the airlines and trucking companies that eventually took away the railroad's passenger and freight business?

The railways certainly had the available capital reserves built up over the years that 'rail was king'. The infant businesses that grew to be Pan Am, TWA and the national carriers struggled for their early existence. Levitt provides the following answer.

Notes

A : They let others take customers away from them because they assumed themselves to be in the railroad business rather than in the transportation business. The reason they defined their industry wrongly was because they were railroad oriented instead of transportation oriented; they were product oriented instead of customer oriented.

Whilst the railway industry went into decline, the transportation market continued to grow by leaps and bounds. By adopting an industry focus the railways did not take on the new enterprises because they were not seen as being any part of the railroad business.

Not all North American railways followed such a 'myopic' stance. Canadian Pacific had a very clear idea of its operations in the transportation market. The company expanded into trucking, shipping and airlines. Later it moved into telecommunications and telex to adopt the most suitable technology for transporting data. Canadian Pacific is today one of the world's largest transportation businesses.

Exercise 8

Another often quoted example of this phenomenon is the US movie industry, which reacted with hostility to the development of television. Analyse this reaction along the line suggested by Levitt's example, and try to identify its shortcomings.

The strategic message is clear. Adopting a marketing orientation concentrates the attention on the needs of the customer. If these needs change or a better technology emerges that more closely attends to these needs then the company will perceive such events as its business. Only by adapting to such changes is the company's future assured. Applying the marketing concept as the basic philosophy that underpins corporate strategy is therefore widely accepted as essential good practice.

The marketing concept: a critical review

Not all commentators accept that the increasing use of the term marketing rather than selling represents a real shift in the basic philosophy followed by organisations. Some suggest that the use of marketing simply reflects that the task of bringing in revenue is now more complex and that it is now rational to use advanced techniques in advertising and market research that were previously not available. Others argue that today's 'sophisticated' consumers are more critical and more aware than their forefathers. Companies therefore need a battery of so called marketing techniques in order to continue the same old process of persuasion in order to sell products.

The most strident critic from this school of thought is the economist J K Galbraith who summarised his views as follows:

> 'So called market orientated companies have merely adopted more sophisticated weapons for selling the product.'

Approval of the marketing concept is not universal even amongst those who accept that the adoption of a market orientation represents a real change in philosophy and practice. Thus, the widespread and often uncritical acceptance of marketing orientation as the established wisdom within large elements of both the commercial and academic communities has, itself, been the subject of debate.

Notes

Exercise 9

Before reading on, think carefully about how a marketing orientation can cause problems that would not occur in a sales-led or production-led organisation. Much of this book attempts to show that the problems are outweighed by the benefits, but try to stay alert to the downside of marketing orientation.

There are two main arguments against the influence of the marketing concept.

(a) A bias is introduced into the organisation that favours marketing activities at the expense of production and technical departments. This bias then directs insufficient energies into the development of technically superior products that subsequently offer better product value to customers.

(b) Secondly, in addition to attending to customers' current needs, organisations must focus on producing goods and services for anticipated changes in future customer requirements. Slavishly focusing new product development on satisfying immediate customer perceptions of what is needed can, the argument runs, stifle real innovation.

These points are forcibly made by Bennett and Cooper.

> 'A market orientated R & D strategy necessarily leads to low-risk product modifications, extensions, and style changes. Product proliferation, a disease of the seventies, has been one result. Market driven new product ideas will usually result in the ordinary. Market researchers have become expert at encouraging consumers to verbalise their wants and needs, but people tend to talk in terms of the familiar, about what is around them at a particular moment. For example, ask a commuter what new product ideas he would like to see in the area of rapid transit and, chances are, he will list a number of improvements to his bus or subway system - tinted glass windows, air conditioning, better schedules, and the like. Rarely will he be able to think in terms of totally new and imaginative urban transportation systems. The latter are the domain of the engineer, scientist and designer.'

In defence of Levitt's views, outlined earlier, one might consider the case of the collapse of Rolls Royce in the early 1970s. The reason for this failure is well documented. The company had embarked on the production of a new generation of large turbo-fan jet engines. All three major competitors in the international market for civil aircraft engines were producing such engines. The Rolls Royce response was the RB211. The RB211 differed from competitors' engines in its use of advanced carbon fibre technology in the manufacture of its turbine blades. The introduction and development of the new technology turned out to be an extremely costly business. Rolls Royce chose to show this expenditure as an asset on its balance sheet, rather than to adopt the prudent principle of writing off development costs against current revenues. Research and development expenses exceeded budgeted levels and Rolls Royce encountered severe cash flow problems resulting in the company's liquidation.

The focus on engineering excellence is a clear indication of the production orientation then being followed by Rolls Royce. Pratt & Whitley and General Electric appeared to follow a product development strategy that more closely accorded with a marketing

Notes

orientation. The demand for the new generation of engines was generated by a change in airlines' requirements. The environmentalist lobby against aircraft noise in the late 1960s and 1970s had culminated with restrictions on night flying and regulations covering permitted noise levels from all new civil aircraft. The oil crisis and rising energy prices created the need for greater fuel efficiency. The new generation of wide-bodied jumbo jets created the need for a range of powerful jet engines.

The needs of the customers were therefore clearly defined. The airlines needed larger, more powerful, more economical and quieter jet engines. Provided that engines met this criteria then customers would be interested. The Rolls Royce engine was proving to be more expensive largely because they offered a product feature, carbon fibre technology, that airlines did not need. The American competitors gave customers what they wanted without having to develop a new metallurgical competence. In the event the technical innovation became a major impediment to sales of the RB211 as airlines became aware of teething problems with the carbon fibre turbines.

It would be uncharitable to accuse Rolls Royce of completely ignoring market conditions. All companies have to take risks, and the RB211 project was on such a scale that failure would have inevitably jeopardised the company's future. However, the suspicion remains that with Rolls Royce the company's history of engineering excellence had produced too great a bias towards production and too little concern for the marketing concept. The Rolls Royce case illustrates the need for a balanced view. Whilst the technical competence and manufacturing skills of companies cannot be ignored, it can be fatal not to follow closely what is required by customers.

General Electric, one of Rolls Royce's major competitors, made its commitment to the marketing concept as long ago as 1952.

> '(The marketing concept) ..... introduces the marketing man at the beginning rather than at the end of the production cycle and integrates marketing in each phase of business. Thus marketing, through its studies and research, will establish for the engineer, the design and manufacturing man, what the consumer wants in a given product, what price he is willing to pay, and where and when it will be wanted. Marketing will have authority in product planning, production scheduling, and inventory control, as well as in sales distribution and servicing of the product.'
>
> 1952 Annual Report : US General Electric Company

Exercise 10

Have you come across any products which have failed in similar circumstances to the Rolls Royce example above?

2 The marketing mix

The concept of a marketing mix, sometimes known as the marketing offer, was first used by Professor Neil Borden of Harvard Business School in 1965, who summarised the concept of the marketing mix as:

'a schematic plan to guide analysis of marketing problems through utilisation of:

Notes

(a) a list of the important forces emanating from the market which bear upon the marketing operations of an enterprise; and

(b) a list of the elements (procedures and policies) of marketing programmes.'

Borden's concept of the market forces embraced factors *outside* the control of the organisation (such as government control over products and over competitive practices), as well as factors *within* the organisation's control.

The current, most common, definition of the marketing mix concentrates on the variables under the firm's control that the marketing manager manipulates in an attempt to achieve tactical marketing objectives.

Marketing mix variables are usually summarised into the four Ps of *product, price, place and promotion*. These four variables are the heart of a marketing plan. It should be noted that the marketing mix variables are highly interactive. A decision with respect to one variable is likely to have an effect on other elements of the mix. There is a need for a highly co-ordinated approach if the company is to maximise profitable sales to its customers.

The marketing function is concerned with identifying and analysing markets; understanding how consumers are motivated and how they behave in those markets as well as identifying groups of consumers which are of particular interest to the business. To build the link between the business and its consumers requires the development of an appropriate marketing mix. The four Ps may be elaborated on as follows.

Product/service
Features
Quality
Brand
Packaging
Durability
After-sales service

Price
Price level
Credit terms
Discounts
Allowances
Trade-ins

Promotion
Advertising
Personal selling
Merchandising
Publicity

Place
Channels of distribution
Intensity of coverage
Location
Stockholding
Freight/insurance

Exercise 11

In the spring of 1981 Hammerite, the all-in-one rust proofing paint, ran what appeared to be a highly successful advertising campaign. Timing was immaculate, the advertisements in both national press and the DIY magazines co-incided exactly with a break in the winter weather. All over the country avid do it yourselfers were ready to go out into the garden to repair the ravages of rust that the British winter had wreaked on swings, wrought iron gates and the like.

The problem was that the campaign was too successful. Dealers rapidly stocked out. As a result shopkeepers, rather than lose a sale, recommended other perhaps inferior products. Try to analyse this failure in terms of elements in the marketing mix.

Notes

The marketing of services

Some commentators have argued that three other 'Ps' also exist and are of particular relevance to service industries.

(a) People. Inclusion of 'people' in the marketing mix reflects the fact that the consumer's perceived quality of a service depends heavily on the persons giving the service.

(b) Processes (eg ease with which loan application forms can be completed if they are well designed).

(c) Physical evidence (eg logos, uniforms, branch or shop layout).

The marketing mix elements must be managed to ensure that the right type of product is available, at the right price, and in the right place and that the consumer is aware of this.

In current business environments, marketing is arguably far too important to be left solely to marketing departments. *It is an approach to business and an attitude to consumers which must permeate the structure of an organisation.* The successful marketing orientated company will be successful only if the philosophy underlies all activities, not just at senior management level but also among employees at all levels.

Services in general differ from goods in a number of respects and as a consequence certain aspects of the marketing approach will also differ.

Four features distinguish services from (work) products

(a) Services are intangible - they cannot be touched
(b) Services are inseparable - production and consumption are linked
(c) Services are perishable - they cannot be stored
(d) Services are variable - much depends on the personnel involved.

Exercise 12

Try to think of a service you have 'consumed' and analyse it in terms of the four characteristics linked above.

Intangibility. A service cannot be seen, touched or displayed. A customer may purchase a particular service but typically has nothing physical to display as a result of that purchase. Insurance and solicitors' fees are services which customers pay for, but the customer *does not obviously have anything to show as a result.*

Some services are often *difficult for the consumer to understand* and the mechanisms which underlie the production of the service may not always be obvious to the consumer. For example, most consumers are aware of the importance of pension plans and realise that money paid now will lead to money in the future, but rather fewer actually understand the mechanisms underlying the operation of a pension plan.

Notes

Inseparability. In general, it is impossible to separate the production and consumption of a service. Most goods are produced and subsequently sold to consumers; by contrast, the service product is typically sold and then produced.

Perishability. As a result, services are *perishable* - they cannot be stored, they must be produced on demand and often can only be produced in the presence of the customer.

Inevitably these will create problems with levels of demand and the issue of how to react in situations when demand is greater than supply or vice versa. For example, when interest rates are low and the economy is prosperous, demand for mortgages will be high but institutions may often experience difficulties in raising the funds to finance the demand for mortgages. They cannot simply 'store' mortgage funds from a period when savings were high and mortgage demand low.

Variability. The quality of the service product is typically highly dependent on the quality of the personnel conducting the transaction. As a result, the potential for variability is high and quality management and control is difficult. The quality of service a customer receives from a bank when making a loan application will be dependent on the performance of the loan assessor; the bank will be judged on that rather than the quality of the resulting loan.

Not-for-profit organisations

It is worth very briefly looking at the particular marketing issues facing such organisations as charities, research associations and others whose primary aim is not the generation of profit.

It would be a mistake to assume that marketing is irrelevant to the needs of such organisations. At the most basic level, they need to raise funds in order to pay salaries and administration costs, and of course to finance the activities in which they engage. But the absence of a profit motive can easily lead to a mixed set of objectives, fatal to the sense of direction which is essential to effective marketing.

The main reason for this is that such organisations are commonly staffed by people with a sense of mission towards non-commercial aims; while the success or otherwise of their activities will depend on 'commercial' decisions by potential 'consumers' of their products or services. The curator of a museum may be a dedicated historian or anthropologist, for example, whose motivation is the preservation and study of the exhibits under his care. He may not see the importance of a marketing strategy aimed at raising income from entrance fees, or may see such a policy as an unwelcome diversion from his main interests.

A more detailed examination of these problems is beyond the scope of this book, but you should bear in mind during your reading of marketing texts that the assumption of a profit objective is not always a valid one.

The three Cs

The four Ps of the marketing mix have long been a feature of the literature on marketing. More recently, students of the subject have begun to recognise the impact on marketing of the 'three C's' or 'strategic triangle' identified by Kenichi Ohmae in *The mind of a strategist*.

Notes

Ohmae's book is primarily concerned with strategic planning, but his theories can be brought to bear upon marketing. By the three Cs Ohmae means the three main players in the construction of a business strategy, namely:

(a) the company itself;
(b) the customer; and
(c) the competition.

On this view, the task of a strategic planner is to match the *company's* strengths to the *customer's* needs more effectively than the *competition* can do.

Ohmae stresses the need for a broad scope in defining each of these three key players. For example, if a strategic plan is formed at too low a level in the company it may not be able to address all of the issues which have a bearing on the formulation of strategy; indeed, it is arguable that, properly speaking, it would not be a 'strategic' plan at all. Similarly, in respect of customers the plan must be able to address the whole of the potential market, not just some sections of it. If it does not, the company may be operating at a disadvantage compared with its competitors.

This does not mean that a company will only be successful if it aims its products at the entire market place. Quite the contrary; the success of 'niche' suppliers in recent years makes it clear that effective market segmentation can be a key to corporate success. Ohmae's argument is that companies can effectively segment the market only if they have a clear understanding of *all* the groups of customers in the market.

Further coverage of these issues is given in the chapter on market segmentation.

3 The marketing department

Marketing management is the function of the marketing department. The function involves analysis, planning and control. As we have seen, a marketing orientation begins and ends with the customer. Thus *analysis* in marketing management involves identifying for example who are the customers, why do they buy and are they satisfied with it, having bought it? This process includes *market research*, and can also include quantitative analysis (How many customers? What is our market share? How many competitors?) and qualitative analysis (Why do people buy? What are their motivations, attitudes, personality?)

In sophisticated companies, sources of market information are integrated into a *marketing information system* which can be used by managers in making marketing decisions.

Marketing management also involves using the information gained from marketing analysis to *plan* the organisation's marketing response - *the strategic marketing plan.*

The strategic marketing plan will involve:

(a) identification of selected target markets;
(b) forecasting future demand in each market;
(c) setting the levels of each element of the marketing mix for each target market.

The third main component of marketing management is to *control* the implementation of the marketing plan. Control involves setting measurable targets for the plan and then checking performance against these targets. If necessary, remedial action must be taken to ensure that planned and actual performance are brought into line.

Notes

We will now discuss how marketing can be organised within a company's organisational structure.

The development of marketing departments

Although every organisation is different, it is often suggested that common patterns appear in the structure of organisations. The position occupied currently by departments of marketing is widely recognised as having evolved from the existence of sales departments. Traditionally all dealings with a marketplace would have been the responsibility of a sales director who would typically report direct to senior management. At this stage a marketing orientation was probably absent and the organisation would usually have been production or sales orientated. When the need for a marketing orientated approach became more apparent a marketing director might appear in parallel to the sales director, but with two distinct functional departments. With fuller recognition of the marketing approach to business, sales and marketing would become a single functional department, but with sales as a sub-group within marketing as opposed to marketing being a sub-group within sales.

Thus the emphasis within organisational structures has generally moved from a sales department to a marketing department as the business philosophy changes.

In its current format, the marketing department in any organisation plays a key role in co-ordinating marketing activities. The marketing manager in particular has to take responsibility for planning, resource allocation, monitoring and controlling the marketing effort. In fact, in order to ensure that the marketing effort has maximum effectiveness, this co-ordinating role is crucial, involving co-ordination of marketing efforts for different products in different markets as well as ensuring that individual marketing campaigns are themselves co-ordinated and consistent. As such, the marketing function tends to be thought of as a staff management function with a co-ordinating role, rather than a line management function.

Organising marketing departments

In the same way as the development of marketing within organisations has varied, so will the present organisation of marketing departments. There is no one format which can be described as 'best' or 'most effective'; rather the format chosen will depend on the nature of the existing organisational structure, patterns of management and the spread of the firm's product and geographical interests. Whatever the format, the marketing department must take responsibility for four key areas:

(a) functions (promotion, pricing etc);
(b) geographical areas;
(c) products;
(d) markets.

By considering these four areas of responsibility we can gain some insight into the different forms which a marketing department may take.

Functional organisation. The department is headed by a marketing director who is responsible for the overall co-ordination of the marketing effort. A number of functional specialists such as a market research manager and a sales manager are found in the second tier of management and they take responsibility for all activities in their functional specialism across all products and markets. This format has the benefit of great simplicity and is relatively straightforward in administrative terms. It allows individuals to develop their particular specialisms, but also imposes a burden on the marketing director who will be required to perform co-ordinating and arbitrating activities to ensure the development of a coherent marketing mix for elements of the product range.

With a limited range of products, the burden on the marketing director may not be a problem. However, as the organisation's range of products and markets expands it will tend to be less efficient. When this occurs there is always the danger that a particular product or market may be neglected because it is only one of a great variety being handled by a specific functional manager who will find it difficult to be a specialist for all products.

Geographical organisation. This is an extension of the functional organisation with responsibility for some or all functional activities being devolved to a regional level, through a national functional manager. This type of organisation would probably be more common in firms operating internationally where the various functional activities would be required for each national market or group of national markets.

Product-based organisation. Product managers take responsibility for specific products or groups of products. This type of approach is likely to be particularly appropriate for organisations with either very diverse products or with a large range of products.

The individual product manager takes responsibility for developing plans for specific products and ensuring that products remain competitive, drawing on the experience and guidance of functional managers. The product manager is effectively responsible for all the marketing activities relating to a particular product group and must therefore draw on and develop skills in relation to promotion, pricing and distribution. This approach allows the individual product managers to develop considerable experience and understanding of particular product groups and as such may be of particular importance in a rapidly changing competitive environment. At the same time because these managers have to undertake a variety of functional activities, there is always the danger that they will become 'jacks of all trades and masters of none'. In spite of this possible problem, the product-based approach is one that is becoming increasingly important because the benefits of managers with particular responsibility and experience for specific product groups is seen to outweigh the costs associated with a loss of functional specialisation.

Market management. This is a variant on the product management structure, but instead of individual managers taking responsibility for particular products they will instead take responsibility for particular markets. The advantage of this approach arises when an organisation sells a variety of different products into particular markets and the understanding of the product is perceived to be slightly less important than the understanding of the market.

Matrix management. In simple terms matrix management can be thought of as an integration of the product and market management approaches. In an organisation dealing with a variety of products in a variety of markets the product based approach will require managers to be familiar with a wide variety of different markets while the market-based approach will require managers to be familiar with a wide variety of products. In either case, however, expertise may not be fully or efficiently utilised. The matrix-based system combines the two with a series of managers dealing with markets and a further series dealing with products. The market managers will take responsibility for the development and maintenance of profitable markets while the product manager will focus on product performance and profitability. The system is interlinked with each product manager dealing with a variety of market managers and each market manager dealing with a variety of product managers.

Notes

Exercise 13

Before reading on, try to identify advantages and disadvantages of a matrix management structure.

The *advantages* of a matrix structure are said to be as follows.

(a) Greater flexibility.

(i) *People*. Employees develop an attitude geared to accepting change, and departmental monopolies are broken down.

(ii) *Tasks and structure*. The matrix structure may be short term (as with project teams) or readily amended.

(b) Reorientation. A functional department will often be production-oriented. Project management will create a market orientation.

(c) A structure for allocating responsibility to managers for end results.

(d) Interdisciplinary cooperation and a mixing of skills and expertise.

(e) Arguably, motivation of employees by providing them with greater participation in planning and control decisions.

The *disadvantages* of matrix organisation are said to be as follows.

(a) Dual authority threatens a conflict between functional managers and product/project managers. Where matrix structure exists it is important that the authority of superiors should not overlap and areas of authority must be clearly defined. A subordinate must know to which superior he is responsible for a particular aspect of his duties.

(b) One individual with two or more bosses is more likely to suffer stress at work.

(c) Matrix management can be more costly, for example product management posts are added, meetings held etc.

(d) It may be difficult for the management of an organisation to accept a matrix structure and the culture of participation, shared authority and ambiguity that it fosters.

Divisional marketing organisation. So far we have considered the organisation of marketing within a unitary organisation, but there are many organisations where the larger product groups are developed into separate divisions (what is often called a multi-divisional or 'M' form organisation). These divisions will have a high degree of autonomy, but ultimately are responsible to head office. Within this arrangement, marketing activity will often be devolved to divisional level as is shown below. This is not always the case, since some marketing activities will be the responsibility of corporate headquarters, but the extent of corporate involvement can vary from none at all to extensive. There is no obvious indication that any one particular level of corporate involvement is desirable;

however, it is often suggested that corporate involvement will tend to be more extensive in the early stages of the organisation's development when the divisions are individually quite weak, but as divisions increase their strength, the extent of corporate involvement in marketing begins to decline.

Relationship with other departments

It can be claimed (and often is by marketing managers) that marketing involves every facet of the organisation's operations. The philosophy of a customer orientation, central to marketing, can be argued to be a central business function which is a prerequisite to success. It is easy to get carried away with this argument and thus to understate the role of finance, production, personnel and other business functions. A strongly held conviction by the marketing department that customer orientation is all important can lead to conflict with other departments.

The table below shows potential conflicts which can arise with other departments in the organisation. Again this can only be a typical list and is intended as a warning of potential dangers. The top management of the organisation needs to take a strong line on any conflicts which arise and to ensure that departmental heads have clear instructions as to the organisation's priorities.

Summary of organisational conflicts between marketing and other departments

Other departments	*Their emphasis*	*Emphasis of marketing*
Engineering	Long design lead time Functional features Few models with standard components	Short design lead time Sales features Many models with custom components
Purchasing	Standard parts Price of material Economic lot sizes Purchasing at infrequent intervals	Non-standard parts Quality of material Large lot sizes to avoid stockouts Immediate purchasing for customer needs
Production	Long order lead times and inflexible production schedules Long runs with few models No model changes Standard orders Ease of fabrication Average quality control	Short order lead times and flexible schedules to meet emergency orders Short runs with many models Frequent model changes Custom orders Aesthetic appearance Tight quality control
Inventory management	Fast moving items Narrow product line Economic levels of stock	Broad product line Large levels of stock

Notes

Other departments	Their emphasis	Emphasis of marketing
Finance	Strict rationales for spending Hard and fast budgets Pricing to cover costs	Intuitive arguments for spending Flexible budgets to meet changing needs Pricing to further market development
Accounting	Standard transactions Few reports	Special terms and discounts Many reports
Credit	Full financial disclosures by customers Lower credit risks Tough credit terms Tough collection procedures	Minimum credit examination of customers Medium credit risks Easy credit terms Easy collection procedures

Source: Philip Kotler, 'Diagnosing the marketing takeover', *Harvard Business Review*, Nov-Dec 1965 (70-72)

A continual problem is the relation between research and development (R&D) and marketing. This has already been touched on in this chapter in the context of objections to the marketing concept.

(a) Part of the problem might be cultural. To the marketing department, the R&D department is filled with scatty boffins; to the R&D department, the marketing department would be full of intellectually vacuous wideboys. Furthermore the R&D department may have an 'academic' or university atmosphere, as opposed to a commercial one.

(b) Part of the problem is organisational. If R&D consumes substantial resources, it would seem quite logical to exploit economies of scale by having it centralised.

(c) Finally, marketing work and R&D work differ in many important respects. R&D work is likely to be more open-ended than marketing work.

That being said, there are many good reasons why R&D should be more closely co-ordinated with marketing.

(a) If the firm operates the marketing concept, then the 'identification of customer needs' should be a vital input to new product developments.

(b) The R&D department might identify possible changes to product specifications so that a variety of marketing mixes can be applied.

Chapter roundup

(a) In this chapter we have looked at the historical development of marketing and the growth of a concept of 'marketing orientation'. Marketing orientated organisations are those which base their strategy on identifying and meeting the needs of customers. They are distinguished from sales orientated and production orientated organisations.

(b) Four definitions of marketing have been given.

(c) Although the marketing concept is accepted, at least in principle, by a large number of UK organisations it is important to remember that many others have a sales or production orientation. Even amongst those that claim to be marketing orientated, the reality may not always match the aspiration.

(d) The marketing mix is a schematic plan to guide analysis of marketing problems. The four elements in the mix are product, price, promotion, place.

(e) We have examined how a marketing department may be structured and controlled, and looked at its relationships with other departments.

Quick quiz

1 Give two possible definitions of marketing.

2 Distinguish between sales orientation, production orientation and marketing orientation

3 Maximising sales revenue will maximise profit. True or false?

4 What was the main argument put forward by Theodore Levitt in his article 'Marketing myopia'?

5 Write down two objections to the current widespread adoption of the marketing concept.

6 The '4Ps' of the marketing mix are well known but what are the three additional 'Ps' that apply to the marketing of services?

7 What are the three Cs?

8 What is meant by a matrix management structure?

Notes

Solutions to exercises

2 This is an example of how the problems facing firms have changed. Production of toothpaste is not a problem: there are many different manufacturers in the market. The problem now is to get the customer to buy *your* toothpaste rather than the next one. One approach is to focus on the differences between one toothpaste and another. Emphasis on such differences is one of the reasons for the proliferation of brands.

3 You might have thought about your initial contacts with various colleges who tried to 'sell' you an educational course or qualification. Or you might have thought of a telephone call to a public utility - perhaps a query about your telephone bill. Did you find the receptionist's manner a good selling point or the opposite?

4 (a) is fairly straightforward - the gardener is trying to get a task done (mowing the lawn), presumably with the minimum of effort and at economical cost.

(b) is more complicated. The purchaser of life insurance may be trying to remove a feeling of financial insecurity, or to fulfil a duty of providing for dependants. There may be more immediate problems involved; for example, taking out life insurance is often a pre-condition of getting a mortgage.

(c) is in some ways the trickiest of all. Although there are some simple facts involved (the need to get from A to B cheaply and conveniently), there are also subtle points of self-image and status in the choice of a particular model of car.

5 This point is covered more fully later. For now it is enough to say that the objectives of a production department do not always coincide with those of a marketing department.

7 (a) The organisation is unlikely to be the only potential supplier. It will therefore be necessary to convince customers to buy from the company and not from a competitor who may also have attempted to match the customer's needs and wants.

(b) Customers may need to be reassured about the benefits of owning or using the company's product or service. In industrial markets buyers will require evidence that technical specifications and appropriate industry standards are met.

(c) It may not be economical or technically feasible to meet the exact requirements that in an ideal world are required by each specific customer. This is particularly true when mass production techniques are targeted at the average customer's requirements, for, as we all know, none of us are average.

Notes

(d) Customers' requirements might have changed since market-led production decisions were made. In some markets, such as basic commodities, customer requirements are stable over considerable periods. Other markets are very dynamic in terms of changing consumer needs. This is particularly true of markets subject to rapid changes in taste or fashion such as designer clothing and the latest trends in leisure and entertainment. We have all heard stories of the warehouses full of unsold skateboards or the like that were delivered a few weeks after another craze evaporated.

8 The fundamental problem was that the big studios saw themselves as being in the movie business, rather than the entertainments business. Instead of worrying that audiences would be attracted away from the cinema, they should have seen that television was opening up a wider audience for their products. Through licensing fees and, later, through the development of videos there were opportunities for the studios in the growth of what appeared to be a competitive threat.

10 One example which may have occurred to you is the C5 electric motor car, developed by Sir Clive Sinclair and launched to media fanfares. It flopped disastrously. Although as an engineering project it must have seemed an exciting development to its designers, and although it attempted to address public concerns about the excessive use of fossil fuels, it ignored very basic consumer requirements (such as being able to travel reasonable distances without a pit stop, and being visible to other drivers for safety reasons).

11 Hammerite did not fully co-ordinate their marketing activities. Their marketing mix lacked balance between 'promotion' and 'place' elements.

2 THE MARKETING ENVIRONMENT

> *Your objectives*
>
> After completing this chapter you should:
>
> (a) understand how working activities are influenced by factors in the operating environment of an organisation;
>
> (b) understand the clarification of environmental factors as micro or macro, and the implications of the distinction in setting a marketing agenda

1 The micro environment: the market environment

The previous chapter highlighted the importance for an organisation of understanding its operating environment. This understanding is crucial in providing the opportunity to exploit changing market conditions which is the essence of a successful marketing strategy. We will now consider specifically that part of the environment which can be described as the micro environment. This environment includes all factors which impact directly on a firm and its activities in relation to a particular market or set of markets in which it operates. It also incorporates any internal aspects of the organisation such as corporate culture which will influence the development of a marketing strategy. We will consider the market environment and the internal environment in turn.

The nature of the market environment is outlined in the diagram below. In essence the market environment concerns itself with all aspects of a market which affect the company's relationship with its customers and the patterns of competition. The importance of the market environment should not be underestimated, not only because it will have a major impact on the operation of a business, but also because it is an aspect of the environment that the business can, in part, control and change. The understanding of suppliers, distributors, consumers, competitors and interest groups have been identified as key elements of the market environment.

The micro environment

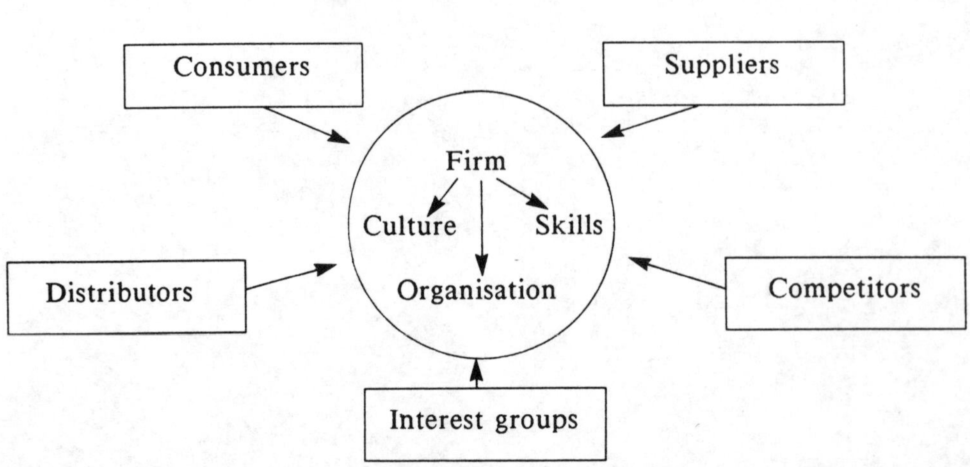

Notes

By attempting to understand the interactions and the behaviour of these groups, the firm can use its marketing strategies to encourage loyalty, obtain preference from suppliers/distributors, and influence what competitors do and what consumers think. Equally, through the development of corporate image, it can influence perceptions held by various interest groups. In that sense the understanding of and reactions to the market environment can be a key factor in ensuring longer term competitive success.

We will now consider each of the key elements of the market environment in turn.

Suppliers. For most organisations this would require some consideration of the number, size and bargaining strength of their suppliers; their ability to guarantee regular supplies, stable prices and quality.

Distribution network. Although the nature and structure of the distribution network is generally treated as a marketing mix variable which can be controlled by an organisation, it is nevertheless a feature of the market environment. There are few instances where an organisation can enter a market which is so new that there are no existing distribution systems. Where these systems are in place, as is normally the case, then they will impose some constraints on what an organisation can do. This may arise partly because of consumer familiarity with existing systems and partly because of the degree of market power which is held by the distribution network.

Exercise 1

Try to think of industries where a highly developed and visible distribution network exists.

Consumers. Understanding consumers is clearly of considerable importance in terms of developing a marketing strategy and the behaviour and motivation of these consumers will be examined in more detail in Chapter 5.

Interest groups. Any analysis of the market environment must give some consideration to the role of interest groups (sometimes referred to in marketing literature as 'publics'). These refer to a variety of groupings whose opinions and attitudes will have some bearing on the success or otherwise of an organisation. An understanding and awareness of the attitudes of these groups will enable the organisation to consider how best to present itself to them.

Competition. The importance of marketing as an aid to establishing a competitive position in the market place has already been stressed; clearly then there is a need for any organisation to develop an awareness and understanding of its competitors, their strengths and weaknesses and the essence of their strategic approach to their markets.

Porter suggests that there are five basic competitive forces which influence the state of competition in an industry. He calls these the 'structural determinants of the intensity of competition' which collectively determine the profit potential of the industry as a whole. Some industries have a bigger profit potential than others, since keener competition means lower profits.

Notes

These five competitive forces are as follows.

(a) The threat of new entrants to the industry.
(b) The threat of substitute products or services.
(c) The bargaining power of customers.
(d) The bargaining power of suppliers.
(e) The rivalry amongst current competitors in the industry.

The threat of new entrants. A new entrant into an industry will bring extra capacity. The new entrant will have to make an investment to break into the market, and will want to obtain a certain market share.

The strength of the threat from new entrants is likely to vary from industry to industry, depending on two factors.

(a) The strength of the *barriers to entry.*

(b) The likely *response of existing competitors* to the new entrant. If a new prospective entrant thinks that firms which are already in the industry would respond to a new competitor by reducing their prices and starting a price war, the new entrant would be more likely to think twice before deciding to make its entry into the market.

The threat from substitute products. The products or services that are produced in one industry are likely to have substitutes that are produced by another industry. Railway travel is a substitute for private motor travel, vegetarian foods are a substitute for meat foods, coffee is a substitute for tea, and so on.

'Substitutes limit the potential returns of an industry by placing a ceiling on the prices firms in the industry can profitably charge. The more attractive the price-performance alternative offered by substitutes, the firmer the lid on industry profits.' (Porter)

When firms in an industry are faced with threats from substitute products they are likely to find that demand for their products is relatively price-elastic. An important threat that they must watch out for is any improvement in the price-performance characteristics of these substitutes.

Exercise 2

A recent example of barriers to entry was provided by a report in the *Financial Times* (21 March 1991) relating to the sale of disposable razors and wet shaving equipment in the UK. The Monopolies and Mergers Commission (MMC) forced Gillette to sell its stake in its main competitor in the UK market. Analyse the MMC's problem in the light of the issues discussed above.

The bargaining power of customers. Customers should want better quality products and services at a lower price, and if they succeed in getting what they want, they will force down the profitability of suppliers in the industry. The profitability of an industry is therefore dependent on the strength of the bargaining power of its customers.

Exercise 3

What factors do you think are important in determining the bargaining power of customers?

The bargaining power of suppliers. Just as buyers can influence the profitability of an industry by exerting pressure for higher quality products or lower prices, so too can suppliers influence profitability by exerting pressure for higher prices.

The ability of suppliers to get higher prices depends on the following factors.

(a) Whether there are just one or two dominant suppliers to the industry, able to charge monopoly prices.

(b) Whether the suppliers are threatened by new entrants to the market, or by substitute products.

(c) Whether the suppliers have other customers outside the industry, and do not rely on the industry for the majority of their sales.

(d) The importance of the supplier's product to the buyer's business.

(e) Whether the supplier has a differentiated product which buyers need to obtain.

(f) Whether switching costs for buyers would be high.

Case example: suppliers and customers: the computer industry

The computer industry provides a good example both of the bargaining power of suppliers and the bargaining power of customers, as the balance has changed in recent years.

Until the advent of microcomputers, the computer industry was dominated by a number of large suppliers, led by IBM, followed by companies like Burroughs, Sperry and Data General. The equipment supplied by each manufacturer was generally incompatible, so that an IBM mainframe could not be used with a Data General machine and so forth. Nor were software applications easily transportable across ranges and makes of machines.

The computer firms were able to 'lock in' their customers, as *switching costs* were so high, and could charge high prices for upgrades. Customers could not mix and match, and so competition as to price was largely irrelevant when it came to system upgrades.

Recently, however, user organisations, supported sometimes by government agencies (the DTI in the UK, and also the EC) have banded together in support of *open systems* so that machines can be connected, through the use of a common set of standards. This process has been aided by other changes in competitive conditions (eg the reduction in the cost of processing power, changes in microchip technology). Customers now have more bargaining power.

Notes

The rivalry amongst current competitors in the industry. The intensity of competitive rivalry within an industry will affect the profitability of the industry as a whole. Competitive actions might take the form of price competition, advertising battles, sales promotion campaigns, introducing new products for the market, improving after sales service or providing guarantees or warranties.

Competition can do one of two things.

(a) It can help the industry as a whole to expand, stimulating demand with new products and advertising. In this situation, the industry as a whole will benefit from the competition.

(b) It can leave demand unchanged, in which case individual competitors will simply be spending more money, charging lower prices and so making lower profits, without getting any benefits except maintaining or increasing market share.

2 The micro environment: the internal environment

Clearly, the internal environment is the area in which the firm can exercise greatest control and should possess the greatest knowledge. Nevertheless, as was emphasised above, it should not be overlooked because the internal capabilities of the organisation are a key factor in generating marketing success. At a very general level, the analysis of the internal environment requires an understanding of the nature of the *corporate culture* - the attitudes and beliefs of personnel at all levels. The strategies available and appropriate for an organisation with a culture orientated towards rapid innovation and risk taking may be quite different to those available to a company orientated towards high quality and an exclusive image, and different again from those which could be pursued by an organisation which sees itself as a low risk, market follower with a reliable, if traditional, product range to offer.

Equally important is an understanding of the strengths and weaknesses of the structure of the company and of the personnel within the company. In many instances, internal structures are changing and reflect the increased pressures of a competitive market place.

The use of *marketing audits* is one technique which is of considerable use in helping an organisation (and the individuals involved in the planning process) to understand the internal environment. A marketing audit is simply a systematic analysis and evaluation of the organisation's marketing position and performance. According to need, it may cover all activities which are either directly or indirectly connected with the marketing function, or it can simply focus on specific products/markets or specific marketing functions. Further distinctions are often drawn between audits which take place at the corporate level, those which take place at the divisional level and those which take place at the level of the product/market.

Although a marketing audit will focus on all the relevant marketing activities, the following may be singled out as being of particular importance.

Marketing capabilities. This includes trying to identify the aspects of marketing in which the company may be considered to have particular strengths and weaknesses. Questions to ask include the following.

(a) How flexible/responsive is the organisation of the marketing department?
(b) What is the company's image/reputation?
(c) How strong are particular product lines?

Notes

(d) What is the extent of brand loyalty among customers?

Although many of these are subjective assessments, their importance cannot be overstated because they will often form the basis of future marketing campaigns.

Performance evaluation. This is essentially the process of comparing the actual achievements of marketing with what was expected - are sales meeting forecasts? Is advertising presenting the desired/planned message? Is the distribution system getting the product to consumers as anticipated? This evaluation will identify weaknesses and strengths of current marketing campaigns which can then be modified when reconsidering the campaign for that product and considering marketing campaigns to be used for new products.

Competitive effectiveness. Essentially this focuses on evaluating the source of an organisation's competitive advantage. This will require some analysis and understanding of competitors, the markets they are targeting and the particular features they use to their advantage.

There are a number of tools available for marketing audits; while not exploring these in depth, we should note that the marketing audit should be systematic, should canvass a wide variety of opinions and is frequently based on questionnaire analysis.

3 The macro environment

The macro environment consists of broad trends and patterns which are taking place in society as a whole which will affect all markets, but will be more relevant to some than others. Many environmental changes, if identified and carefully analysed, can provide invaluable assistance in the process of evolving marketing strategies, identifying profitable products and determining the best routes to reach consumers. Equally, careful monitoring of this environment can enable an organisation to identify developments which may be harmful to its business and will enable it to adopt a *proactive* rather than a *reactive* stance in the action it takes.

The macro environment can usefully be broken down into four key components: political/legal, economic, social/cultural, and technological (PEST factors). The diagram below shows these factors.

The macro environment

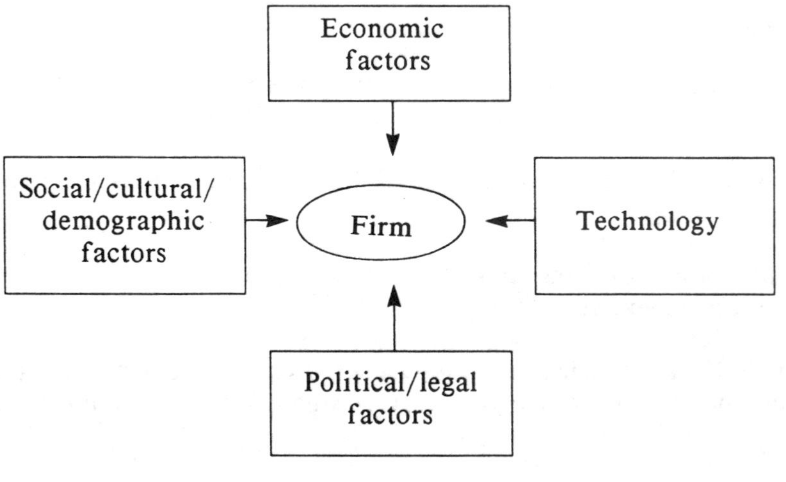

Notes

The political/legal environment. The political/legal environment is primarily the interaction between organisations and government or regulatory bodies. It incorporates a variety of legal restrictions which governments impose to regulate the pursuits of businesses in a formal sense. Equally important are the less formal aspects of government relations with industry such as government attitudes to business and willingness to support initiatives. Increasingly, international developments, including the EC, need to be considered in the context of the legal environment.

The economic environment. Economic conditions are perhaps the key component of the macro environment. Attention is focused on developments within the economy which are likely to have an impact on businesses either directly or as a result of their impact on consumer spending. Key aspects of the economic environment usually include inflation, unemployment, economic growth, consumer income and wealth, interest rates, balance of payments and currency fluctuations.

The social/cultural environment. The social cultural environment concerns itself with a variety of factors including demographic change and changing attitudes and perception. The UK, like many other developed countries, has an ageing population, and this of course has many implications for organisations. The changing role of women may also have implications for the marketer. For instance, as more women work, more convenient shopping times have been introduced.

Exercise 4

In recent years 'green' issues have come into considerable prominence. How have green issues affected the way in which products are marketed?

The technological environment. This fourth component of the macro environment focuses on the way in which technology (both the level and the rate of change) will affect the way an organisation undertakes its business.

When developing marketing strategy the firm must look at both the micro and macro environmental factors. Ultimately a successful marketing strategy needs to be consistent with the external operating environment, but at the same time consistent with internal attitudes and capabilities. One trend that affects businesses is consumerism which will be looked into in further detail below.

Ethics/consumerism

A trend which has increased the importance of customer care is consumerism. A number of consumer rights have developed, including the following.

(a) The right to be informed of the true facts of the buyer-seller relationship, for example:

- (i) the true cost of loans (annualised percentage rates must now be published in any advertisement for loans);
- (ii) truth in advertising (watchdog bodies vet any advertisement and consumers complain about advertisements to the Advertising Standards Authority).

(b) The right to be protected. Consumers' trust in organisations must not be abused. For example, the sale of mailing lists to third parties can lead to consumers receiving vast quantities of 'junk' mail.

(c) The right to ensure quality of life. This right is focused increasingly on environmental protection which should awaken suppliers to the social implications of their actions.

Suppliers need to take careful note of these consumerist pressures. Their reputations must be protected at all cost. This requirement may well militate against aggressive marketing tactics and so, despite competitive pressures, the need to consider the best interests of customers should be paramount in a marketing strategy. The long-term view is necessary rather than attempting to maximise short-term profits.

Chapter roundup

(a) Marketing strategy depends on factors within the micro environment of an organisation and the macro environment.

(b) The micro environment includes the market environment and the internal environment of an organisation.

(c) Competitors are one element of the market environment. We have looked at Porter's analysis of competition, which he breaks down into five competitive forces.

(d) A key tool in understanding the internal environment of an organisation is the marketing audit.

(e) Analysis of the macro environment is often systematised by analysis into PEST factors.

Notes

Quick quiz

1 List five external elements in the market environment of an organisation.

2 In the content of the marketing environment, what is meant by 'interest groups'?

3 Porter refers to five forces influencing the state of competition in an industry. List them.

4 What factors determine the bargaining power of a supplier?

5 What is meant by the term 'marketing audit'?

6 What is meant by the acronym PEST?

7 What do you understand by the term 'consumerism'?

Solutions to exercises

1 There are of course many possibilities: the food industry (grocers shops and supermarkets); motor cars (the network of motor dealers); mortgage lending (the building societies), postal services (post office branches); and so on.

2 'There are few suppliers and a number of practical *barriers* to anyone wishing to achieve entry to the UK market as a manufacturer of razor blades and razors. *Distribution channels* do not encourage entry and strong customer loyalty makes it more difficult. There are no *close substitutes* for wet-shaving products ...One of the key disputed questions [in the report] was the height of the entry barriers.'

The report carried on to mention the different estimates of *capital investment* required to enter the market (which varied widely from £6m to £80m), the numbers of blades sold to make entry worthwhile (100m-500m pa).

3 Just how strong the position of buyers will be depends on a number of factors.

(a) Whether the buyer's purchases represent a substantial proportion of total sales by the producer. If they do, the buyer will be in a strong position relative to the seller.

(b) Whether the buyer's purchases from the industry represent a large or a small proportion of the buyer's total purchases. If most of a buyer's supplies come from a single industry, the buyer will be in a weaker bargaining position than if only a small proportion did so.

(c) Whether switching costs are high or low. (Switching costs are a barrier to entry).

Notes

(d) Whether the products supplied by the industry are standard items and undifferentiated. Suppliers may try to increase their bargaining power over buyers by creating a strong brand image. Thus, a supermarket chain may feel obliged to stock leading brands of a product because its own customers might *expect* to find these brands in any supermarket.

(e) Whether the buyers make low profits. A buyer who makes low profits will be forced to insist on low prices from suppliers.

(f) The threat that buyers might take over sources of supply, if suppliers charge too much.

(g) The skills of the buyer's purchasing staff, or the price-awareness of consumers.

(h) The importance of *product quality*. When product quality is important to the buyer, the buyer is less likely to be price-sensitive, and so the industry might be more profitable as a consequence. For example, although the Ministry of Defence may wish to keep control over defence spending, it is likely as a buyer to be more concerned that the products it purchases perform satisfactorily than with getting the lowest price possible for everything it buys. As a consequence, profitability in the defence industry is likely to be high.

4 There are many points to make because every stage of a product's life is affected by environmental issues - how it is made, what it is made of, how it gets to the customer, what it is used for, what is the effect of its use, and how it is disposed of. 'Green' issues have affected the *product* itself ('ozone-friendly', 'dolphin-friendly'), its *packaging* (recyclable), its *price* (organically produced vegetables are more expensive, for example), and its *promotion* (BMW got a good deal of mileage out of the idea that their cars are almost totally recyclable for the next generation of car drivers).

3 MARKETING RESEARCH

> *Your objectives*
>
> After completing this chapter you should:
>
> (a) understand the scope of marketing research and the main techniques it embraces;
>
> (b) be aware of the main sources of marketing research data, including computerised databases.

1 The purpose and approach of marketing research

Exercise 1

As in the previous chapter, begin by asking yourself what you understand by 'marketing research'. Is it the same as market research?

Marketing decisions are inevitably made under conditions of uncertainty and risk. The use of marketing research cannot eliminate risk but can reduce it by indicating the likely outcome of a certain course of action.

Markets are dynamic and competitive; success in business depends on greater investment and more frequent innovation so as not to lose ground to competitors. Important decisions have to be taken frequently, and in order to make decisions with confidence management needs relevant and comprehensive information. It is the task of marketing research to provide this information.

Marketing information may be needed for: strategic decision-making (such as product life cycle estimates, information to help with decisions about diversifying or to segment a market); tactical decisions (such as planning sales territories, setting short-term marketing cost budgets); or preparing a marketing database (such as for market share analysis, competitor analysis, substitute product analysis).

The information system for marketing is referred to as *marketing research.*

Definitions of marketing research

'Market research' and 'marketing research' are often used interchangeably although it would be more correct to say that market research is just an aspect of marketing research.

(a) Market research refers to finding out information about the market for a particular product or service.

(b) Marketing research was defined more broadly by the American Marketing Association as 'the systematic gathering, recording and analysing of data about problems relating to the marketing of goods and services'. A similar definition, by the UK Chartered Institute of Marketing, refers to the 'objective gathering, recording and analysing of all facts about problems relating to the transfer and sale of goods and services from producer to consumer or user'.

Within this definition, there are a few points to note.

(a) Marketing research should provide a regular *information* system to aid planning and control decisions by marketing and senior management.

(b) Marketing research is concerned with all types of customer and user (industrial, government and resellers) not just the consumer.

(c) Marketing research provides information which enables managers to make decisions about the marketing mix - product, place, price and promotion. It is not simply 'market research'.

Marketing research is therefore a very broad concept. It embraces not only market research but also product research, price research, sales promotion research and distribution research.

The table below shows a number of activities falling into each of these categories of research. It is not intended to be exhaustive.

Type of research	*Examples of activities*
Market research	Analysing the market potential of existing products Forecasting likely demand for new products Forecasting sales for all products Analysing market shares Studying market trends
Product research	Estimating customer acceptance of proposed products Forecasting new uses for products Comparing competitive products Test marketing
Price research	Analysing elasticity of demand Estimating the effect on demand of changes in credit policy Analysing customer perceptions of price
Sales promotion research	Analysing the effectiveness of advertising Analysing the effectiveness of salesmen Establishing sales territories
Distribution research	Planning the location and design of distribution centres Analysing dealer supply requirements Analysing the costs of different methods of transportation and warehousing.

Notes

The most important of these are product research and market research, which we will now examine in more detail.

Product research

This aspect of marketing research attempts to make product development customer-oriented. Product research is concerned with the product itself, whether new, improved or already on the market, and customer reactions to it.

Exercise 2

Where might the ideas for new products come from? Try to think of likely sources within and outside the firm.

Research and development is carried out by company scientists, engineers or designers; much wasted effort can be saved for them, however, if new ideas are first tested in the market; that is, if product research is carried out.

New ideas are first screened by a range of specialists (market researchers, designers, research and development staff etc) and are rejected if they:

(a) have a low profit potential or insufficient market potential;
(b) have a high cost and involve high risk;
(c) do not conform to company objectives;
(d) cannot be produced and distributed with the available resources.

Ideas which survive the screening process should be product tested and possibly test marketed. Test marketing in a selected area will give a better indication of how well the product will sell if produced for a wider market, but it also gives competitors an early warning of what is happening.

Typical considerations in product research for a *new* product are:

(a) the combination of quality, price, value and associated image, together with the shape, colour and size of product, which will appeal most successfully to customers;

(b) the extent to which a new product will encroach on the market for existing lines;

(c) whether the new product extends or improves the existing product range of the company;

(d) the extent to which action by a competitor forces a firm to develop a new product.

Typical considerations for improving an *existing* product are:

(a) customer (or dealer) reaction to the existing product and the possibility that this could be improved by changing the product itself, its size, colour or packaging and so on;

(b) customer reaction to after-sales service and the possibility that this could be improved.

Notes

Product research also includes the need to keep the product range of a company's goods under review for the following reasons.

(a) *Variety reduction* may be desirable to reduce production costs, or when there are insufficient sales of certain items in the product range to justify continued production. In practice, there is often strong resistance, both from within a company and from customers, to the elimination of products from the market.

(b) *Product diversification* increases a product range by introducing new items, and a wide range of products can often improve a company's market image.

(c) *Segmentation* is a policy which aims at securing a new class of customers (a new market segment) for an existing range of products, perhaps by making some adjustments to the products to appeal to the new segments.

Product research also involves finding *new uses* for existing products, and this could be considered a means of extending a product range.

Exercise 3

Without going into the detail of individual brands, can you think of some broad product areas where this kind of extension has been apparent in recent years?

As in all aspects of marketing research, it is important to be aware of the activities of competitors in product research because:

(a) it is necessary to know what new or improved products they are making and what their product range is;

(b) a company must also be aware of the advantages and disadvantages, both real and imaginary, of a competitor's products, and attempt to maintain the advantages and reduce the disadvantages of its own products in relation to these.

These points are covered in more detail in the final section of this chapter.

Market research

The information for market research can be collected directly (for example, from sample market results or questionnaires filled in by customers) or from secondary sources (such as analyses of past sales, or external information such as the *Nielsen index*, which gives summary information on sales by products and geographical areas).

The information should reduce the risk involved in marketing decisions and thus increase the chances of making the right choice. But the quantity and quality of information provided by market research has an associated cost and the trade-off between cost and accuracy is important, particularly because risk cannot be eliminated. There is no such thing as perfect information when dealing with decision making in an uncertain world. Market research can provide information which should help to reduce the risk in decision making but, usually, the more accurate the information, the higher the cost. Market research should always be cost effective.

Notes

A distinction which will be explored more fully later is that between *primary research* and *secondary research*. At this point it is sufficient to say that primary research is carried out for a specific purpose and is used for that purpose (for example, a manufacturer seeking to improve his product might circulate a questionnaire to his customers or potential customers); secondary research is research which is being used for a purpose other than that for which it was intended (for example, a manufacturer might derive information from government statistics originally compiled for quite a different purpose). As a generalisation, one can say that primary research will usually be more expensive, but the better focus it provides can make it more effective.

We will now look at some specific market research techniques:

(a) market forecasts;
(b) sales forecasts;
(c) research into potential sales;
(d) information on concentration ratios;
(e) market signals.

Market forecasts

These are forecasts for the market as a whole. It is mainly involved in the assessment of environmental factors, outside the organisation's control, which will affect the demand for its products/services. Often it consists of three components.

(a) An *economic review* (national economy, government policy, covering forecasts on investment, population, gross national product, and inflation).

(b) *Specific market research* (to obtain data about specific markets and forecasts concerning total market demand).

(c) Evaluation of *total market demand* for the firm's and similar products - including such factors as profitability and market potential.

Sales forecasts

These are estimates of sales of a product in a future period:

(a) at a given price;
(b) using a stated method of sales promotion which will cost a given amount of money.

Unlike the market forecast, a sales forecast concerns the firm's activity directly. It takes into account such aspects as sales to certain categories of customer, sales promotion activities, the extent of competition, product life cycle, performance of major products.

Sales forecasts are expressed in volume, value and profit, and in the case of national and international organisations regional forecasts are usual, by product.

Research into potential sales

Sales potential is an estimate of the part of the market which is within the possible reach of a product. The potential will vary according to the price of the product and the amount of money spent on sales promotion, and market research should attempt to quantify these variations. Sales potential also depends on:

(a) how essential the product is to consumers;
(b) whether it is a durable commodity whose purchase is postponable;
(c) the overall size of the possible market;
(d) competition.

Whether sales potential is worth exploiting will depend on the cost of sales promotion and selling which must be incurred to realise the potential.

Exercise 4

Market research has led a company to the opinion that the sales potential of product X is:

	Sales value	*Contribution* earned before selling costs deducted*	*Cost of selling*
either	£100,000	£40,000	£10,000
or	£110,000	£44,000	£15,000

*Contribution is an accountancy term which means sales revenue less variable costs.

What use can the company make of this information?

Sales potential will influence the decisions by a company on how much of each product to make: its *production mix*. A company might decide, for example, that maximum profits will be earned by concentrating all its production and sales promotion efforts on one segment of a market. Action by competitors might then adversely affect sales and market research might reveal that another market segment has become relatively more profitable. The company might therefore decide to divert some production capacity and sales promotion spending to the new segment in order to revive its profits.

Estimates of sales potential are required in deciding whether to invest money in the development of a new or improved product.

Market research, to be comprehensive, must show an awareness of the economic, fiscal, political and social influences which may affect supply and demand for a product. Changes within this framework should wherever possible be anticipated.

Other aspects of market research include investigation of:

(a) the expansion or decline of demand within a particular market segment;
(b) the expansion or decline of demand within a particular geographical area;
(c) the timing of demand - is there a cyclical or seasonal pattern of demand?

Notes

Information on concentration ratios

To develop a market share strategy, an organisation might want to obtain information about the concentration ratios in the market, that is, what proportion of firms hold most of the market.

One way of expressing concentration ratios is to assess the percentage of the market that is held by the top five firms, say, and the top ten firms.

A more detailed concentration ratio analysis can be charted on a Lorenz curve. This is a graph which maps the number of units in a population against the market share for which they account.

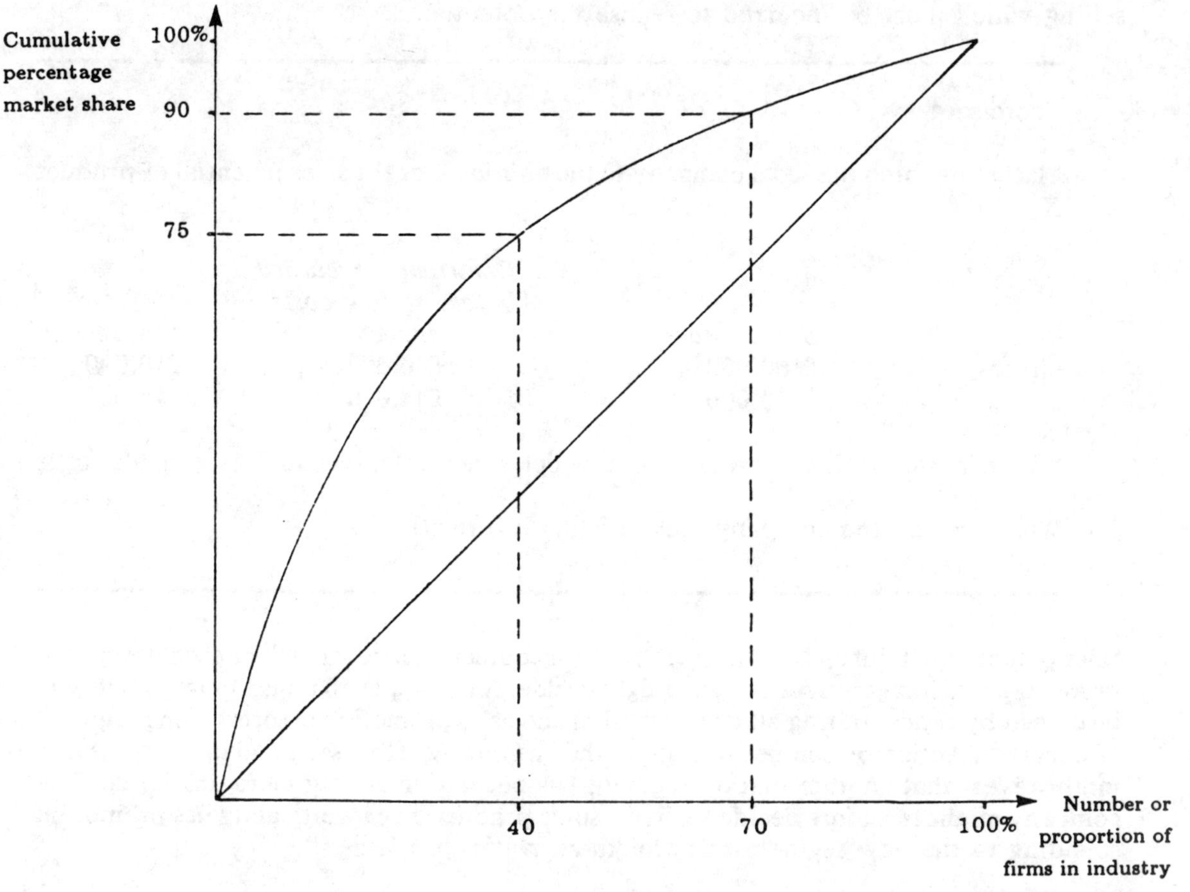

In this example, for instance, the top 40% of the firms in the industry have 75% of the total market, and the top 70% have 90% of the market. The greater the bend on the curve away from the straight line the greater is the concentration of the firm in the hands of the market leaders.

Exercise 5

To test your understanding of the Lorenz curve, suppose that for a particular industry the 'curve' is in fact the diagonal straight line indicated in the above diagram. What would that imply about the concentration ratios in the industry?

Market signals

Market signals are information that comes to light about competitors' actions in the market. They may be 'honest' or they may be 'bluffs'; nevertheless, they are significant for making decisions about market strategy.

Market signals can take any of the following forms.

(a) A competitor makes an announcement of what he intends to do, but before he has done it. Prior announcements are publicity measures intended to warn off competitors from trying to do the same and to test competitors' reactions. They might also be intended to win support from the investing public or as a threat of retaliatory action against something another competitor has already done.

(b) A competitor makes an announcement of what he has done, after the event; such as signing a major contract with a supplier or customer, or making a takeover bid for another company.

(c) Competitors adopt a particular course of action when they would have been expected to do something else. What does their unexpected action signal?

(d) An aggressive marketing action by a competitor. When a firm's competitor takes an aggressive marketing action directed specifically against the firm, it might be a signal that the competitor thinks the firm is gaining too much market share, and the aggressive action might be the first stage in an intensification of competition.

Marketing research procedure

Marketing research involves the following five stages of work.

(a) *Definition of the problem.* An individual research project cannot be undertaken successfully until the marketing problem which management wishes to resolve has been properly defined.

(b) *Design of the research.* Once the research team knows what problem it must help to resolve, it will establish the type of data, the collection method to be used (postal questionnaire, personal interview), the selection of a research agency (if appropriate) and if a sample is to be taken, the design of the sample. Any questions put to respondents must be carefully designed.

(c) *Collection of the data.*

(d) *Analysis of the data.*

(e) *Presentation of a report* which should then lead to a management marketing decision.

2 Sources of marketing research information

The sources of marketing research information are secondary data and primary data. Primary data will be discussed later. First we will look briefly at secondary data.

Notes

Secondary data is 'data neither collected directly by the user nor specifically for the user, often under conditions that are not well known to the user' (American Marketing Association). The collection of secondary data as part of a marketing research project is sometimes known as *desk research.*

Desk research involves collecting data from internal and external sources.

(a) Records inside the firm, gathered by another department or section for its own purposes, may be useful for the research task in hand.

Exercise 6

What sort of internal data might be useful in a marketing research project?

(b) Published information from external sources includes:

(i) publications of market research agencies, such as the Nielsen Index;
(ii) government statistics;
(iii) publications of trade associations;
(iv) professional journals.

Sources of secondary data for marketing vary according to the needs of the organisation.

The *government* is a major source of economic information and information about industry and population trends. Examples of UK government publications are:

(a) the Annual Abstract of Statistics and its monthly equivalent, the Monthly Digest of Statistics, containing data about manufacturing output, housing, population etc;

(b) the Digest of UK Energy Statistics (published annually);

(c) Housing and Construction statistics (published quarterly);

(d) Financial Statistics (monthly);

(e) Economic Trends (monthly);

(f) Census of Population;

(g) Census of Production (annual), which has been described as 'one of the most important sources of desk research for industrial marketers' and provides data about production by firms in each industry in the UK;

(h) Department of Employment Gazette (monthly) giving details of employment in the UK;

(i) British Business, published weekly by the Department of Trade and Industry, giving data on industrial and commercial trends at home and overseas;

(j) Business Monitors, giving detailed information about various industries.

Non-government sources of information include:

(a) the national press (Financial Times etc) and financial and professional magazines and journals;

(b) companies and other organisations specialising in the provision of economic and financial data (eg the Financial Times Business Information Service, the Data Research Institute, Reuters and the Extel Group) and research organisations who analyse certain markets and publish and sell the results (eg Mintel, Euromonitor);

(c) directories and yearbooks;

(d) professional institutions (eg Chartered Institute of Marketing, Industrial Marketing Research Association, British Institute of Management, Institute of Practitioners in Advertising);

(e) specialist libraries, such as the City Business Library in London, collect published information from a wide variety of sources;

(f) trade sources: many industries have an industry body which provides useful market research data. The Association of British Insurers (ABI) provides market share data on the life insurance industry; the Society of Motor Manufacturers and Trades (SMMT) provides detailed data on the registration of new vehicles by brand on a regular basis. In addition trade press is often a valuable source of information about competitors.

Primary data

The collection of primary data is sometimes known as *field research.*

Field research may be carried out in a number of areas, notably customer research, advertising research, product research, packaging research and distribution research. There are several techniques involved in the collection and analysis of primary data and we shall consider in detail:

(a) experimentation;
(b) observation;
(c) sampling;
(d) questionnaires;
(e) consumer panels;
(f) trade audits, such as retail audits;
(g) pre-testing and post-testing;
(h) attitude scales and methods of analysis.

Experimentation

In a *controlled experiment,* a controlled research environment is established and selected stimuli are then introduced. To the extent that 'outside' factors can be eliminated from the environment (and therefore depending on the degree to which a controlled environment is established) the observed effects can be measured and related to each stimulus. Controlled experiments have been used to find the best advertising campaign, the best price level, the best incentive machine and the best sales training method.

Observation

Observation can be used as a means of obtaining sample data where quantitative data is required.

Notes

Exercise 7

Most people have seen this process - the collection of research data by physical observation- in action. Can you recall an example of it?

Observation can also be used to study consumer behaviour, although this is usually within a controlled experiment.

(a) Direct observation involves the examination by an observer of how people behave in particular situations. This is important in retail trade research (such as watching how customers react to product displays and promotions).

(b) Recording devices can be used to monitor the responses of individuals:

  (i) an *eye camera* records eye reactions and is sometimes used to test response to advertisements;

  (ii) a *psychogalvanometer* measures perspiration (which is in turn a measure of involuntary physical response) and is also used in advertising testing;

  (iii) a *tachistoscope* exposes material for a brief moment, and measures the visual impact of an advertisement or its legibility when exposed for this short time.

Sampling

In marketing research for consumer goods, it will be impossible to obtain data from every consumer in the market, because not only would this take too much time and cost too much money, but it would also be impracticable in any case. (In a small market, however, such as an industrial market or government market, a census might be practicable and preferable to a sample survey.) To obtain data, it is therefore usually necessary to obtain a sample to provide an estimate of the characteristics of the entire 'population' and the accuracy of the sample will depend on:

(a) how the sample is taken;
(b) the amount of variability in the population;
(c) the size of the sample.

The larger the sample, the greater the likelihood that the sample will provide an accurate reflection of the population as a whole.

To make a truly random sample we need a *sampling frame*. This is a list of every member of the target 'population'. If we wished to obtain a sample of opinions among people eligible to vote in an election, a sampling frame would be provided by the Electoral Register. If a sampling frame is prepared which excludes any 'members' or items, a sample chosen by reference to the sampling frame cannot be truly random.

A complete sampling frame is difficult to obtain in practice because:

(a) comprehensive lists of a population get out of date as soon as they are published, since new members join and existing members leave, retire or die;

(b) a comprehensive sampling frame would not be justified if the benefits from greater confidence in the accuracy of sample estimates are less than the cost of obtaining or maintaining the sampling frame. For example, if a company manufacturing snack foods wished to obtain data about the reaction of potential customers to a new product, a comprehensive sampling frame would need to consist of every potential customer in the entire market. This would not be justified on grounds of cost (as well as on grounds of practicality).

Exercise 8

Suppose you are developing a new product: a piece of computer software designed to simplify the completion of an income tax return. You wish to assess demand for the product by sampling potential users. How would you go about obtaining a sampling frame?

For these reasons, various techniques of sampling (methods of sample design) have been developed so that samples which are 'nearly' random ('quasi-random') can be obtained. You must have some understanding of these techniques and which of them might be used in certain circumstances.

A *random sample* is one selected in such a way that every item in the population has an equal chance of being included. To obtain a random sample, we need a sampling frame, which has already been described. A random sample can be selected from the sampling frame by two main methods:

(a) the 'lottery method' (picking numbers out of a hat);

(b) the use of random number tables, which is to be preferred as it provides a high guarantee against bias.

In many situations it is either not possible or else undesirable to use a random sample. The main methods of *non-random sampling* are as follows:

(a) systematic sampling;
(b) stratified sampling;
(c) multistage sampling;
(d) quota sampling;
(e) cluster sampling.

Some of these methods try to approximate the random sampling technique, and are 'quasi-random' sampling methods.

Systematic sampling may provide a good approximation to random sampling. Select every nth item after a random start. For example, if it was decided to select a sample of 20 from a population of 800, then every 40th (800 ÷ 20) item after a random start in the first 40 should be selected. The starting point could be found using the lottery method or random number tables. If (say) 23 was chosen, then the sample would include the following items:

23rd, 63rd, 103rd, 143rd 783rd

The gap of 40 is known as the *sampling interval.*

Notes

Exercise 9

Can you see a possible logical flow in this method? Can you see how the difficulty might be overcome?

A typical example of systematic sampling might be quality control checking where every nth item produced is selected for a control inspection.

In many situations *stratified sampling* is the best method of choosing a sample. It is another 'quasi-random' sampling method. The population must be capable of being divided into strata, which may conform to a consumer characteristics or a market segment.

For example, a manufacturer of machine equipment may know that 40% of its sales come from one industry A, 30% from another industry B, 10% from industry C and so on. A stratified sample would aim to obtain 40% of its respondents from industry A, 30% from group B, and 10% from C. If all potential customers in each industry are known, the sample within each group could then be selected by random sampling methods using a sampling frame.

Multistage sampling is normally used to cut down the number of investigations and the costs of travelling etc. Again an example will serve to illustrate the principles.

A national survey of cheese consumption is to be carried out. The country is divided into a number of areas and a small sample of these is selected at random. Each of the areas selected is subdivided into smaller units and again, a small number of these is selected at random. This process is repeated as many times as necessary and finally, a random sample of the relevant people living in each of the smallest units is made. A fair approximation to a random sample can be obtained.

Thus we might choose a random sample of 8 areas and from each of these areas, select a random sample of 5 towns. From each town, a random sample of 200 people might be selected so that the total sample size is $8 \times 5 \times 200 = 8{,}000$ people.

Using *quota sampling,* investigators are told to interview all the people they meet up to a certain quota. However, a large degree of bias can be introduced. For example, an interviewer may fill up his quota by only meeting housewives out shopping. In practice, this problem is partially overcome by subdividing the quota into different types of people, eg on the basis of age, sex and social class. For example, an interviewer might be expected to take a sample of 100 people, but told that the total must be made up of 50 men and 50 women, and that each sub-total of 50 should contain, say, 5 people from socio-economic group A, 10 from each of B, C1, C2 and D, and 5 from group E. It should be clear that one major advantage of quota sampling is that, although a fairly detailed knowledge of the characteristics of a population are required, it is not necessary to establish a sampling frame.

Using *cluster sampling,* the field under examination is cut down in much the same way as for a multistage sample. The investigators are then told to examine every item in the small areas which fit the required definition. The purpose of multistage sampling is to cut down costs but the purpose of cluster sampling is to find a sample. Like quota sampling, it will normally only be used when no sampling frame is available. Cluster sampling has the advantage of low costs in the same way as multistage sampling.

Notes

A cluster sample might be gathered as follows: by use of map references, a geographical area might be broken down into smaller areas. Some of these smaller areas will then be selected by random sampling. The 'sampling unit' is *every* person or household within the selected small area (in most samples, the 'sampling unit' selected is an individual or household).

A possible problem with cluster sampling is that if the individuals in the selected small areas show a similarity to one another, the findings of the sample (perhaps because they live in the same block of flats) may not be representative of the population as a whole.

Instead of interviewing every individual in the small area, the sample may select one in every 'n' individuals - say 1 in 5. This would be a type of two-stage sampling.

Exercise 10

This is a more lengthy and complex exercise than most. Try to think it through carefully and jot down some workings for your calculations.

A large retailing group wishes to evaluate the effect upon store sales of using window space for advertising purposes. Given the following data, show how a 20% sample of its stores should be drawn.

Type size	*No. of stores*	*Range of window sizes*	*Average window*
A	150	$4m^2$ - $10m^2$	$8m^2$
B	80	$11m^2$ - $17m^2$	$15m^2$
C	50	$18m^2$ - $25m^2$	$20m^2$
D	20	More than $25m^2$	$30m^2$
	300		

There are several faults or weaknesses which might occur in the design or collection of sample data.

(a) *Bias:* in choosing a sample, unless the method used to select the sample is the random sampling method, or a quasi-random sampling method, there will be a likelihood that some 'units' (individuals or households) will have a poor, or even zero chance of being selected for the sample. Where this occurs, samples are said to be biased.

A biased sample may occur when:

(i) the sampling frame is out of date, and excludes a number of individuals or 'units' new to the population; or

(ii) some individuals selected for the sample decline to respond. If a questionnaire is sent to 1,000 households, but only 600 reply, the failure of the other 400 to reply will make the sample of 600 replies inevitably biased; or

(iii) a questionnaire contains leading questions, or a personal interviewer tries to get respondents to answer questions in a particular way.

Notes

(b) *Insufficient data:* the sample may be too small to be reliable as a source of information about an entire population.

(c) *Unrepresentative data:* data collected might be unrepresentative of normal conditions. For example, if an employee is asked to teach a trainee how to do a particular job, data concerning the employee's output and productivity during the time he is acting as trainer will not be representative of his normal output and productivity.

(d) *Omission of an important factor:* data might be incomplete because an important item has been omitted in the design of the 'questions'.

(e) *Carelessness:* data might be provided without any due care and attention. An investigator might also be careless in the way he gathers data.

(f) *Confusion of cause and effect (or association):* it may be tempting to assume that if two variables appear to be related, one variable is the cause of the other. Variables may be associated but it is not necessarily true that one causes the other. For example, in a period of hot weather both sales of swimwear and ice creams are likely to rise. However, one is not causing the other; they are both caused by the hot weather.

(g) Where questions call for something more than simple 'one word' replies, there may be difficulty in interpreting the results correctly. This is especially true of 'depth interviews' which try to determine the reasons for human behaviour (*motivation research*).

One method of checking the accuracy of replies is to insert *control questions* in the questionnaire, so that the reply to one question should be compatible with the reply to another. If they are not, the value of the interviewee's responses is dubious, and may be ignored.

Questionnaires

Questionnaires may be administered by personal interview, telephone or post. By their nature postal questionnaires tend to be highly structured, whereas questionnaires that are used to support an interview (by acting as an aide memoire) may be relatively open ended. In common with all other forms of marketing research it is important to attempt to survey a relatively large representative sample. It would be a mistake to assume that the need to obtain a large sample for statistically significant results necessarily favours the use of a postal survey.

Postal surveys have the additional problem in that whilst the mail out may be to a representative group the subsequent response is likely to be biased towards those who responded because they found the topic of particular interest. Postal surveys tend to attract a relatively low response rate, with unsolicited questionnaires often obtaining only a 2% or 3% return. Under these circumstances great care should be taken when extrapolating from such results.

Exercise 11

Try to think of some simple techniques which might improve the response rate to a postal survey.

It can be seen that it is a mistake to assume that using a postal survey will always be the most cost effective means of conducting a survey.

There are two main considerations in designing questionnaires.

(a) Questions should generate valid and reliable information on the matter being surveyed. Respondents must therefore find the questions comprehensible. Questions that are likely to produce biased answers should also be avoided.

(b) The questionnaire should be designed to facilitate the subsequent data analysis.

The following guidelines should therefore be adopted.

(a) Leading questions should be avoided.

(b) Questions should be short and unambiguous.

(c) No calculations should be required.

(d) Questions should fall in a logical sequence.

(e) The working language of the target group should be used.

(f) *Filter questions* should be used to avoid wasting time. For example: do you own a car? YES/NO. A no response then enables questions on garages to be skipped.

(g) *Funnelling*, a technique of moving from general to restricted questions more directly related to the research objectives, can be applied. This technique is sometimes reversed to check limited responses.

(h) Personal questions on sex, politics, religion and personal habits should only be asked in exceptional circumstances. Before attempting such questions interviewers need to have established goodwill.

However carefully the questionnaire design has been conducted, it is still necessary to pilot the questionnaire, by surveying a limited number of respondents in some depth, before going to the cost of launching a survey that might produce some meaningless results. As an example, a question that appeared obvious to the design team might be found in practice to be highly confusing or misleading.

It is often important, especially when identifying potential market segments, to classify individuals, often by socio-economic grouping or age. Questions to establish these groupings should be treated with care as they can subsequently colour the individual's response to other questions. Socio-economic groupings are still determined by the occupation of the 'head of the household', the man in the case of a couple. This is a remarkably archaic notion now that so many women work full or part-time. However, if asked at the outset of the interview what her husband's occupation is, a woman may spend the rest of the interview trying to portray her household as belonging to a higher socio-economic grouping than it actually does. No, she rarely buys baked beans, and yes, she usually purchases sirloin in preference to cheaper cuts of meat. If questions on occupation and the like are to be asked they should be left to the end of the interview. Often it is safer even then to allow a trained market researcher to infer such classifications using their subjective appraisal.

Notes

Consumer panels

Some research firms have created consumer panels consisting of a cross-section of consumers who have agreed to give information about their attitudes or buying habits (through personal visits or mail questionnaires) at regular intervals of time. Consumer panels with personal visits are called *home audit panels* and panels which send data by post are called *diary panels*. Panels might be established for either the long term or the short term.

Consumer panels provide a useful illustration of the difficulties which exist in obtaining reliable market research findings. The advantages of consumer panels are that they provide continuous information over time from willing guinea pigs. The problems, however, are as follows.

(a) It is difficult to select a panel which is a representative sample. The panel must be representative of:

   (i) all the customers in the target market;
   (ii) the decision making units who will make the purchase decision (husbands as well as wives, for example).

(b) Panel members tend to become sophisticated in interviewing techniques and responses.

(c) It is difficult to maintain a stable personnel; turnover of members may be high and this will affect results as new members are enlisted.

Trade audits or retail audits

Trade audits are carried out among panels of wholesalers and retailers, and the term 'retail audits' refers to panels of retailers only. A research firm sends auditors to selected outlets at regular intervals to count stock and deliveries, thus enabling an estimate of throughput to be made.

The audits provide details of:

(a) retail sales for selected products and brands, sales by different type of retail outlet, market shares and brand shares;

(b) retail stocks of products and brands (enabling a firm subscribing to the audit to compare stocks of its own goods with those of competitors);

(c) selling prices in retail outlets, including information about discounts.

Exercise 12

How can the data from a retail audit be of any value to a manufacturer who is not making retail sales?

A well-known example of a retail audit is the *Inventory Audit of Retail Sales*, also called the *Nielsen Index* (after its originator) which has operated since 1939. This monitors sales and stock levels for three product groups: food, drugs and pharmaceuticals. The Nielsen Food Index audits about 800 grocers bi-monthly and reports on each brand, size, flavour etc specified by the client, together with an 'all other' category, showing:

(a) consumer sales in units and £;
(b) retailer purchases in units;
(c) the source of delivery (co-operatives, multiple stores depot, independent wholesalers);
(d) retailers' stocks and stock cover (in days/weeks);
(e) prices;
(f) details of out of stock items;
(g) press, magazine and TV expenditure.

The report is subdivided into shop types (all grocers, cooperatives, multiples, major multiples and independents) and television regions.

Pre-testing and post-testing

Marketing research may be carried out before, during and after marketing decisions are implemented. Such research is often directed at attempting to measure the effectiveness of advertising campaigns. However, whereas the effects of sales promotions (coupons, three for the price of two and the like) are directly measurable in terms of sales, the effectiveness of advertising often needs to be inferred.

The reason for these difficulties is that the advertising effect might be swamped by other more powerful influences in the market place, such as price cuts and sales promotions by competitors. The impact of these and other marketing activities can then mask the true effect of the company's advertising campaign. Much research therefore focuses on the effectiveness of the campaign in communicating with its target audience, the logic being that any beneficial changes in awareness and attitudes will later be reflected in increased sales.

It therefore follows that measurement of the *communication effect* is more reliable than attempts to measure the *sales effect* attributable to a particular advertising campaign.

Some examples of pre-testing are given below.

(a) Before the advertisement copy is finalised, *motivational research* may be carried out on a sample of potential customers. Members of the public might be invited to watch a film show which includes new TV advertising, and a measure of the shift in their brand awareness would be taken after the show. *Copy research* might involve showing members of the public a number of press advertisements and then asking questions about them (in order to measure the impact of different slogans or headlines).

(b) *Laboratory tests* have been carried out to measure the physiological reactions of people watching advertisements (eg heart beat, blood pressure, dilation of the pupil of the eye, perspiration). Such tests measure the arousal power or attention-drawing power of an advertisement, but cannot measure its effectiveness in communicating the message.

(c) *Ratings tests* involve asking a panel of target consumers to look at alternative advertisements and to give them ratings (marks out of ten) for attention-drawing power, clarity, emotional appeal and stimulus to buy.

Notes

Exercise 13

In 1979, when Ford launched the Fiesta, their advertising agency, Ogilvy, Benson, Mather, abandoned their first creative idea after motivational research. The proposed copy for the advertisement focused on the theme of Ford's 'new baby'. An expectant father was seen pacing up and down outside his garage. Suddenly, from inside the garage came the sounds of a new born baby crying. The garage door was opened to reveal a proud wife with the new Fiesta.

Why do you think this idea was received unfavourably?

The purpose of *test marketing* is to obtain information about how consumers react to the product - will they buy it, and if so, will they buy it again? Will they adopt the product as a regular feature of their buying habits, and if so, how frequently will they buy it? With this information an estimate of the total market demand for the product can be made.

A test market involves testing a new consumer product in selected areas which are thought to be 'representative' of the total market. This avoids a blind commitment to the costs of a full-scale launch while permitting the collection of market data. In the selected areas, the firm will attempt to distribute the product through the same types of sales outlets it plans to use in the full market launch, and also to use the advertising and promotion plans it intends to use in the full market. A test marketing exercise can be expensive, but it enables the company to 'test the water' before launching the product nationally. Not only does it help to make sales forecasts, it can also be used to identify flaws in the product or promotional plans which can then be dealt with before the product is launched nationally.

Other forms of product testing include the following.

(a) *Simulated store technique* (or laboratory test markets). In these tests, a group of shoppers are invited to watch a selection of advertisements for a number of products, including an advertisement for the new product. They are then given some money and invited to spend it in a supermarket or shopping area. Their purchases are recorded and they are asked to explain their purchase decisions (and non-purchase decisions). Some weeks later they are contacted again and asked about their product attitudes and repurchase intentions. These tests help to assess advertising effectiveness as well as to forecast sales volumes; in addition the results are made available relatively quickly.

(b) *Controlled test marketing*. In these tests, a research firm pays a panel of stores to carry the new product for a given length of time. The research firm can decide on shelf locations, point-of-sale displays and pricing etc; the sales results are then monitored. This test (also known as 'minimarket testing') helps to provide an assessment of 'in-store' factors in achieving sales as well as to forecast sales volumes for the new product.

There are several drawbacks to test marketing.

(a) The marketing staff may become so involved in the testing that they develop an 'emotional' commitment to the product's success and seek every reason to justify a full market launch.

(b) The test markets may be unrepresentative of the total market, so that predictions of market sales will be biased and inaccurate. 'Despite the various claims of media owners, it is clear that no perfect microcosm exists and that test marketing is of dubious value if undertaken for predictive purposes alone' (Baker).

(c) Test marketing invites the attention of competitors who are given advance warning of the new product and can then develop aggressive counter-tactics in order to prevent a successful launch of the new product (eg expensive advertising or price reductions may be planned). If the counter-tactics are introduced during the test marketing phase, the test will then fail to obtain reliable predictions of future sales volumes, due to the abnormal trading conditions during the test. If the test market is for an entirely new product, it will give competitors time to study it and develop their own substitutes.

For these reasons, test marketing is only used occasionally in Britain. Many firms rely on marketing mix tests, and then proceed to a full market launch without test marketing.

During an advertisement campaign attempts can be made to measure the resulting changes in sales. However, as noted above with the exception of responses to mail order advertisements, such direct effects might not be easy to assess. *Post-testing* will therefore concentrate on the following measures of the communication effect of advertisements.

(a) *Recall tests* ask the interviewee to remember, unaided, advertisements which have been seen before the interview.

(b) *Recognition tests* involve giving the interviewee some reminder of an advertisement, and testing his/her recognition of it.

The recording and use of *electronic point of sales* (EPOS) data is still in its infancy with the exception of advanced retailing systems in companies such as Sainsbury's and Next. Information from smart tills will provide a real opportunity in the near future to directly measure the effect of, say, local radio advertising on the immediate sales of a brand in the media's catchment area. The use of such disaggregated tactical data will overcome the problems of external effects distorting aggregated sales figures.

EPOS will therefore enable major retailers, such as the supermarkets, to measure directly the performance of competitive brands. Hitherto, this information has had to be inferred from the use of consumer purchasing audits conducted by organisations like Audits of Great Britain (AGB).

Recording data about attitudes

When a survey collects data about customer attitudes, it is necessary to use some method of recording differing attitudes for analysis and evaluation. (*Note*: it has been suggested earlier that favourable consumer attitudes to a product do not necessarily cause the consumer to buy the product; nevertheless, the causal link possibly exists, and attitude surveys are fairly common in marketing research.)

Attitudes are measured by means of attitude scales, and there are three common types used in marketing research.

(a) *Thurstone scales*. A Thurstone scale contains 7, 9 or 11 statements which appear to cover a range of attitudes in equal intervals. Respondents are then asked to select the statement which most closely reflects their attitude.

Notes

(b) *Likert scales.* A respondent is asked to indicate his measure of agreement or disagreement with a series of statements put to him, such as 'strongly agree, agree, uncertain, 'disagree, strongly disagree'.

(c) *Semantic differential scales* are based on extreme objectives (strong-weak, good-bad, always-never) with perhaps intermediate attitudes as well (eg. extremely good, very good, fairly good, neither good nor bad, fairly bad, very bad, extremely bad).

Exercise 14

Cast your mind back to when you last completed a questionnaire. It is very likely that some or all of the questions invited you to respond in the way mentioned above. How appropriate do you think this format was in the light of the questionnaire's objectives?

Evaluating data

The evaluation of data collected in a survey will be carried out using statistical techniques. Some forms of analysis are:

(a) *multiple regression analysis:* this might be used, for example, to analyse the effect on sales of changes in a variety of other variables such as price and advertising;

(b) *discriminant analysis:* this might be used when the researcher wants to know what consumer traits (eg socio-economic groupings, lifestyle, age and sex) are associated with frequent, or infrequent purchase of a particular product or brand;

(c) *tests of statistical significance,* eg chi-squared tests and calculation of standard errors.

The reliability of sample data

The results of a sample are intended to indicate the attitudes or behaviour of a population as a whole. This is usually done by making statistical tests of significance. For example:

(a) A sample survey might show that 35% of people in Britain prefer coffee to tea. From the sample data, it might then be possible to predict with a certain degree of confidence (typically, a 95% level of confidence is used by researchers) that the percentage of the total population who prefer coffee to tea is, say, 35% plus or minus $1\frac{1}{3}$%.

(b) Suppose that young people are seen as a market segment with its own different characteristics. A subsequent sample might show that, say, 45% of young people in Britain prefer coffee to tea. In comparison with the results of the sample in (a), this would indicate that there is a significant statistical difference between the preferences of young people and the preferences of the community as a whole.

Sampling can be used to identify consumer attitudes and behaviour, but also to identify potential market segments. To be reliable, however, sample data must be random or quasi-random.

Notes

Example: statistical significance

A manufacturer of frozen foods decided to plan a national TV advertising campaign for a particular product and to assess the results in terms of sales achieved. A sample survey undertaken before the campaign over a period of four weeks revealed the following:

		Sales (units)	
Channel	*Product A*	*Product B*	*Total*
Multiple stores	160,250	71,300	231,550
Independent stores	40,500	18,160	58,660
Total	200,750	89,460	290,210

The advertising campaign (for Product B) lasted for four weeks, and, immediately thereafter, a further sample survey over a period of four weeks showed the following changes:

		Sales (units)	
Channel	*Product A*	*Product B*	*Total*
Multiple stores	176,275	89,125	265,400
Independent stores	42,525	20,430	62,955
Total	218,800	109,555	328,355

(a) What conclusion can be drawn from these results?

(b) What other information would you require before making any positive statements on the effect of the campaign?

Solution

Workings

Method 1

	Increase in sales of A		*Increase in sales of B*		*Increase in total sales*	
Channel	*Units*	%	*Units*	%	*Units*	%
Multiple stores	16,025	10	17,825	25	33,850	14.6
Independent stores	2,025	5	2,270	12.5	4,295	7.3
Total	18,050	9	20,095	22.5	38,145	13.1

Method 2

	Product A		*Product B*	
	Period 1	*Period 2*	*Period 1*	*Period 2*
% of total sales in multiple stores	69.2	66.4	30.8	33.6
% of total sales in independent stores	69.0	67.5	31.0	32.5
% of total sales	69.2	66.6	30.8	33.4

Discussion

Sales of both products increased between one period and the next, but sales of B increased by a greater percentage amount. B accounts for about 22% more of total sales in period 2 than in period 1. Without statistical analysis it is impossible to state whether there is any statistical significance in the difference between the periods.

Notes

A superficial assessment, even so, might lead us to predict that the difference is significant.

However, we have no evidence to link the greater increase in B sales with the advertising campaign.

Before we can make any positive statements about the connection between the higher growth in B sales and the advertising campaign, we need the following information.

(a) What was the aim of the campaign? The purpose of the campaign might have been to maintain B's existing share of the market, rather than to increase unit sales.

(b) Are there any seasonal factors or other factors which might explain the higher growth in B sales? The campaign was a national campaign: in practice, many firms select a control area such as a TV region in which to launch a campaign, and then to compare sales results in the region with the rest of the country. If sales are better in the TV region, the advertising campaign might then be judged successful, and extended to a national coverage.

(c) A market research team might carry out a post-testing exercise to measure consumer response to the campaign.

(d) Is the sample reliable and unbiased?

(e) Since we are dealing here with consumer products, the sample shows sales by stores to their customers. The manufacturer's customers are the stores. An advertising campaign would only be judged successful if higher consumer sales resulted in higher purchases of goods by stores from the manufacturer. No data is provided in the question about this.

(f) An advertising campaign's effects are likely to be greatest in the short term. However, the effect of the campaign should be measured over a period of longer than just four weeks.

(g) Are there any other elements in the marketing mix which might explain the higher sales of B? For example, the price of B might have been cut, or a sales promotion offer might have been made (such as money off next order coupons).

(h) Might the growth in sales of B have had an adverse effect on sales of A? For example, if B is frozen beans and A is frozen peas, higher sales of beans might result in lower sales of peas.

Marketing research in non-consumer products industries

There are particular aspects of marketing research that apply in industries other than those for consumer products.

(a) *Service industries.* Research on behalf of financial institutions such as banks or insurance companies requires data which may be considered personal and confidential. For example, it may be necessary to know details of the respondents' income. Given that respondents may be wary about the improper use of confidential information, great care and tact are required to conduct a survey.

(b) *Industrial marketing research.* The researcher must have some understanding of the industry or industries in order to design a research survey. In addition, it may be possible to carry out a census instead of a sample. It may be difficult to identify the person (or persons) in a customer firm who makes the buying decisions, therefore care must be taken to ensure that the researcher goes to the 'real' buyer.

(c) *Non-profit making organisations.* A considerable amount of market research is carried out on behalf of the national or local government. Social problems concerning the old, disabled, unemployed etc may call for information about their opinions and circumstances so that marketing research can help government officials to make policy decisions.

Exercise 15

In practice, marketing research by non profit making organisations is less common than in the commercial sector. What are the reasons for this?

The value of research information

Information is only worth having if the benefits derived from it exceed the costs of its collection. The greater the accuracy of information provided, the more it will cost. At high levels of accuracy the marginal costs of collection will probably exceed the marginal benefits of the extra accuracy obtained.

It is also worth noting that it is only worth paying for market research that provides additional information. Marketing research that merely confirms information that is already widely known has little real value.

Interpretation of results takes great care. There is some controversy as to how much interpretation market researchers should offer clients. One school of thought suggests presentation of the facts only, leaving the client to draw conclusions. A contrasting approach is for the researcher to interpret results and suggest conclusions or interpretations based on evidence in the findings. The guiding principle should be the brief given to the researcher at the outset of the project.

The use of marketing research consultants

Marketing research has been a growing source of organisation expenditure in recent years. Very few organisations believe that they can shoulder the cost of a large full-time staff of marketing research workers, especially a 'field force' of researchers spread around the country. It is quite probable, therefore, that the organisation will have a small full-time marketing research department, and will also use the services of external marketing research consultants for specific projects. In addition to market research agencies, there are market research departments in many of the large UK advertising agencies.

An external agency would bring *expertise* in marketing research which an organisation might not be able to supply in-house, although it would need to liaise with the organisation through its marketing research department.

Notes

A further advantage of marketing research agencies is that they may bring together their general knowledge of a particular market and supply this information to all clients or subscribers. An examples of such information provision is the Television Consumer Audit.

Overseas research

A UK company is able to obtain considerable help and advice in its attempts to research foreign markets. Informal contacts may be made with a variety of organisations including the following.

(a) Overseas agents and distributors
(b) Banks
(c) Trade and professional organisations
(d) Chambers of Commerce
(e) Department of Trade and Industry
(f) UK and foreign embassies and consulates
(g) Academic institutions.

In carrying out desk research 'in-house' there are a number of sources that may be consulted. The appropriate source is generally only found by experience and the initial exercise may be time consuming until the appropriate sources are located. Most publicly available sources can be found in the following places.

(a) Public reference libraries
(b) Business school libraries
(c) Major Chambers of Commerce
(d) Overseas Trade Services (OTS) offered by the DTI and the Foreign Office.

The most commonly consulted sources are listed below.

(a) The Bank of England and the major UK banks' booklets on trade prospects for various countries.

(b) The major 'serious' newspapers produce periodic surveys on various countries.

(c) The Economist Intelligence Unit produces reports on various industries, countries and long-term developments.

(d) Most major trade associations and Chambers of Commerce hold data on trade fairs, visits and market intelligence for various countries.

(e) There are numerous trade directories for overseas markets including Kompass, Dun and Bradstreet, Kluwer and Crone.

(f) The EC and OECD produce numerous reports on trade statistics and prospects for member countries.

(g) The Department of Trade and Industry and the British Overseas Trade Board provide many publications, statistical summaries and intelligence reports. Special mention should be made here of the Statistical and Market Intelligence Library, the Product Data Store, the Market Prospects Service, and the Export Intelligence Service (all OTS).

(h) The CBI produces a monthly report on foreign markets.

(i) Many Anglo-foreign Chambers of Commerce and major Chambers of Commerce based on foreign countries provide regular market reports.

(j) The Central Statistical Office produces regular data on international trade.

(k) Many reference libraries subscribe to syndicated market research and abstract services including ANBAR, Keynote, Mintel, Extel, and Euromonitor.

Among the more commonly available and used data sources are the following.

(a) Guide to official statistics
(b) Monthly digest of statistics
(c) Overseas trade statistics

Various international bodies including the United Nations, the European Community, the European Coal and Steel Community, the Organisation for Economic Co-operation and Development and the International Monetary Fund produce publications such as the following.

(a) International finance statistics.
(b) International labour reviews.
(c) International travel statistics.
(d) United Nations yearbook of national account statistics.
(e) United Nations yearbook of international trade statistics.
(f) United Nations demographic yearbook.
(g) United Nations directory of international trade.
(h) United Nations national statistic yearbook.

The small company entering a foreign market for the first time

According to surveys carried out as recently as 1991, most small firms do not carry out any market research, including foreign research, at all.

Exercise 16

What do you think are the reasons for this?

Whilst this is acceptable initially, the lack of market knowledge, and reliance on the expertise of an intermediary, will limit the ability of the company to expand in the longer term. For this reason most countries, including the United Kingdom, have sources of low cost advice and assistance targeted at the small business to encourage the company to develop and expand international trading operations.

The medium sized company wishing to extend its export business

A company in this situation will be faced with problems of finding new markets, representation, and distribution. Unlike the initial market entry where the company was mostly reactive and responding (probably) to enquiries, the company has to be proactive. Options include:

Notes

(a) using existing channels of distribution to obtain intelligence. Cooperation may or may not be forthcoming, depending on the benefit to the channel member;

(b) use the assistance and advice services outlined earlier; and

(c) should the potential business be sufficiently large, engage an international marketing research agency.

The larger company with overseas presence wishing to increase its foreign market operations

Larger companies in international marketing terms. They:

(a) tend to be exporting on a regular basis;
(b) gain between 10% to 30% turnover from export operations;
(c) have some 'in house' expertise, usually in the form of an export department.

Most forms of general marketing research for international markets will be within the capability of the company and its own experts; thus collation and analysis of information from published sources and channel members will be done 'in house'. Where the research involves technically difficult techniques (such as a survey in a foreign country) the company will contract out such requirements to an agency.

Major multinationals introducing new products

The multinational corporation generally tries to introduce products that have a global appeal. Generally such products will be either made under contract, licensed, or made by a subsidiary. In many cases the production units will be in or near the markets they serve. This local presence means that the multinational can call upon the expert resources of its own employees in that market. All the international market research activities are usually conducted 'in house'.

3 Databases

In simple terms, a database is a large file or files of data, with the file structured in such a way that the data can be processed by different users in a large number of different ways. A database is, by implication, a computer file, and the collection of programs that are written to process data on the file in the many different ways is referred to as a database management system (DBMS). These systems provide managers with support for their decision making. Marketing data can be analysed using statistical techniques, in models on anything from media mix to new site locations. The manager is presented with marketing evaluations to help in the task of decision making.

A database can provide an organisation with a 'mine of information' about its customers. Databases can reveal correlation relationships between different types of customer, which allows companies to identify market segments and to target them effectively.

Every purchase made by a customer provides two benefits to the seller: an increase in the sales revenue and an increase in information about future market opportunities.

Examples are given below (reported in the *Financial Times* 4 July 1991).

(a) *Littlewoods* keeps a database record of every transaction a customer makes, and applies statistical techniques to predict customers' buying habits. This has revealed that 'people who have bought black ash furniture, it seems, are 20 times more likely to respond to a fashion promotion than those who have not'.

(b) GE-Capital's database collects;

(i) demographic information from credit card applications;
(ii) shopping records;
(iii) payment data;

so that former customers can be 'targeted' with appropriate material.

(c) Eagle Star sells motor insurance policies. It uses a database to build up information on each customer, including the customer's age, sex and post code. The post code is used as a guide to socio-economic data. Each customer has a reference number, independent of the policy number, so that the database is a *database of customers* not just a file of policy details. (This is similar to the *customer information system* being introduced by high street banks). The database is used to help design products and analyse why launches failed.

Internal and external databases

Data can be generated in two ways.

(a) It can be built up by the business itself in its own internal database system.
(b) It can be obtained from an external database that is operated by another organisation.

Exercise 17

What kind of information might a motor vehicle components supplier be interested in having on a database?

Much environmental data is likely to be secondary data, in other words data not collected for the specific purposes of a particular data user. We have already seen some of the limitations of secondary data earlier in this chapter.

In particular, secondary data can never be as relevant and focused as primary data and for this reason internally generated databases have an edge in terms of information value (though this has to be weighted against the relative cheapness of secondary data).

Public databases

It is now possible to access large volumes of generally available information through databases held by public bodies. A variety of such services are available.

(a) Some newspapers offer computerised access to old editions, with search facilities looking for information on particular companies or issues. FTPROFILE, for example, provides on-line business information.

Notes

(b) A variety of public databases are also available for inspection. An example of an on-line legal database is JUSTIS. Another public database is *Spearhead*. This is run by the DTI and is an on-line database of information relating to the Single European Market.

Chapter roundup

(a) We began by looking at definitions which bring out the essential features of marketing research. Note in particular that the term describes a broad area of activity, embracing market research, product research, price research, sales promotion research and distribution research.

(b) The raw data for a marketing research project can come from either primary or secondary sources. Primary data has the advantage of relating directly to the problems under scrutiny, but it is often expensive to assemble. Secondary data is available cheaply from numerous sources but must be treated with caution when used for a purpose other than that for which it was collected.

(c) We looked at a number of ways of collecting data and examined the techniques - and the pitfalls - of sampling.

(d) We also examined ways of evaluating the data collected and assessing its statistical significance.

(e) Many sources of secondary data are now available in computerised form.

Quick quiz

1 Give a definition of marketing research.

2 List three activities falling into the category of product research, and two in the category of distribution research.

3 What is a market forecast?

4 What is meant by the term 'concentration ratio'?

5 What is meant by the term 'desk research'?

6 List six techniques of field research.

7 Describe (a) stratified sampling and (b) cluster sampling.

8 Describe the workings of a consumer panel.

9 Explain what is meant by the 'simulated store technique'.

10 Name three common types of attitude scale.

11 List six sources of marketing data that might accessed by a UK firm entering an overseasmarket.

12 What is a database?

Solutions to exercises

1 Most of this chapter is a solution to this exercise. In particular, it will be emphasised that marketing research is *not* the same as market research.

2 The possibilities are endless, but you might have thought of research and development personnel; marketing and sales personnel; competitors; customers; ideas springing from new scientific or technological discoveries.

3 Again, there are many possibilities. You might have thought of the vast expansion in the range of uses for man-made materials such as plastics or nylon. Or you might cite the proliferation of computer hardware: where twenty years ago computer usage was confined to the mainframe installations in large companies, nowadays even very small organisations have a PC or two to streamline their operations.

4 An extra £5,000 of selling spend generates £10,000 of extra sales, but only £4,000 of extra contribution. Other things being equal, it is preferable to take the first option: contribution of £40,000 from selling spend of £10,000.

5 It would indicate that each firm in the industry had an equal market share.

Notes

6 Amongst many other ideas you might have listed:

- production data about quantities produced, materials and labour resources used etc.
- data about stock levels (inventory)
- data about sales (analysed by geographical area, by salesman, by distribution outlet
  etc
- data about sales promotions

7 It is common to see researchers logging details of traffic passing along a particular road at certain times of the day. This enables local authorities to improve services (by introducing traffic lights, constructing roundabouts or whatever). Users of public transport will often see researchers counting the number of passengers passing through, say, a railway station at a particular time, again with a view to assessing and possibly improving service levels.

8 Potential users might conceivably include individuals daunted by their own tax returns, but a sampling frame for all such individuals would be almost impossible to obtain. It would be better to reflect that most people with complicated tax affairs use the services of an accountant. Targeting firms of accountants is much easier: they are all registered with a professional body, and the membership lists of these bodies provide a convenient sampling frame.

9 You need to ensure that there is no regular pattern to the population which, if it coincided with the sampling interval, might lead to a biased sample. In practice, this problem is often overcome by choosing multiple starting points and using varying sampling intervals whose size is selected at random.

10 A stratified sample should be obtained. If the effect of using window space for advertising is the object of the research, the sample should relate to the total window size of the population.

Workings

Type	*No. of stores*	*Average window size*	*Total window size*	*% of total*
		m^2	m^2	
A	150	8	1,200	30
B	80	15	1,200	30
C	50	20	1,000	25
D	20	30	600	15
			4,000	100

The sample should consist of 30% of store type A, 30% of B, 25% C and 15% D. Since the total sample will be 20% of the number of stores (ie 20% of 300 = 60 stores) then the sample should consist of 18 stores of type A, 18 of type B, 15 of C and 9 of D.

Notes

Workings

Type	*Total number*	*Number in sample*	*% of total in sample*	*% of window size*
A	150	18	6	30
B	80	18	6	30
C	50	15	5	25
D	20	9	3	15
	300	60	20	100

The stores in the sample should be randomly selected - eg the stores of type A should be randomly selected from the total of 150 type A stores.

11 (a) Write to a named individual.
(b) Ensure details such as job titles are up to date.
(c) Send a covering letter, emphasising confidentiality and anonymity.
(d) Include a stamped addressed envelope for the reply.

12 Such data can be valuable for many reasons.

(a) Problems in retail sales provide an early warning of coming problems in factory gate sales.

(b) Retail audits indicate long-term trends in the market place, so assisting in strategic marketing planning.

(c) In the shorter term, they may indicate a need for changes in pricing policy, sales promotion, distribution policy etc.

13 Women reacted very unfavourably to the advertisement which was shown in its pre-production animatic form (drawings with soundtrack). They expressed uncomfortable feelings and anxiety at the thought of a baby being locked up in a garage. Wisely the advertisement was reformulated to a high technology theme.

15 The possible disadvantage of marketing research for smaller non-profit making bodies such as universities or charities is the cost of conducting a research project. There might be a temptation for an organisation to use its own inexperienced staff to do research, with the result that findings might be incomplete, or biased and misleading.

16 (a) Small firms generally use indirect means of exporting, and hence tend to rely on the channel intermediary for market intelligence.

(b) They often lack the available resources.

(c) The amount of foreign business does not warrant significant expenditure on market research.

17 (a) PRS, the consultancy group, has built up a database which can provide a detailed breakdown of the constituent parts of motor vehicles produced worldwide, making it possible for component suppliers to identify trends in their market.

Notes

(b) Another PRS database holds data about new car registrations in Europe for at least the last ten years. This should be of interest to component suppliers who supply replacement parts to the 'aftermarket'.

(c) A database available from James McArdle and Associates, another consultancy firm, provides data about commercial vehicle production.

'It is possible, as just one example, to ask the database to show, over a five-year rolling period, manufacturers and their country of origin of commercial vehicles defined by the number of axles, vehicle weight, torque or power output, or cubic capacity - or a combination of these.' (*Financial Times)*

Such databases could be used by component suppliers to take much of the guesswork or number-crunching out of their planning, and to assess the likely future demand both for replacement parts and for original equipment.

4 MARKET SEGMENTATION

> *Your objectives*
>
> After completing this chapter you should:
>
> (a) understand the meaning of, and the reasons for, market segmentation;
> (b) be aware of some of the different bases on which markets may be segmented;
> (c) understand how segmentation is used to identify target markets.

1 Requirements for effective market segmentation

It is obvious that not all of an organisation's customers are the same. Market segmentation is an attempt to take different customer characteristics into account. It is thus the subdivision of a market into subsets of customers. Within each subset, customers have similar needs which differ in some definable way from those in other subsets.

The major reason for segmenting markets is that, by using different marketing approaches to each segment, it should be possible to increase profit contribution when compared with using an undifferentiated marketing approach for the whole market. The marketing approach used for each segment should reflect the particular needs of customers and potential customers in that segment. It is akin to using a rifle (to aim at specific targets) rather than a shotgun (to aim at all targets at the same time).

Exercise 1

Think back to three or four items that you have purchased recently - anything from a takeaway pizza to a compact disc to a ticket for a sporting event. Now put yourself in the position of the person you purchased from. What criteria might he use to segment his market and in which segment do you yourself belong?

Clearly there are many possible characteristics of buyers which could be used as a basis for segmenting markets and there are criteria to be used to identify the most effective characteristics for use in market segmentation decisions.

(a) *Measurability*
The degree to which information exists or is obtainable cost effectively in respect of the particular buyer characteristic. Whilst a bookshop may be able to obtain information on sales relatively easily, it is more difficult for shops to obtain information about the personality traits of buyers.

Notes

(b) *Accessibility*
The degree to which the organisation can focus effectively on the chosen segments using marketing methods. Thus whilst educational establishments in a bookshop's catchment area can be identified easily and approached using direct mail or telemarketing, individuals with income over £30,000 per annum in the catchment area might be more difficult to isolate effectively.

(c) *Substantiality*
The degree to which the segments are large enough to be worth considering for separate marketing cultivation. Devising different marketing approaches is expensive, and so a minimum size of segment can be set and measured, perhaps by potential profitability. Thus, whilst a large number of people in social group DE aged over 65 could be identified, their potential profitability to a bookshop is likely to be less in the long term than a smaller number of 17-18 year old students. This latter group might be worth cultivating using a specially devised marketing approach whereas the former might not be.

Benefits of market segmentation

Besides the overall aim of improved contribution to profits, a number of other benefits may result from successful market segmentation.

(a) The organisation will be in a better position to spot new marketing opportunities. This benefit should flow from a better understanding of customer needs in each segment.

(b) Specialists can be used for each of the organisation's major segments. Thus, small business counsellors can be employed by banks to deal effectively with this market segment, and a computer consultancy can have specialist sales staff for, say, shops, manufacturers, service industries and local authorities.

(c) The total marketing budget can be allocated to take into account the needs of each segment and the likely return from each segment.

(d) The organisation can make fine adjustments to the product and service offerings and to the marketing appeals used for each segment.

(e) The organisation can try to dominate particular segments, thus gaining competitive advantage.

(f) The product range can more closely reflect differences in customer needs.

2 Bases for market segmentation

A number of different bases for segmenting a market will now be considered which could be (either alone or in combination) suitable for use by many organisations.

Geographic segmentation
Here, the basis for segmentation is location. Consider the example of a national chain of supermarkets: geographic segmentation interacts closely with the chain's outlet strategy. Each branch or group of retail outlets could be given mutually exclusive areas to service and so the method enables the supermarket chain to make more effective use of target marketing. The obvious advantage to customers is convenience of access, which is a

Notes

primary motivation to retailers when considering ways of segmenting the grocery shopping market. Of course this customer benefit needs to be considered against the cost of provision of retail branches, but research has shown that one of the major reasons why customers choose particular stores in which to shop is convenience of access.

Demographic segmentation

Here the market is divided on the basis of age, gender, socio-economic group, housing, family characteristics or family life cycle stage, or by some combination of these factors.

A good example of *age segmentation* in target marketing is the attempt by the High Street banks to attract 18 year olds as customers, especially new students in the higher education sector. Working on the premise that customers are unlikely to switch accounts between competing suppliers, banks expect long-term relationships (and profit) to result from success in this target marketing effort. It is a highly competitive market segment.

Many products are targeted by *gender*. Cosmetics, clothing, alcohol, cars and even financial services are all products in which the market can be perceived to be segmented by gender.

Exercise 2

Think of examples you have noticed of holiday firms segmenting their market so as to appeal to different age-groups and interest-groups.

The UK market research industry uses standardised social groupings which are based entirely on occupation.

Socio-economic groups in the UK

Social grade	*Description of occupations*	*Example*
A	Higher managerial and professional	Company director
B	Lower managerial and supervisory	Middle manager
C1	Non-manual	Bank clerk
C2	Skilled manual	Electrician
D	Semi-skilled and unskilled manual	Labourer
E	Those receiving no income from employment/casual	Unemployed workers

This classification is very commonly used in marketing and market research in the UK, yet it is simplistic. For example, in terms of disposable income (the take-home pay of workers) C2 members often have more money than do C1, which obviously affects buying capability. Also there is class mobility in that individuals and their families can move between groups, although their underlying influences may remain as they were or change only slowly.

However, socio-economic groups are a useful and usable way of segmenting markets for the following reasons.

(a) They provide a generally reliable picture of the relationship between occupation and income.

Notes

(b) They indicate differences in purchase and consumption patterns even where the total disposable income between two groups may be similar.

(c) The categories are stable and enduring.

(d) Each group carries identifiable attitude patterns. For instance, ABCI groups tend to be more 'future orientated' than do C2DE groups which are more 'present orientated'. Such attitudes are clearly highly significant for the marketing of endowment policies or private education, for example.

Exercise 3

As stated earlier, the socio-economic classification is, like all generalisations, simplistic. How would you assess your own socio-economic grouping (or that of your parents)? Do you conform to the generalisations suggested above?

Because of criticisms of the A-E classification, more sophisticated measures of socio-economic and group membership have been devised. Housing type and ownership are particularly important methods of segmentation for many types of good. The use of this method is made much easier by the major categorisation scheme for all housing types in the UK, known as ACORN (A Categorisation Of Residential Neighbourhoods), which enables precise target marketing based on housing type to be conducted by suppliers.

This system introduces house type into the classification and every UK household has been classified in ACORN groups. Other work has cross-referenced ACORN with postcodes for every address in the UK making specific identification of customer types more flexible.

1985 ACORN profile of Great Britain

ACORN Groups		*1985 Population*	%
A	Agricultural areas	1,837,585	3.4
B	Modern family housing, Higher incomes	9,056,851	16.8
C	Older housing of intermediate status	9,519,639	17.7
D	Older terraced housing	2,309,097	4.3
E	Council estates - category I	7,015,875	13.0
F	Council estates - category II	4,892,746	9.1
G	Council estates - category III	3,935,124	7.3
H	Mixed inner metropolitan areas	2,088,892	3.9
I	High status non-family areas	2,265,371	4.2
J	Affluent suburban housing	8,531,179	15.9
K	Better-off retirement areas	2,048,658	3.8

Notes

ACORN Types		1985 Population	%
A1	Agricultural villages	1,404,704	2.6
A2	Areas of farms and smallholdings	432,881	0.8
B3	Post-war functional private housing	2,276,963	4.2
B4	Modern private housing, young families	1,805,955	3.4
B5	Established private family housing	3,173,195	5.9
B6	New detached houses, young families	1,475,680	2.7
B7	Military bases	325,058	0.6
C8	Mixed owner-occupied and council estates	1,877,008	3.5
C9	Small town centres and flats above shops	2,185,911	4.1
C10	Villages with non-farm employment	2,523,830	4.7
C11	Older private housing, skilled workers	2,932,890	5.5
D12	Unmodernised terraces, older people	1,349,349	2.5
D13	Older terraces, lower income families	752,530	1.4
D14	Tenement flats lacking amenities	207,218	0.4
E15	Council estates, well-off older workers	1,879,887	3.5
E16	Recent council estates	1,460,237	2.7
E17	Better council estates, younger workers	2,642,427	4.9
E18	Small council houses, often Scottish	1,033,324	1.9
F19	Low rise estates in industrial towns	2,498,587	4.6
F20	Inter-war council estates, older people	1,607,711	3.0
F21	Council housing, elderly people	786,448	1.5
G22	New council estates in inner cities	1,075,117	2.0
G23	Overspill estates, higher unemployment	1,678,631	3.1
G24	Council estate with some overcrowding	839,998	1.6
G25	Council estates with greatest hardship	341,378	0.6
H26	Multi-occupied older housing	204,279	0.4
H27	Cosmopolitan owner-occupied terraces	577,592	1.1
H28	Multi-let housing in cosmoplitan areas	388,292	0.7
H29	Better -off cosmopolitan areas	918,729	1.7
I30	High status non-family areas	1,132,770	2.1

Notes

I31	Multi-let big old houses and flats	833,500	1.5
I32	Furnished flats, mostly single people	299,101	0.6
J33	Inter-war semis, white collar workers	3,056,752	5.7
J34	Spacious inter-war semis, big gardens	2,671,266	5.0
J35	Villages with wealthy older commuters	1,560,179	2.9
J36	Detached houses, exclusive suburbs	1,242,982	2.3
K37	Private houses, well-off older residents	1,204,778	2.2
K38	Private flats, older single people	843,880	1.6
U39	Unclassified	294,080	0.5
Area Total		**53,795,097**	**100.0**

Another method of segmentation is based on the family type: the size and constitution of the family unit. There have been changes in the characteristics of the family unit in the last few decades; this is shown in the table below.

Households by type

	1961		*1971*		*1981*	
	Million	*% of total*	*Million*	*% of total*	*Million*	*% of total*
One person, under retirement age	0.7	4	1.1	6	1.5	8
One person, over retirement age	1.2	7	2.2	12	2.8	14
Two or more persons (non-family)	0.8	5	0.7	4	0.9	5
Married couple alone	4.1	26	4.9	27	5.0	26
Married couple + dependent child(ren)	6.1	38	6.3	34	6.0	31
Married couple + independent child(ren)	1.7	10	1.6	8	1.6	8
Lone parent + dependent child(ren)	0.4	2	0.5	3	0.9	5
Lone parent + independent child(ren)	0.7	4	0.7	4	0.7	4
Two or more families	0.4	3	0.3	1	0.2	1
Total	16.2		18.3		19.5	

Percentages may not add up due to rounding. *Source: Social Trends 15.*

Notes

Exercise 4

'Married couple with dependent child(ren))' is still the most common household type in the above figures, but it only accounts for 31% of total households (compared with 38% 20 years earlier). Try to think of some of the social trends accounting for this change.

An increase in the divorce rate is one of the factors which has led to an increase in single parent families and a decline in the 'traditional' family of working husband, housewife and dependent children. The increase in unemployment in the early 1980s was weighted towards males in traditional industries and the subsequent increase in employment in the late 1980s was weighted towards females in service-orientated industries, often involving part-time rather than full-time work. Thus one would now expect to find more households in which the sole or main breadwinner is female rather than male.

These household structural changes have been accompanied by other important social trends:

(a) later marriage and delayed childbearing;

(b) house price rises have meant that newly formed households contain partners who both work;

(c) the 'enterprise economy' has encouraged a greater interest in career development;

(d) greater financial independence for women caused by recent economic and social changes;

(e) products aimed at the increased number of 'single person of pensionable age' households are also likely to increase.

The implication for marketing is that new niche markets are likely to grow whilst traditional markets may be declining. The use of customer databases to direct more specific target marketing may be one solution, as may product proliferation.

The *family life cycle (FLC)* is a summary demographic variable; that is, it combines the effects of age, marital status, career status (income) and the presence or absence of children. Herein lies its appeal, for it is able to identify the various stages through which households progress. The table below shows features of the family at various stages of its life cycle. It is clear that particular products and services can be target-marketed at specific stages in the life cycle of families.

Notes

The family life cycle

I	II	III	IV	V	VI	VII	VIII	IX
Bachelor Stage: young single people not living at home	Newly married couples; young, no children	Full nest I: youngest child under six	Full nest II: youngest child six or over	Full nest III: older married couples with dependent children	Empty nest I: older married couples, no children living with them, head of family still in labour force	Empty nest II: older married couples, no children living at home, head of family retired	Solitary survivor in labour force	Solitary survivor(s) retired
Few financial burdens. Fashion/ opinion leader led. Recreation orientated. Buy: Basic kitchen equipment, basic furniture, cars, equip- ment for the mating game holidays. Experiment with patterns of personal financial management and control.	Better off financially than they will be in the near future. High levels of purchase of homes and consumer durable goods. Buy: Cars, fridges, cookers, life assurance, durable furniture, holidays. Establish patterns of personal financial management and control.	Home purchasing at peak. Liquid assets/savings low. Dissatisfied with financial position and amount of money saved. Reliance on credit finance, credit cards, overdrafts etc. Child dominated household. Buy necessities: washers, dryers, baby food and clothes, vitamins, toys, books etc.	Financial position better. Some wives return to work. Child dominated household. Buy necessities: foods, cleaning material, clothes, bicycles, sports gear, music lessons, pianos, holidays etc.	Financial position still better. More wives work. School and examination dominated household. Some children get first jobs; others in further/higher education. Expenditure to support children's further/higher education. Buy: New, more tasteful furniture, non-necessary appliances, boats etc: holidays.	Home ownership at peak. More satisfied with financial position and money saved. Interested in travel, recreation, self-education. Make financial gifts and contributions. Children gain qualifications; move to Stage I. Buy luxuries, home improvements eg. fitted kitchens etc.	Significant cut in income. Keep home. Buy: medical appliances or medical care, products which aid health, sleep and digestion. Assist children. Concern with level of savings and pension. Some expend- iture on hobbies and pastimes.	Income still adequate but likely to sell family home and purchase smaller accom- modation. Concern with level of savings and pension. Some expend- iture on hobbies and pastimes. Worries about security and dependence.	Significant cut in income. Additional medical requirements. Special need for attention, affection and security. May seek sheltered accommodation. Possible dependence on others for personal financial management and control.

Exercise 5

Think of a few families with which you are familiar (including your own). Where does each of them fit in the family life cycle? Do their general attitudes and consumption patterns correspond with the predictions of the model?

Demographic segmentation methods are powerful tools to specify target market segments. This conclusion is particularly true when each of the bases is used in combination with other methods, since it is clear that the bases for demographic segmentation are not independent but are interdependent. Age and family life cycle stage are linked, as are housing and socio-economic groups. By using bases in combination it is possible to be highly specific in selecting targets for marketing campaigns.

Psychographic segmentation

Psychographics or *lifestyle segmentation* is a method which seeks to classify people according to their values, opinions, personality characteristics and interests; by its inherent nature it should be very dynamic. In today's competitive world, where innovation is the key to improved organisational performance, a system which is able to introduce new perspectives is worthy of investigation. Lifestyle segmentation fits this criterion because it deals with the person as opposed to the product and attempts to discover the particular unique lifestyle patterns of customers, which will give a richer insight into their preferences for various products and services. Lifestyle refers to 'distinctive ways of living adopted by particular communities or subsections of society.' Lifestyle is a manifestation of a number of behavioural factors, such as motivation, personality and culture. Its use in marketing depends on accurate description, and the numbers of people following a particular lifestyle must be quantified. Then marketers can assign and target products and promotion at particular target lifestyle groups. Lifestyle is a controversial issue, and a full analysis of the arguments is beyond the scope of this text. Its implications for marketing, and the problems of definition involved, can perhaps best be illustrated by some examples.

One simple example generalises lifestyle in terms of four categories, as follows.

(a) *Upwardly mobile, ambitious:* seeking a better and more affluent lifestyle, principally through better paid and more interesting work, and a higher material standard of living. A customer with such a lifestyle will be prepared to try new products.

(b) *Traditional and sociable:* compliance and conformity to group norms bring social approval and reassurance to the individual. Purchasing patterns will therefore be 'conformist'.

(c) *Security and status seeking:* stressing 'safety' and 'ego-defensive' needs. This lifestyle links status, income and security. It encourages the purchase of strong and well known products and brands, and emphasises those products and services which confer status and make life as secure and predictable as possible. These would include insurance, membership of the AA or RAC etc. Products that are well established and familiar inspire more confidence than new products, which will be resisted.

Notes

(d) *Hedonistic preference:* placing emphasis on 'enjoying life now' and the immediate satisfaction of wants and needs. Little thought is given to the future.

Two more complex lifestyle analyses are shown in the table below. These sets of analysis are based on empirical attitude research, and the agencies that have constructed them use them to advise their clients on how best to design and position existing and new products at target segments made up of people who have similar lifestyle patterns.

Life-style categories

McCann-Erikson Men	McCann-Erikson Women	Taylor Nelson
Avant Guardians. Concerned with change and well-being of others, rather than possessions. Well educated, prone to self righteousness.	*Avant Guardians*. 'Liberal left' opinions, trendy attitudes. But outgoing, active, sociable.	*Self-explorers*. Motivated by self-expression and self-realisation. Less materialistic than other groups, and showing high tolerance levels.
Pontificators. Strongly held, traditional opinions. Very British, and concerned about keeping others on the right path.	*Lady Righteous*. Traditional, 'right-minded' opinions. Happy, complacent, with strong family orientation.	*Social resisters*. The caring group, concerned with fairness and social values, but often appearing intolerant and moralistic.
Chameleons.Want to be contemporary to win approval. Act like barometers of social change, but copiers not leaders.	*Hopeful seekers*. Need to be liked, want to do 'right'. Like new things, want to be trendy.	*Experimentalists*.Highly individualistic, motivated by fast-moving enjoyment. They are materialistic, pro-technology but anti-traditional authority.
Self-admirers. At the young end of the spectrum. Intolerant of others and strongly motivated by success. Concerned about self-image.	*Lively ladies*. Younger than above, sensual, materialistic, ambitious and competitive.	*Conspicuous consumers*. They are materialistic and pushy, motivated by acquisition, competition, and getting ahead. Pro-authority, law and order.
Self-exploiters. The 'doers' and 'self-starters', competitive but always under pressure and often pessimistic. Possessions are important.	*New unromantics*. Generally young and single, adopting a hard-headed and unsentimental approach to life. Independent, self-centred.	*Belongers*. What they seek is a quiet, undisturbed family life. They are conservative, conventional rule followers.
Token triers. Always willing to try new things to 'improve their luck', but apparently on a permanent try-and-fail cycle. Includes an above average proportion of unemployed.	*Lack-a-daisy*. Unassertive and easy-going. Try to cope but often fail. Not very interested in the new.	*Survivors*. Strongly class-conscious, and community spirited, their motivation is to 'get by'.
Sleepwalkers. Contented underachievers. Do not care about most things, and actively opt out. Traditional macho views.	*Blinkered*. Negative, do not want to be disturbed. Uninterested in conventional success - in fact, few interests except TV and radio.	*Aimless*. Comprises two groups, (a) the young unemployed, who are often anti-authority, and (b) the old, whose motivation is day-to-day existence.
Passive endurers. Biased towards the elderly, they are often economically and socially disfranchised. Expect little of life, and give little.	*Down-trodden*. This group is shy, introverted, but put upon. Would like to do better. Often unhappy and pressurised in personal relationships.	

Notes

Exercise 6

Try to think of examples of each of these categories amongst your own friends, acquaintances and family. If you find this easy, you must have a very wide circle of acquaintances! It is more likely that most of your close friends, at least, fall into a fairly limited number of the classifications.

It is possible to gain further insights into lifestyle behaviour by cross-referring demographic variables to observed behaviour which indicates lifestyle types. The table below gives one example relating to leisure, social and travel facilities.

Profiles by sex, age and social grade, of users of various leisure, social and travel facilities.

	all adults	*travel by air (in past 3 years)*	*use London underground*	*visit cinemas*	*visit pubs*	*visit licensed clubs*	*visit rest-aurants (day)*	*visit rest-aurants (evenings)*	*used Yellow Pages in last 4 weeks*	*listen to Radio Luxembourg*
Population (in 000's)	44,150 %	15,333 %	13,397 %	15,749 %	30,300 %	16,411 %	17,590 %	22,881 %	16,990 %	4,417 %
All adults	100.0	100.0	100.0	100.0	100.0	100.0	100.0	100.0	100.0	100.0
Men	47.9	49.1	52.9	50.2	52.6	54.1	43.3	49.6	51.7	53.6
Women	52.1	50.9	47.1	49.8	47.4	45.9	56.7	50.4	48.3	46.4
15–24	20.0	20.8	22.2	35.6	24.5	28.7	16.0	22.2	21.0	42.7
25–34	17.0	19.1	18.6	23.6	21.6	19.4	15.8	22.4	21.6	20.8
35–44	16.3	16.5	18.6	19.2	19.0	17.0	17.9	20.2	19.6	12.9
45–54	13.8	15.2	15.2	10.9	13.7	13.0	15.0	15.7	14.3	8.2
55–64	14.5	14.9	13.3	7.0	11.4	11.8	15.5	11.5	12.1	6.7
65 or over	18.4	13.5	12.1	3.8	9.8	10.0	19.7	8.0	11.4	8.7
AB	16.7	26.5	28.9	23.9	18.3	13.1	24.1	23.6	23.1	10.9
C1	22.1	27.6	27.9	26.3	24.6	23.0	26.8	26.6	24.9	20.8
C2	28.8	26.7	24.8	28.4	30.1	33.1	25.5	29.6	29.0	33.7
D	18.1	12.3	11.4	14.2	17.1	19.6	13.4	13.6	14.4	20.1
E	14.3	7.0	7.1	7.3	10.0	11.2	10.2	6.6	8.5	14.4

Geo-demographic segmentation

Geo-demographics is a segmentation technique which was introduced in the early 1980s, but came into its own in the late 1980s and early 1990s. Basically, it is an approach which classifies people by where they live. It is rooted in the belief that households within a particular neighbourhood exhibit similar purchasing behaviour, outlook and so on: 'birds of a feather flock together'.

The central themes of geo-demographics were outlined by one leading market research expert as:

> '... that two people who live in the same neighbourhood, such as a Census Enumeration District, are more likely to have similar characteristics than are two people chosen at random. The second is that neighbourhoods can be categorised in terms of the characteristics of the population which they contain, and that two neighbourhoods can be placed in the same category, that is they can contain similar types of people, even though they are widely separated'.

Notes

Geo-demographics is thus able to target customers in particular areas who exhibit similar behaviour patterns. The implication for organisations is very significant, as this system allows them to profile the users or potential users of a product or service and then proceed to target customers who match these profiles. This of course should increase the profitability and take-up of the offered product/service.

Customer database

It should be clear from the above discussion of segmentation methods that for large scale usage of the more sophisticated methods to be effective, computerised systems have to be adopted. These systems can often be used by organisations which actually hold detailed data on customers, such as banks, building societies and insurance companies. The systems are based on the array of data held about each customer in a relational database. In other words, a sub-sample of customers could be formed by the use of any one specifying variable (or combination of variables). Thus all customers aged 18-24 could be identified, for the development of long-term relations, as discussed above, as could all customers aged 25-34 with incomes over £20,000 pa and who live in ACORN type B6 housing.

Such customer database systems allow highly specific target marketing. The most obvious marketing use is by direct mail methods, the particular advantage of which is the capability for exact monitoring of results using the computer system. The costs of each mailshot can be related to the increase in business which results and the types of customers who do buy can be used to refine the target marketing further.

Exercise 7

C2 met C1 and fell in love. They moved to FLC II and lived in a C11. He was a belonger and she was lady righteous; it would not be long before they reached FLCI.

What are we talking about?

---

3 Target markets

Because of limited resources, competition and large markets, organisations are not usually able to sell with equal efficiency and success to the entire market: that is, to every market segment. It is therefore necessary for the sake of efficiency to select target markets. The marketing management of a company may choose one of the following policy options.

(a) *Undifferentiated marketing:* this policy is to produce a single product and hope to get as many customers as possible to buy it; that is, ignore segmentation entirely.

(b) *Concentrated marketing:* the company attempts to produce the ideal product for a *single* segment of the market (eg Rolls Royce cars, Mothercare mother and baby shops).

(c) *Differentiated marketing:* the company attempts to introduce several product versions, each aimed at a different market segment (for example, the manufacture of several different brands of washing powder).

The major disadvantage of *concentrated marketing* is the business risk of relying on a single segment of a single market; for example, the de Lorean sports car firm ran into irreversible financial difficulties in 1981-82 when the sports car market contracted in the USA. On the other hand, specialisation in a particular market segment can give a firm a profitable, although perhaps temporary, competitive edge over rival firms.

The major disadvantage of *differentiated marketing* is the additional cost of marketing and production (more product design and development costs, the loss of economies of scale in production and storage, additional promotion costs and administrative costs and so on). When the costs of further differentiation of the market exceed the benefits from further segmentation and target marketing, a firm is said to have 'overdifferentiated'. Some firms have tried to overcome this problem by selling the same product to two market segments (so, for example, Johnson's baby powder is sold to adults for their own use; in the fairly recent past, many hairdressing salons switched from serving women only to serving both sexes).

The choice between undifferentiated, differentiated or concentrated marketing as a marketing strategy will depend on the following factors.

(a) How far can the product and/or the market be considered homogeneous? Mass marketing may be 'sufficient' if the market is largely homogeneous (eg safety matches).

(b) Will the company's resources be overextended by differentiated marketing? Small firms may succeed better by concentrating on one segment only.

(c) Is the product sufficiently advanced in its 'life cycle' to have attracted a substantial total market? If not, segmentation and target marketing is unlikely to be profitable, because each segment would be too small in size.

The potential benefits of segmentation and target marketing are as follows.

(a) A feature of a particular product might appeal to one segment of the market in such a way that the product is thought better than its rivals. To other customers in different segments of the market, there may be no value in this distinguishing feature, and they would not buy it in preference to a rival product.

(b) The seller will be more aware of how product design and development may stimulate further demand in a particular area of the market.

(c) The resources of the business will be used more effectively, because the organisation should be more able to make products which the customer wants and will pay for.

Ohmae's ideas on market segmentation

We referred in Chapter 1 to the views of Kenichi Ohmae on the three Cs (or the strategic triangle). Central to Ohmae's position is the importance of effective market segmentation.

He distinguishes between two broad approaches to segmentation:

(a) segmenting by objectives
(b) segmenting by customer coverage.

Notes

Segmenting by objectives means differentiating between the ways in which customers use a given product. For example, not everyone who drinks coffee does so merely to enjoy the taste or to stay alert; for some, it is a means to relax or socialise (coffee breaks in the workplace, going to a cafe with a friend). If these differences are significant, it may be worthwhile for the producer to offer a differentiated service or product.

Segmenting by customer coverage means targeting some customers but not others. This may be enforced (because the costs of reaching all potential customers outweigh the likely benefits), or it may reflect a perception by the company that it has a competitive edge in one segment of the market, while lagging behind its competitors in others.

Whichever segmentation a company adopts, it must recognise that over time the reasons for doing so may change. In other words, it will be desirable to re-segment the market. And at the same time is is necessary to recognise that market segments themselves may change over time (either through geographic or demographic changes).

Exercise 8

Try to think of products which exemplify the change in customers' objectives over time. In other words, try to think of products which have been adapted in order to meet changing objectives of the people who use them.

According to this view, the danger for companies is not so much that of head-on competition, as that of changes in the market segment that they target. It is easy to see that if a company is forced by strong growth in a segment where it is weak, while other segements in which it is strong are in decline, the effects could be disastrous. This emphasises the need for companies to keep a very close eye on changes in market segments over an extended time period.

Notes

Chapter roundup

(a) The requirements for effective segmentation have been identified as measurability, accessibility and substantiality.

(b) We have looked at a number of different bases for market segmentation. These include geographic segmentation, demographic segmentation (by socio-economic group, by family type etc), psychographic segmentation and geo-demographic segmentation.

(c) Effective segmentation is an aid to selecting target markets. Targeting policies, including concentrated marketing and differentiated marketing, have been discussed.

Quick quiz

1 What is the major reason for segmenting markets?

2 What are the benefits of market segmentation?

3 What is meant by a social grade of B? Or C2?

4 What does the acronym ACORN stand for?

5 The family life cycle is a summary demographic variable. What individual variables does it summarise?

6 In the context of psychographic segmentation, list four categories of lifestyle.

7 Describe a McCann-Erikson self-exploiting man, and a Taylor Nelson self explorer.

8 What is meant by geo-demographic segmentation?

9 Distinguish between concentrated marketing and differentiated marketing.

10 Which two approaches to segmentation are analysed by Ohmae?

Notes

Solutions to exercises

2 The range of package holidays available today is far greater than it was say, 20 years ago. This reflects the realisation by tour companies that effective segmentation can boost appeal and, eventually, profits. Segmentation may be based on age (18-30 holidays, over 60 holidays); special interests (bridge cruises, art tours); adventure holidays (trekking, mountain ascents) and so on.

3 Apart from the factors mentioned in the text, you might have noticed the increased prevalence of households with 'one person, over retirement age'.

7 Just refer back to the various market segmentations you have read about in the last few pages.

8 Ohmae cites the case of motor cars. Since the late 1960s, the cost/benefit objectives of many car owners have changed. Whereas before high-speed travel and prestige were the objectives, nowadays people are looking increasingly for convenience, economy and utility.

5 BUYER BEHAVIOUR

Your objectives

After completing this chapter you should:

(a) be aware of the influences that shape a consumer's behaviour, and of their importance to achieving marketing objectives;
(b) be aware of the particular features influencing organisational buyers;
(c) be aware of the importance of national differences and similarities.

1 Influences on customer behaviour

It is important that each customer who deals with an organisation is left with a feeling of satisfaction. This outcome is important since it can lead to increased purchases and/or to a willingness to pay higher prices and thus to higher profits. If customers are satisfied they may:

(a) buy again from the same supplier;
(b) buy more of the same item or of more expensive items;
(c) advise their friends to buy from the supplier.

Making a purchase necessarily involves taking a risk. Everyone likes to get value for money, but the risk in buying a new product or buying from a new supplier increases the risk of dissatisfaction. It is important that the supplier helps to reduce this risk for new customers so that they are more likely to become regular customers.

Customer loyalty is important for several reasons.

(a) It means that customers will support the supplier when times are hard, making it difficult for competitors to attract them away from their favoured supplier.

(b) Regular customers provide regular and reliable income and turnover.

(c) It is possible to build rapport with customers over time which helps the supplier understand their needs more easily, thus making the sales process more straightforward.

(d) Customer loyalty is a source of goodwill and will enhance the supplier organisation's image. It can be a source of very potent advertising in that loyal customers may recommend the supplier to their friends or colleagues.

Customer dissatisfaction is the reverse of customer loyalty in the sense that it may dissipate established goodwill and can adversely affect the company image. The added complication is that bad news travels faster than good news. It is easier by far for new customers to be put off by a negative recommendation than for a company to attract new customers with positive recommendations.

Notes

Understanding customer behaviour can be a major help in effective marketing management. However, there are many influences on customer behaviour and so the outcome in terms of purchasing decisions can be very difficult to understand from a rational viewpoint. Emotional and rational influences intertwine and lead to purchase outcomes which can seem illogical even to the buyer. We are all purchasers, and even organisational buying is conducted by individuals who have their own preferences and preconceptions which still affect them in the work environment.

We will now consider influences on customer purchasing decisions, namely needs, motives, culture, socio-economic groups, family and other reference groups.

Needs

There are many classifications of need. The simplest is to split needs into two main types.

(a) *Physiological needs* concern physical well-being and include needs for food, drink, warmth, sex and sleep.

(b) *Psychological needs* concern emotional or mental wellbeing and include needs for belonging (to groups), acceptance (by those regarded as important) and affection (of others).

We are born with these needs. In addition, we learn other psychological needs as we grow in society. These are secondary or learned needs and include:

(a) appreciation (by others);
(b) respect (by others regarded as important);
(c) recognition (of accomplishments);
(d) achievement.

Exercise 1

What has all this got to do with marketing? According to economists, purchasers (a) behave rationally, and (b) spend money in order to maximise utility. Try to think of examples where this economic approach appears inadequate to explain a purchasing decision.

Motives

Motives sit between needs and action. A need motivates a person to take action. Motives are derived from needs. The differences between needs and motives are as follows.

(a) *Motives activate behaviour*. Being thirsty (need) causes (motivates) us to buy a drink (action). If the need is sufficiently intense, we are motivated to act.

(b) *Motives are directional*. Needs are general but motives specify behavioural action. A need to belong may lead to a motivation to join a badminton club.

(c) *Motives serve to reduce tension.* Essentially man aims to be in an equilibrium state. This aim is known as the concept of *homeostasis*. If we are too cold, we are motivated to reduce the tension in our bodies that this causes by seeking a source of warmth. If we are not accepted by those we regard as important, we aim to reduce the tension this causes by seeking to change our behaviour so as to gain acceptance by those we value. This tension is also known as *dissonance*. When it exists, we aim to reduce it.

For example, dissonance may arise when an item is purchased which does not give satisfaction. The buyer may feel that he has not 'done the right thing'. This tension has to be reduced. The buyer may convince himself that he has bought the right thing by rereading the sales brochure or revisiting the sales people who sold it to him. Alternatively, he may get rid of the item and reduce the tension in this way. Importantly, what remains is likely to be a negative image of the supplier.

Exercise 2

Have you ever bought something on impulse or been talked into buying something that you were not quite convinced that you needed? Try to remember how you reconciled yourself to the purchase.

Culture

Motives arise from needs and can lead to purchasing actions. However, motives do not tell us how consumers choose from the options available to satisfy needs. Other influences are clearly at work.

Culture represents a group's common interests. It is about values and characteristic ways of living in a society. Culture varies widely and has many influences as shown in the following lists.

The impact of culture

Language
- spoken
- written
- official
- linguistic
- pluralism
- hierarchy
- foreign languages
- mass media

Religion
- sacred objects
- philosophical systems
- beliefs
- norms
- prayer
- holidays
- rituals
- taboos

Values and attitudes
- time
- achievement
- work
- wealth
- change
- scientific methods
- risk taking
- health
- 'green' issues

Law
- equity
- common law
- codes
- foreign laws
- international law

Politics
- nationalism
- sovereignty
- imperialism
- power
- national interests

Education
- formal
- vocational
- primary
- secondary
- higher
- university
- scientific
- literary

Notes

Technology	*Social organisation*
transportation	kinship
energy systems	social institutions
tools	authority
communications	structures
urbanisation	interest groups
invention	social mobility
science	social satisfaction
	status systems

Culture varies between countries but also within countries (subculture). Not only do we have restaurants in the UK offering ethnic food (such as Chinese or Indian) but within the UK there are certain (although declining) regional differences in the food we eat - laver bread in Wales, lardy cake in the West and potato bread in Northern Ireland being examples.

Language differences raise obvious marketing implications when brand names have to be translated, often leading to entirely different (and sometimes embarrassing) meanings in the new language.

Cultural differences raise many purchasing issues influencing every facet of life. Cultural differences can affect purchasing in several ways.

(a) *What* is bought (style, colours, types of goods/service)?
(b) *When* are things bought (for example, is Sunday shopping approved of)?
(c) *How* are things bought (bartering, haggling about price)?
(d) *Where* are things bought (type of retail outlet)?
(e) *Why* are things bought (influence of culture on needs and hence motives)?

Socio-economic groups

Marketing interest in socio-economic groups (as already discussed in Chapter 4) stems from the observable fact that members of specific groups have similar lifestyles, beliefs and values which can and do affect their purchasing behaviour.

Socio-economic classification is very commonly used in marketing and market research in the UK, despite its somewhat simplistic basis. As we discussed in Chapter 4, more sophisticated measures of socio-economic group membership have been devised. An example is the ACORN system (A Classification of Residential Neighbourhoods).

Further, more sophisticated, classifications based on socio-economic groups have been developed which add the person's activities, interests and opinions to the analysis. These analyses (known as psychographics) enable the identification of specific clusters of individuals who share similar activities, interests and opinions and hence, by association, purchasing behaviour. The 'He Man' cluster of young, aggressive, sporting men is one psychographic group. This group is a target group for lager advertising and sportswear, for example.

Family

Family background is a very strong influence on purchasing behaviour. It is in family groups that we learn how to be members of society and how to behave in different settings. Having learnt, it is difficult to forget. Family influences remain strong through the rest of our lives.

In the UK family structure is changing. There are more single person and single family households as the divorce rate has increased and as the population ages. There are now more single person households of young unmarried people than of older widows/widowers. The traditional nuclear family of husband, wife and two children beloved of TV advertisements actually represents a small proportion of all families.

The family is important in purchasing behaviour because it is often a 'purchasing unit' with one member (the buyer) buying on behalf of all members (users) but others in the family influencing the decision (influencers). Joint husband and wife purchasing decisions for major items are common.

Exercise 3

These terms are taken from Kotler's identification of the following participants in the buying process.

(a) The initiator - who suggests the idea
(b) The influencer(s) - anyone with a say in the decision
(c) The decider - who finally takes the decision
(d) The buyer - who actually makes the purchase
(e) The user - who consumes the product

Suppose your own family (or any other family if you prefer) was considering the purchase of a family saloon from a motor dealer. Identify the people who would fill the Kotler roles above.

Other reference groups

The family is a reference group in that in marketing decisions we use it as a reference point. Socio-economic groups are also reference groups in this sense. The immortal phrase 'keeping up with the Jones's' is a useful reminder of a further point: that other groups to which a person belongs or aspires can be strong influences on purchasing and other behaviour. Examples abound. Yacht clubs are synonymous with a particular style of dress (club blazer, for example) whereas working men's clubs conjure up different but no less potent images (such as the cloth cap). Different marketing approaches by suppliers would be necessary for each type of reference group.

Other influences on customer behaviour

There are other influences on customer behaviour in relation to suppliers.

(a) *Economic influences*
  (i) Income
  (ii) Occupation

Notes

(iii) Career prospects
(iv) House type

(b) *Social influences*
  (i) Family
  (ii) Socio-economic group
  (iii) Culture
  (iv) Reference groups
  (v) Education

(c) *Psychological influences*
  (i) Needs
  (ii) Motivation
  (iii) Personality
  (iv) Attitudes

(d) *For organisational buyers: organisational influences*
  (i) Company needs
  (ii) Inter-departmental rivalries
  (iii) Performance
  (iv) Buying committee/purchasing officer.

To get a better idea of how these factors can influence purchasing behaviour, we will continue by considering the major steps in the purchasing process.

How do people buy?

People buy not because they want the product/service in itself but because they want to solve problems they have. These problems to be solved are rooted in the lifestyle of the buyer and are influenced by the factors we have discussed in this chapter.

There is an identifiable buying process which consumers follow through, either consciously and logically or, more often, unconsciously and intuitively. This can be summarised as follows:

(a) problem recognition;
(b) information search;
(c) evaluation of alternatives;
(d) purchase decision;
(e) post-purchase evaluation.

The first stage in the process is *problem recognition.* The buyer must recognise a need and be motivated to solve it. A difference exists between the customer's desired state and his or her actual state, and this difference is sufficiently large to persuade the customer to act in order to solve the problem. The recognition, by the customer, of a problem (a need for a particular type of product or service) will be affected by the individual's personal characteristics, social position and relationships, economic circumstances and psychological make up.

The second stage involves *seeking information* which can be used in the decision making process as to how to solve an identified problem. Many sources of information exist and typically the more complex the problem, the more information will be sought. Sources of information include the following.

(a) Memory: if the purchase to be made is of a type which has been made before, then past experience is a potent influence.

(b) Family: reference may be made to past purchasing behaviour by the family unit. A child who has left home, for example, may buy the brands familiar from home.

(c) Friends: especially if a friend is a 'significant other', someone whose view on a particular type of product is respected (for example, a car enthusiast or a hi fi buff may be approached because their views on car or hi fi purchases are valued and seen as independent, and hence highly potent in influencing behaviour). Pharmacists are often asked to recommend patent medicines by mothers, a fact recognised by suppliers who try to convince pharmacists to recommend their brand.

(d) Sales brochures.

(e) Visits to sales outlets.

(f) Watching/listening to/reading advertising messages.

(g) Consumer advice sources, such as Which? magazine.

The process of collecting information regarding the possible purchases which could be made in order to generate a solution to a particular problem may be *internal*, based on past experience of a product/service, or may simply take the form of brand loyalty. Equally, though, the customer may undertake *external* searches, collecting information from manufacturers, distributors, other users, consumers' associations and so on.

Purchasers are at their most receptive to advertising messages at this stage. How to recognise and influence purchasers who are at this stage is an important decision, and making sure persuasive information is available is a key task.

The third stage is to *identify alternative solutions* and to evaluate each option. This process may be as quick and simple as looking at competing brands on a supermarket shelf or it may take months if the purchase is important and the criteria are complicated (such as buying a car). Based on the evaluation of alternatives, the consumer will make a choice to buy, selecting that product which has the most satisfactory performance in relation to the evaluative criteria.

How the options are evaluated will involve both rational and emotional considerations. For example, a car can be evaluated on rational criteria such as price, economy, range of extras and performance but also on emotional criteria such as style, colour quality, image and personality.

The prime task for suppliers is to get their product on the customer's shortlist of options.

The fourth stage is the *purchase decision*. The customer will see this decision as finding a solution to the problem he has identified. It is important that suppliers also take this view and thus express all communications to customers in terms with which the customer can identify.

Based on the evaluation of alternatives, the customer will make a choice to buy, selecting that product which seems to have the most satisfactory performance in relation to the evaluative criteria. In the absence of sudden or unexpected changes in the customer's

Notes

circumstances or in the market place, the purchase decision will lead to actual purchase. It is of course possible that the decision will be not to buy or to postpone purchase until a later date.

The process does not end with the purchase decision. Buyers reappraise their decision.

Exercise 4

Why is this post-purchase re-appraisal important for marketers, given that the sale has already been achieved?

Models of customer behaviour

We have now considered influences on customer behaviour and introduced one type of model of the purchase process.

The use of models for buying behaviour is an attempt to express simply the fundamental elements of a complex process. Such models try to express the interrelationship of those variables which are significant in influencing the outcome of a purchase motivation. Their aim is to help the marketing manager to understand the buying process so as to use a marketing strategy which is most applicable to the specific situation.

Thus the simple model discussed earlier in this chapter attempts to simplify and clarify the purchase decision process by showing it as a series of sequential steps. This type of model is useful to the marketing manager in trying to influence the process. For example, advertising and promotional activity is aimed at the information search stage and after sales service is aimed at the post-purchase evaluation stage.

The other major type of model is the theoretical model which tries to show the interrelationship between the various behavioural and economic factors which are involved. The aim is to give the marketing manager a better understanding of the buying process. Here is an example of a well known theoretical model, the Howard-Sheth model of consumer behaviour.

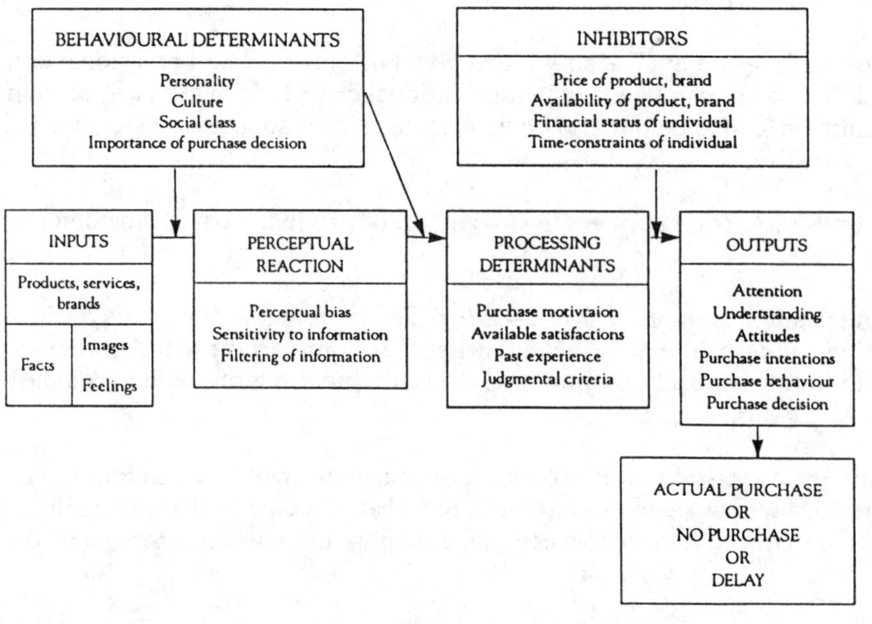

The Howard-Sheth model has a number of elements.

Inputs
Information inputs about the alternative services available include both rational and emotional elements. Thus, the interest rate structure information for a particular type of savings account at a bank or building society (rational or factual data) can be an input, as can the customer's reaction to the organisation's logo (emotional or irrational factor).

Behavioural determinants
These elements (covered earlier in this chapter) include the existing predispositions of the purchaser which have been influenced by culture, socio-economic group, family and personality factors, amongst others. This element will have a larger role for big or otherwise significant purchase decisions.

Perceptual reaction
Information from inputs is not accepted at face value but interpreted. For example, an individual is likely to value information more highly if it has been actively sought than if it has been passively received (from TV advertisements for example). The credibility of information varies according to the credibility of the source, perceived authority and content of the information. The customer will filter out information which is thought to be unimportant or which lacks credibility.

Processing determinants
These are the factors affecting how the information gathered is evaluated. They include motivation (based on perceived needs), the available satisfactions relevant to the purchase motivation and the individual's past experience of the supplier's services. The individual will also have some judgemental criteria with which to evaluate the alternatives. These personal criteria are clearly vital in the process. Organisations can use market research methods to try to identify these criteria so as to try to influence the individual.

Inhibitors
There are external constraints on actual or potential purchase behaviour. For example, for the purchase of a car, constraints could include:

(a) the rate of interest charged for a loan;
(b) legal constraints on credit terms;
(c) the price of petrol and performance criteria of different models of car;
(d) time constraints, such as the duration of a special offer.

Outputs
The outcome of the complex process of interacting elements may be a purchase decision, a decision not to buy or a decision to delay buying.

The Howard-Sheth model has a number of advantages over other models.

(a) It has been validated for practical examples of purchases.
(b) It indicates the complex nature of the buying process.
(c) It emphasises the need for marketing managers to analyse the satisfactions which customers seek in relation to the purchase of goods or services.
(d) It emphasises the need to gain a clear understanding of individual purchase motivations.
(e) It points to the importance of external constraints on the process.

Notes

(f) It suggests that customer satisfactions occur on a number of levels and in a number of forms at the same time. For example, both rational and emotional satisfactions are likely to be sought.

Thus the Howard-Sheth model can help the marketing manager to obtain useful and practical insights into customer behaviour. Like other such models, however, it is not an infallible guide. In particular, its predictive power is obviously limited.

Exercise 5

Using the Howard-Sheth model explain what the inputs, behavioural determinants and so on might be in making the following purchases.

(a) A new suit
(b) A packet of cigarettes
(c) A meal in a restaurant not visited before
(d) A microwave oven
(e) A novel
(f) A weekend break

2 Features of organisational buyer behaviour

All organisational buying decisions are made by individuals or groups of individuals, each of whom is subjected to the same types of influences as they are in making their own buying decisions. However, there are some real differences between personal and organisational buying decision processes.

(a) Organisations buy because the products/services are needed to meet wider objectives: for instance, to help them to meet their customers' needs more closely. However, as individuals do not buy products and services for themselves but for the benefits they convey, it could be argued that both are forms of derived demand.

(b) A number of individuals are involved in the typical organisational buying decision. Again, a personal buying decision may involve several family members, for example, and so may not be very different in some cases.

(c) The decision process may take longer for corporate decisions: the use of feasibility studies, for example, may prolong the decision process. Tendering processes in government buying also have this effect.

(d) Organisations are more likely to buy a complex total offering which can involve a high level of technical support, staff training, delivery scheduling, finance arrangements and so on.

(e) Organisations are more likely to employ buying experts in the process.

There are many examples of different types of organisational buying behaviour ranging from simple reordering (for example, of stationery supplies) to complex purchasing decisions (such as that of a consortium to build a motorway with bridges, tunnels, for example). Although it is difficult to identify a useful overall categorisation scheme there are common features which can be discussed.

Notes

(a) Who buys? Is it an individual or a committee? What is the job title of the buyer? Who influences the process?

(b) How does the organisation buy? Are there discernible stages in the buying process?

(c) Why does the organisation buy? What are the factors which influence the decision process and what is the relative importance of these factors?

Exercise 6

It is sometimes said that one distinction between an organisational buyer and a consumer is that the latter is less likely to act in a completely rational way. What exactly do you think this means, and do you believe it is true?

Complexity of organisational buying

One system of categorisation for corporate buying decisions, devised by Howard and O'Shaughnessy, is based on the complexity of organisational buyer behaviour. They identify three types.

(a) *Routinised buyer behaviour*. This category is the habitual type, where the buyer knows what is offered and is buying items which are frequently purchased. It is likely that the buyer has well developed supplier preferences and any deviation in habitual behaviour is likely to be influenced by price and availability considerations.

(b) *Limited problem solving*. This category is relevant to a new or unfamiliar product/service purchase where the suppliers are nevertheless known and the product is in a familiar class of products, for instance a new model of car in a company fleet.

(c) *Extensive problem solving*. This category relates to the purchase of unfamiliar products from unfamiliar suppliers. The process can take much time and effort and involve the need to develop criteria with which to judge the purchase, for example the construction and refurbishment of new offices where previously buildings were looked after by managing agents.

Large organisational buyers

An extra dimension in the organisational buying process occurs where the customer involved actually or potentially represents a significant proportion of the total sales of the supplier. For marketing purposes the relationship between the supplier and the large customer needs to be managed well. In addition, it is possible that independent intermediaries such as consultants are involved in the process, adding complexity. It is important to identify the dimensions of what is a complex buyer-seller relationship so that the supplier can try to plan and control the relationship.

In a Canadian study of buyers of industrial equipment (Banting 1976) the dimensions of the supplier-customer interface (where there is direct distribution) in order of importance were as follows.

Notes

1 Delivery reliability
2 Promotional activity
3 Technical advice
4 Discounts
5 After sales service
6 Representatives
7 Ease of contact
8 Replacement guarantee
9 Wide range
10 Pattern design
11 Credit
12 Test facilities
13 Machinery facilities.

A study by Schary (1982) of head office buyers for a major UK food product group produced the following hierarchy of customer service elements:

1 Product availability
2 Prompt quotation
3 Representatives
4 Order status
5 Distribution system
6 Delivery time
7 Pricing
8 Merchandising
9 Product positioning
10 Invoice accuracy
11 New product introductions
12 Advertising

Whilst most commentators dismiss the interface between customer and supplier as being primarily concerned with a price-quality trade-off, the above lists illustrate the wide range of dimensions which are considered important in practice by the organisational buyer.

Choosing a supplier

In practice there are two types of dimension to the relationship between organisational buyer and supplier.

(a) Formal dimensions include objectively measurable supplier characteristics such as price, credit terms, delivery speed, documentation and product training.

(b) Informal dimensions include subjectively evaluated supplier characteristics such as technical product responsiveness, producer credibility, perceived sales representative quality and perceived ease of contact.

The reason for making the distinction between formal and informal dimensions is to emphasise the role which marketing can play in the supplier's attempt to influence the interface. In addition the distinction emphasises the importance of customer service in the supplier's marketing mix.

From a marketing perspective, the role of the sales representative is vital to the supplier. As the human face of the supplier company, the sales representative is a key figure in establishing the relationships between the supplier and the customer.

Much of the research work on organisational buyer behaviour stresses the rationality with which buyers defend their purchasing decisions. It is much more difficult to identify and evaluate the weight of informal dimensions of the interface than it is to deal with objectively measurable dimensions.

A further complication is that links between supplier and industrial customers can occur at different levels in the organisation. Indeed, for one-off purchases the decision makers in the buying organisation need to be identified at an early stage in the marketing process.

Notes

Models of the organisational buyer behaviour process

A number of models have been devised to try to encapsulate the essence of the organisational buying process. Here we consider two.

Wind's model: a model of industrial source loyalty

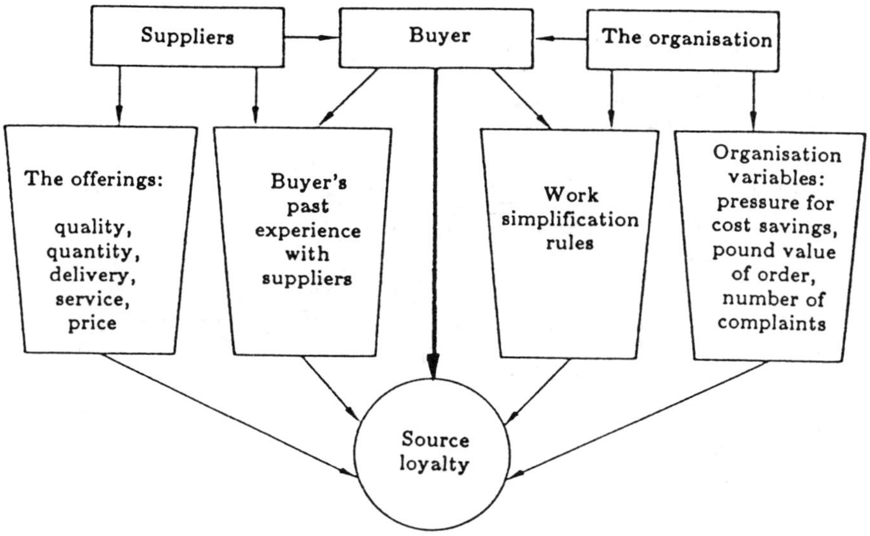

This model stresses *source loyalty:* in other words, the tendency for customers to continue to rely on the same supplier unless there are good reasons not to do so. These reasons are classified by Wind as:

(a) the offerings and dimension of the relationship with the customer;

(b) the past relationship with the supplier;

(c) organisational variables such as the degree of pressure for cost savings, the number of complaints;

(d) ways in which the organisational customer thinks the task can be simplified, such as convenience of access to the supplier, inertia and resistance to change.

Notes

Webster and Wind's model: a model of organisational buyer behaviour

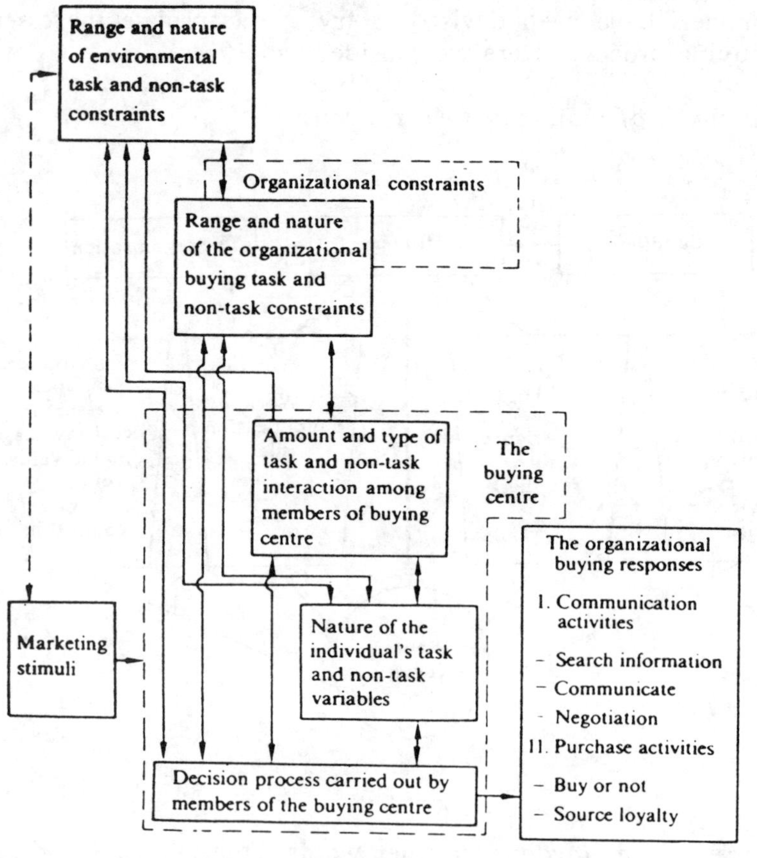

Webster and Wind together see organisational buyer behaviour as influenced by a number of sets of variables.

(a) The *individual characteristics* of the members of the buying centre, such as personality and preference, must be considered. These factors are similar to personal buying processes.

(b) The *relationships* between members of the buying centre are also important.

 (i) The *user* may have influence on the technical characteristics of the equipment (and hence the cost) and on reliability and performance criteria.

 (ii) The *influencer* is particularly useful where the purchase relies on technical knowledge. Unlike personal purchasing behaviour where opinions may be sought from colleagues, friends and family, competitive pressures and trade secret constraints may limit the sharing of information between companies. In this environment the salesman can be a respected technical link with the buyer and so be able to influence the purchasing process. Trade journals and trade associations or professional bodies can often be a good sources of influential information in addition to salesmen of the supplying company. Also, there is a tendency not to copy competitors but to seek one's own solution and thus demonstrate independence.

(iii) The *buyer* or *decider*. As already noted, decisions are, in the final analysis, made by individuals or groups of individuals. These individuals have personal idiosyncrasies, social pressures and organisational and environmental pressures. Thus each has a set of rational factors (task variables) and non-economic factors (non-task variables).

(iv) The *gatekeeper* who controls the flow of information about the purchaser may be senior or junior but is important because he/she influences the communication flow within the organisation.

(c) *Organisational characteristics* including the buying and organisational task, the size and structure of the organisation, the use of technology and so on. The relationships of the buyer within the organisation are particularly important. This post can be senior or junior and can involve power struggles with user departments. To retain and to try and increase organisational status, the buyer might use a variety of techniques designed to stress the buyer's role over that of financial or operational specialists.

(i) Role-orientated tactics involve keeping to the formal rules of the organisation where these rules work in favour of the buyer's intentions.

(ii) Role-evading tactics involve passive resistance to the rules where these rules do not work in favour of the buyer's intentions.

(iii) Personal-political tactics involve manipulating the relationship between informal and formal relationships in the process.

(iv) Educational tactics include using persuasive techniques.

(d) Environmental factors such as the physical, technological, economic and legal factors which affect general competitive conditions.

Exercise 7

Try to position the following groups of people according to the Webster and Wind model, in other words, decide whether they are 'buyers', 'influencers' and so on.

(a) People who control the flow of purchasing information
(b) People who need the product to perform their work duties
(c) People who set specifications for the buying decision.

The decision making unit

We can see that there are four main sets of variables influencing organisational buyer behaviour:

(a) individual characteristics in the buying centre;
(b) group characteristics in the buying centre;
(c) organisational characteristics; and
(d) environmental factors.

Notes

These four sets of variables interact in the decision process carried out by members of the buying centre. This is the *decision making unit* (DMU) of the buying organisation. In marketing terms the DMU is a vital target for the supplier's marketing initiatives. The size and structure of the DMU will vary between organisations, over time in the same organisation and for different types of purchase.

The marketing department of a supplier aiming at corporate clients therefore needs to be aware of:

(a) how buying decisions are made by the DMU;
(b) how the DMU is constructed; and
(c) the identities of the most influential figures in the DMU.

The decision process and the DMU

The diagram shows the decision process and the role of members of the DMU at each stage. Of course the process will vary according to the type of purchase being made.

A decision process model of industrial purchase behaviour

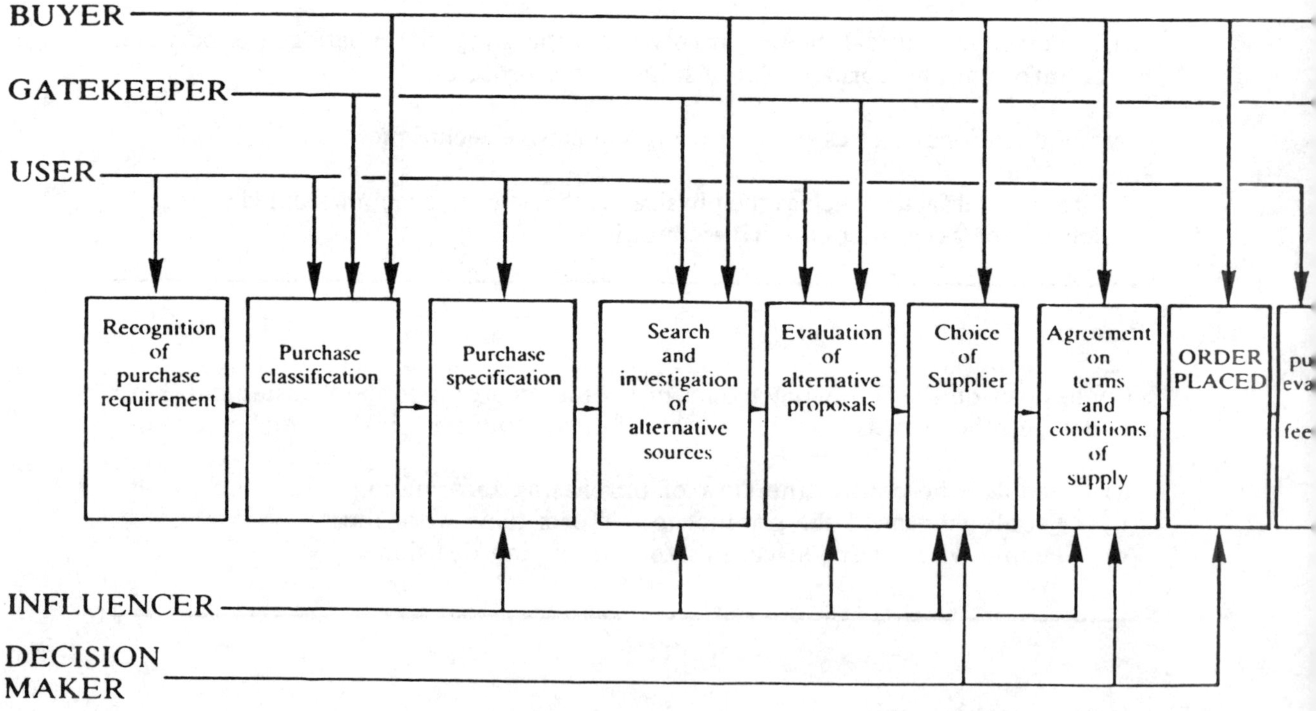

The organisational buying process is complex and needs careful marketing action if the outcome is to be influenced favourably.

3 National differences and similarities

Most cultures are identified with a nation, although some regions have strongly independent cultural identities.

Notes

Cultural segmentation must be considered particularly carefully, therefore, in an international (or *cross-cultural*) context: the marketer would need to understand the beliefs, values, customs and rituals of the countries in which a product is being marketed in order to alter or reformulate the product to appeal to local needs and tastes, and reformulate the *promotional message* to be intelligible and attractive to other cultures.

(a) Nestlé, the Swiss coffee maker, sells different strengths and styles of coffee in Europe than in America.

(b) Board games such as Monopoly are sold worldwide - with nationally-relevant street/area names, money and tokens.

(c) Legal and regulatory provisions with regard to advertising vary from country to country: the showing of cigarettes in ads, for example, the use of comparative advertising, or the use of children in advertising.

(d) Products are positioned as exotic imports with the specific appeal of their country of origin (Australian lager, Italian pizza, French mineral water) - while in the domestic market they are sold on familiarity and cultural loyalty.

There are two ways of looking at cross-cultural marketing.

(a) *Localised marketing strategy* stresses the diversity and uniqueness of consumers in different national cultures.

(b) *Global marketing strategy* stresses the similarity and shared nature of consumers worldwide.

Exercise 8

Try to identify the marketing problems arising from national differences in:

(a) language
(b) consumption patterns
(c) socio-economic factors; and
(d) marketing practices and conditions

A failure to understand cultural differences may thus cause problems with each of the four Ps.

(a) *The product*. Nestlé coffee, Camay soap and a host of similar products are marketed internationally - with different names, flavours, aromas, and other characteristics. Coffee is preferred very strong, dark and in ground form in Continental Europe - but weaker, milder and instant in the USA. Colour is another interesting element in product and packaging: it means different things to different cultures. Blue is said to represent warmth in Holland, coldness in Sweden, purity in India and death in Iran! Product benefits also vary in appeal: Pepsodent apparently tried to sell their toothpaste using the slogan 'You'll wonder where the yellow went!' in South-East Asia - where chewing betel nuts is considered an elite habit (giving status-enhancing brown teeth!).

Notes

(b) *Promotion.* Customs, symbols and language do not always travel well. Apparently the Chevrolet Nova failed to sell in Latin America because in Spanish *'no va'* means 'doesn't run'! 'Come alive with Pepsi' was translated as 'Pepsi brings your dead ancestors back to life' in one Far Eastern country! Advertising practices such as the extent and frequency of nudity used may vary widely from culture to culture, as do government regulations and voluntary guidelines on a number of issues.

(c) *Price.* Large package sizes may not be marketable in countries where average income is low, because of the cash outlay required.

(d) *Place.* Distribution tastes may vary. Supermarkets are very popular in some countries, while others prefer intimate personal stores for groceries and other foodstuffs. Newly-opening markets such as Eastern Europe exhibit poor distribution systems and very low salesperson effort and productivity - compared to Japan, say, which rates very highly.

Global perspectives

However, it should be remembered that culture is dynamic and adaptive: it changes as new values and behaviours are learned. Now that television and other forms of communication, and the speed of air travel, make the world more accessible to more people, cross-cultural exposure is increasing. So, too, is the global perspective encouraged by concerns for peace and the environment, which are global issues.

Consumers are more able to *try out* goods and customs from other national cultures - beyond those which already form subcultures within their own nation. They may experience different customs/products abroad, and adopt them into their lifestyle when they return home - a process made easier by the fact that immigrants from the other countries bring those customs/products with them, so they can also be tried out (and/or subsequently adopted) *at* home. Apart from ethnic foodstores, which have become increasingly fashionable, there are hitherto unfamiliar products in UK supermarkets: Vegemite (yeast extract) from Australia, fromage frais from France, star fruit, papaya, plantain and other exotic fruits/vegetables from all over the world. There are sushi bars and Karaoke clubs from Japan. Meanwhile McDonalds hamburgers have invaded Red Square in Moscow and Coca Cola is everywhere.

Consumers are also encouraged to become positively cosmopolitan and cross-cultural in their *outlooks*. International festivals of culture, foreign holidays, global environmental problems, the European Market completion in 1992 and the opening up of Eastern Europe all contribute to widen people's horizons, and make parochial, narrowly nationalistic viewpoints unfashionable. This is not an easy process: witness the UK's struggle with aspects of the European movement - giving up cultural emblems such as the pint, the mile, or the pound sterling.

Exercise 9

In what ways is an increasingly cross-cultural outlook becoming evident in UK consumers?

Some marketers have argued that standardised marketing strategies are, therefore, becoming more and more feasible, as cultural assimilation makes markets more and more similar. There are *world* or *global brands*, which are manufactured, packaged and positioned in the same way in all the countries in which they are sold: the Marlboro (cigarettes) cowboy, the Coca Cola name and packaging and British Airways.

Given the case histories mentioned earlier, however, it is as well to be cautious about the feasibility of global marketing in general. Global manufacturing and promotion brings efficiencies and economies - where it works. (Hoover (UK) wanted to sell washing machines in Europe, but found that the number of different features wanted by consumers in different countries would have made the expansion plan simply not viable.)

Marketers should distinguish between:

(a) global advertising/promotion/direct mail marketing; and
(b) globally standardised products.

They must understand the distinction between:

(a) global strategy; and
(b) global execution.

Even Coca Cola, with a mainly global strategy, adds an element of local variation in execution. The 'I'd like to buy the world a Coke' song advertisement is international in the people shown, and is featured in 21 languages in 16 countries. Other campaigns, however, show different people, settings and celebrities, according to local culture.

International marketing research

Monitoring is by far the most widespread activity in international marketing research. Studies have indicated that it accounts for about three quarters of all information received by international marketing managers (with research proper accounting for the remaining quarter). It involves passive information gathering in which the organisation or individual manager has identified a particular market or type of information on which information needs to be collected but, as yet, does not warrant active measures. The manager thus 'keeps his eyes open' for relevant information which is then collated and analysed.

Established international marketing companies are often engaged in continuous monitoring. They scan the business environment for changes which affect the products and markets of particular interest to them. In sophisticated companies it may form part of a wider marketing information system, in which information is classified and collated and then made available to managers across the organisation.

For companies with a wholly domestic orientation the position differs. Although a similar exercise may be carried out for the domestic market it is unlikely to extend internationally. A change occurs when a senior manager acquires information, often by chance, which suggests that there may be good marketing opportunities abroad. Such information may come from a very wide range of sources, such as friends, professional colleagues, reports of the success of a competitor or simply a general published analysis of the economy of a particular country.

Notes

If the information that has been acquired indicates the potential for a new market, the manager will proceed to the next stage, investigation. Otherwise he or she will return to scanning the business environment for general information, without any particular focus.

Social and cultural behaviour

Economic prosperity, in other words the ability to pay, accounts only partially for the demand for goods. The desire to acquire the goods is probably more significant. The importance we attach to the ownership of goods and use of services is determined by the learning process we acquire through cultural and social education. We learn how to be consumers by interacting with others and observing their reactions. Thus the comparison of the UK and French attitudes to food may explain why microwave cookers have had less acceptance in France than in the UK but that dishwashers are more popular in France than in the UK.

The development of attitudes and beliefs

We acquire our feelings about the worth of goods and services through a process of cultural and social development. This process establishes in our minds a set of values. In international marketing these differences in values may be quite marked, whereas in domestic markets they may be so subtle as to be unnoticeable. For the international marketeer differences of attitude and belief may affect:

(a) attitude towards ownership of an item;
(b) strength and direction of attitude;
(c) reason for desire/antipathy;
(d) perception of appropriate design/style; and
(e) meaning of colours, symbols and words.

Generally our value system is largely developed in our formative years, when exposure to family influences, education and peers has an important formative influence on our values and attitudes. This exposure inculcates values derived from religious, class and cultural norms.

Such norms form part of an acceptable code of behaviour, and violation of this code is met by social sanctions to ensure correct behaviour is observed.

Motivation and cultural norms

In developed societies, or in those sectors of a developing society which are affluent, most basic, physiological and safety needs are met. The remaining needs are social needs, self respect, respect from others, and 'self-actualisation'. Thus in affluent societies the needs are essentially social and so the value of goods is socially and culturally determined. In underdeveloped societies however the needs are more basic and physiologically determined. The implications are:

(a) similar items may be purchased for different reasons;
(b) in most societies the culture determines the attitude towards a product;
(c) marketers need to understand the cultural norms.

Symbolism

Cultures develop symbols to represent ideas. Thus in Western cultures white is pure, but in Eastern cultures white is death. Logos too form a symbolism. The elephant may have a distinct symbolic value in the far east, whereas it portrays bulk and durability in the West. Colours, logos and other symbolic messages do not translate, they have a local meaning.

Language

Another problem that the international marketeer faces is language. Literal translation often produces unfortunate consequences. Advertising literature is full of literal translation problems. To overcome language problems:

(a) translate into the foreign language;
(b) have a foreign national back-translate into the original language; and
(c) compare the translations.

Taboos

We have already noted that each culture establishes its own norms. These extend to ways of conducting business, and probably more important, excessive behaviour that is beyond the local socially acceptable behaviour. Excessive behaviours are taboo. They extend to:

(a) limiting what is acceptable behaviour in a situation;
(b) topics and subjects that are sensitive.

Often these are derived from religious observance. Thus alcoholic drink, pork, unclad females, men doing housework and so on may all be taboo in certain cultures. What is acceptable in terms of behaviour, promotion or product in one country is not necessarily so in another. A recent example has been the novel *The Satanic Verses* by Salman Rushdie, which has been seen as harmless in most Christian cultures but has caused significant offence in Muslim societies.

Cultural convergence and divergence

For certain product groups, where social exposure is important, and to the social classes where status is also important, the acquisition and adoption of an 'international' lifestyle has led to international products such as Walkman, Coke, Boss etc. Two groups seem to be most affected:

(a) young people, who have an above-average need for social acceptance; and
(b) international travellers, who are exposed to multicultural values.

This convergence process has led to the idea of global products that have an appeal worldwide with little or no modification.

Notes

Divergence

On the other hand, cultural groups which are isolated from exposure to external ideas, or which have strong religious or national affinity, tend to reject 'foreign' goods. The importer has at least to modify the offer to meet local needs.

According to innovation theory, the culturally convergent groups should become the models for other groups and so facilitate the introduction of new ideas. However the spread of fundamentalism can also be postulated by the same mechanism, and hence the processes of divergence and convergence may act concurrently. The implications for international marketeers are:

(a) in any society there will be groups who will accept 'international' products; and

(b) for the remaining groups in that society, products will need modification to meet local needs.

Exercise 10

A firm has developed a drug which can cure Alzheimer's disease. What factors do you think would distinguish its export marketing efforts to a country in the EC from its export marketing efforts to a country in the Third World?

Chapter roundup

(a) Consumer behaviour is influenced by needs, motives, culture, socio-economic groups, family and other reference groups. Some insight into the behaviour of consumers is provided by models such as the Howard-Sheth model.

(b) Additional factors are at work in the case of organisational buyers. Some insight into the process of organisational buying is provided by models such as those of Wind and Webster and Wind.

(c) In international marketing, the choice between a localised strategy and a global strategy can be key to achieving sales success.

Quick quiz

1 For what reasons is customer loyalty important?

2 List as many as you can of the economic, social and psychological influences on the buying behaviour of a consumer.

3 A consumer's buying behaviour was modelled in this chapter as a sequence of five steps. List the five steps.

4 List as many as you can of the elements in the Howard-Sheth model.

5 Describe the differences between the buying process of an individual and that of an organisation.

6 In international marketing what specific problems may arise as a result of national differences in (a) language; (b) consumption patterns; and (c) market segmentation.

Solutions to exercises

1 The problem with the economist's view is that 'utility' has to be very widely defined to explain exactly why some purchases are made in preference to others. To give one example at random, its seems inconceivable that *The Times* would ever be published in a tabloid format, and yet it is hard to think of any logical reason why purchasers would object to it. Indeed if you have ever studied the behaviour of broadsheet readers on a crowded bus or train, you might think that they would positively welcome a more convenient format in their newspapers.

3 Obviously this one you can only answer yourself. In a 'typical' family of 30 years ago, it might have worked as follows.

(a) Initiator - the father and the salesman
(b) Influencers - the mother, other family members, perhaps friends
(c) Decider and buyer - the father
(d) Users - both father and mother, and perhaps grown-up children too.

Today, in an era when family structures are less rigid, your own answer may have differed considerably from the above.

4 (a) If customers are satisfied with their experience of using the product or service then the next time a similar problem arises, they may short-circuit the decision process and buy the same product or use the same service. They become loyal customers.

(b) If a customer is dissatisfied, then not only will the same supplier not be used again but the customer may disseminate negative reports about the supplier and/or its products to others.

Notes

6 The argument is that organisational buyers are more 'rational' in the sense that:

(a) they have more technical buying expertise and product knowledge than the consumer; and

(b) their purchasing decisions are dictated by organisational goals rather than by their own personal goals.

While (a) is usually true, it is very doubtful whether (b) is. Buyers remain humans even if they are acting on behalf on an organisation

7 (a) Gatekeepers
(b) Users
(c) Influencers

8 *Language*
A promotional theme may not be intelligible - or properly translatable - whether in words or symbols

Consumption patterns
One country may not use a product as much as another (affecting product viability), or may use it in very different ways (affecting product positioning)

Socio-economic factors
Consumers in one country may have different disposable incomes and/or decision-making roles from those in another

Marketing practices and conditions
Differences in retail, distribution and communication systems, promotional regulation/legislation, trade restrictions etc may affect the potential for research, promotion and distribution in other countries.

9 Consumers in the UK are starting to learn languages, to drink wine as well as beer, to cook with garlic and herbs, to try other cuisines/music/arts. Newspapers such as *The European* exploit this trend, as do advertisements set in Italy and France: foreign or international 'style' is now recognised as acceptable and desirable, rather than alien.

10 You could write reams, but here are a few *preliminary* ideas.

Western countries

(a) Attitudes to elderly.

(b) Distribution: over the counter? Prescribed by doctors?

(c) Current health care of elderly.

(d) Demographic trends: is the age structure of the country becoming more heavily weighted towards older people?

(e) Drug testing and certification régime.

Notes

Third World country

(a) Is Alzheimer's seen as a major problem, compared to other medical conditions (eg diseases from poor sanitation)?

(b) Would the drug be affordable?

(c) Attitudes to elderly.

(d) Age structure of the country (fewer old people than in the West).

You will doubtless think of more.

6 THE PRODUCT

> ***Your objectives***
>
> After completing this chapter you should:
>
> (a) be aware of the options available to firms exploiting new products and/or new markets;
> (b) understand the main models used in classifying products;
> (c) understand the uses of branding.

1 Product/market decisions

In order to grow, an organisation can decide to use particular combinations of product and market decisions. Ansoff expressed these options in terms of a diagram.

	Existing products	*New products*
Existing markets	Market penetration	Product development
New markets	Market development	Diversification

(a) *Market penetration*
This involves selling more of the existing products in existing markets. Possible options are persuading existing users to use more (so a credit card issuer might try to increase credit card use by offering higher credit limits or gifts based on expenditure); persuading non-users to use (for example, by offering free gifts with new credit card accounts); or attracting consumers from competitors. It should be noted that market penetration will, in general, only be a viable strategy where the market is not saturated.

This aim could be achieved by better *market segmentation* (see Chapter 4), that is by tailoring products more closely to the needs of target groups of customers within the existing market. The danger to be borne in mind with this strategy is of putting all the organisation's eggs in one basket.

(b) *Market development*
This entails expanding into new markets existing products. These may be new markets geographically, new market segments or new uses for products. Since the advent of the Single European Market, the opportunities for market development in the European

Notes

Community are likely to increase significantly in some (although not all) areas of business. As a strategy, it requires effective and imaginative promotion, but it can be profitable if markets are changing rapidly.

(c) *Product development*
This approach requires the organisation to operate in its existing markets but develop modified versions of its existing products to appeal to those markets. Recent developments in the mortgage market provide a good example of product development as the traditional standardised mortgage account is rapidly being supplemented by variants which offer lower starting rates, special terms for particular types of customer, particular mixes of fixed and flexible repayment rates etc.

A strategy of this nature relies on good service design, packaging and promotion and often plays on company reputation to attract consumers to the new product. The benefits are that by tailoring the products more specifically to the needs of some existing consumers and some new consumers the organisation can strengthen its competitive position.

A danger is *cannibalisation:* that is, sales of new products may be achieved at the expense of existing products. Nevertheless, such a strategy may work if the new products make a greater contribution per unit to profit or if there is a danger that, without the new product, customers would switch from the existing product anyway, but to competitors' products.

(d) *Diversification*
The three strategies described above tend to be relatively low risk, since the organisation is operating in areas in which it has some experience. By contrast, the fourth strategy - *diversification* (new products, new markets) is much more risky because the organisation is moving into areas in which it has little or no experience. As a consequence, the instances of pure diversification are rare and its use as a strategic option tends to be in cases when there are no other possible routes for growth available.

Exercise 1

Try to think of at least one example of each of these strategies which you have observed in practice, other than those already cited in the text.

To understand the implications of these strategies, some knowledge is required of the characteristics of different products. Researchers have devised a number of models which attempt to classify products according to their leading characteristics. In the next section we look at some of the important models.

2 Classification of products

A concept frequently met in the marketing literature is that of the product life cycle (sometimes, rather confusingly, abbreviated to plc). The concept has an almost 'biological' basis. Products are born (or introduced), grow to reach maturity and then enter old age and decline. Despite its wide currency, however, it is not without its critics and there is little good empirical evidence supporting its existence.

Notes

Nevertheless, the product life cycle has proved to be a useful control device for monitoring the progress of new products after introduction. As Professor Robin Wensley of Warwick University puts it: 'The value of the product life cycle depends on its use, ie it has greater value as one goes down the scale from a predictive or forecasting tool, through a planning tool to a control tool.'

The profitability and sales position of a product can be expected to change over time. The 'product life cycle' is an attempt to recognise distinct stages in a product's sales history.

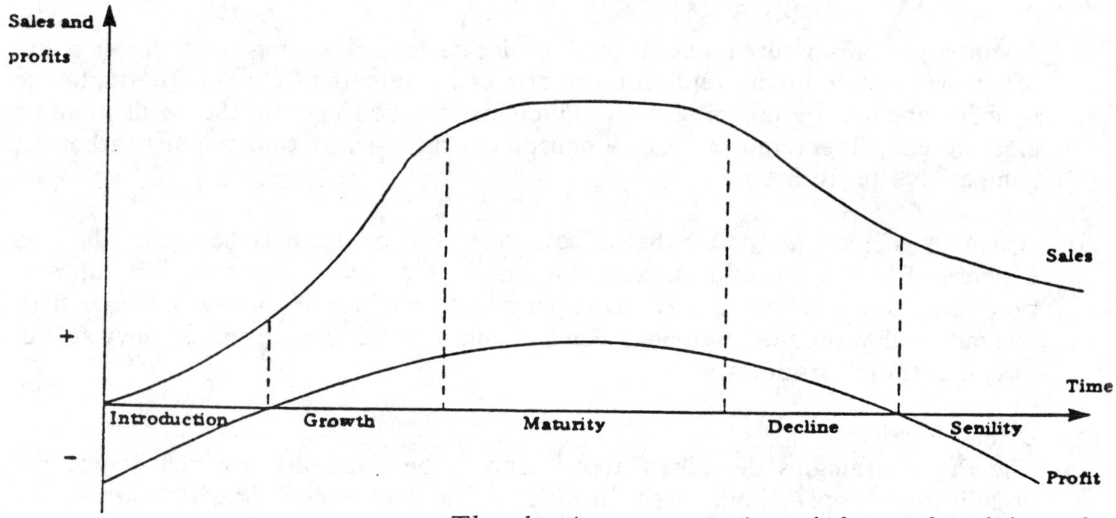

The classic representation of the product life cycle

(a) *Introduction:* a new product takes time to find acceptance by would-be purchasers and there is a slow growth in sales. Only a few firms sell the product; unit costs are high because of low output; there may be early teething troubles with production technology and prices may be high to cover production costs and sales promotion expenditure as much as possible. For example, pocket calculators, colour televisions and video cassette recorders were all very expensive when launched. The product for the time being is a loss maker.

(b) *Growth:* if the new product gains market acceptance, sales will eventually rise more sharply and the product will start to make profits. New customers buy the product and as production rises, unit costs fall. Since demand is strong, prices tend to remain fairly static for a time. However, the prospect of cheap mass production and a strong market will attract competitors so that the number of producers is increasing. With the increase of competition, manufacturers must spend a lot of money on product improvement, sales promotion and distribution to obtain a dominant or strong position in the market.

(c) *Maturity:* the rate of sales growth slows down and the product reaches a period of maturity which is probably the longest period of a successful product's life. Most products on the market will be at the mature stage of their life. Eventually sales will begin to decline so that there is overcapacity of production in the industry. Severe competition occurs, profits fall and some producers leave the market. The remaining producers seek means of prolonging the product life by modifying it and searching for new market segments.

(d) *Decline:* most products reach a stage of decline which may be slow or fast. Many producers are reluctant to leave the market, although some inevitably do because of falling profits. If a product remains on the market too long, it will become unprofitable and the decline stage in its life cycle then gives way to a 'senility' stage.

Buying participants through PLC stages

The introductory stage represents the highest risk in terms of purchasing a new, as yet untested product. Buyers reflect this: they typically consist of the relatively wealthy, to whom the risk of a loss is relatively small, and the young, who are more likely to make risky purchases.

In the growth and mature stages the mass market needs to be attracted. By the time decline sets in the product is well tested with all its faults 'ironed' out. At this stage enter the most risk-averse buyers, termed *laggards*. These are the converse of those who participated in the introductory stage, being the poorer and older sections of the community.

This analysis is based on the research of Everett Rogers (*Communication of innovations*, New York, second edition, 1971). He analysed the people adopting a new product into the following groups.

(a) *Innovators*. These people are in the vanguard of fashion. They are young, wealthy and with wide social connections.

(b) *Early adopters*. These are not so fashion-conscious as the innovators, but enjoy wide respect as opinion formers. These are the people that *must* be reached by promotional activities.

(c) *Early majority*. These adopt the new product early, but not until a firm lead has been given.

(d) *Late majority*. This is a sceptical group, not easily won over. But in the end they are influenced by social pressure from the early majority.

(e) *Late adopters and laggards*. These adopt the product after others have begun to think it obsolete. They are often poor, elderly or both.

Exercise 2

How does word of a new product circulate to the 'innovators'?

How are life cycles assessed?

It is perhaps easy enough to accept that products have a life cycle, but it is not so easy to sort out how far through its life a product is, and what its expected future life might be.

(a) There ought to be a regular review of existing products, as a part of marketing management responsibilities.

Notes

(b) Information should be obtained about the likely future of each product and sources of such information might be:

   (i) an analysis of past trends;
   (ii) the history of other products;
   (iii) market research;
   (iv) if possible, an analysis of competitors.

   The future of each product should be estimated in terms of both sales revenue and profits.

(c) Estimates of future life and profitability should be discussed with any experts available to give advice - for example R & D staff about product life, management accountants about costs and marketing staff about prices and demand.

Once the assessments have been made, decisions must be taken about what to do with each product. The choices are:

(a) to continue selling the product, with no foreseeable intention of stopping production;

(b) to initiate action to prolong a product's life, perhaps by advertising more, by trying to cut costs or raise prices, by improving distribution, or packaging or sales promotion methods, or by putting in more direct selling effort etc;

(c) to plan to stop producing the product and either to replace it with new ones in the same line or to diversify into new product-market areas.

Costs might be cut by improving productivity of the workforce, or by redesigning the product slightly, perhaps as a result of a value analysis study.

Exercise 3

Where do you consider the following products or services to be in their product life cycle?

(a) Mobile telephones
(b) Baked beans
(c) Satellite television
(d) Cigarettes
(e) Carbon paper
(f) Mortgages
(g) Writing implements
(h) Car alarms
(i) Organically grown fruit and vegetables.

Notes

Criticisms of the product life cycle

There have been contradictory papers directed at establishing or refuting the validity of the product life cycle by empirical tests. Polli and Cook (1969) tested 140 categories of non-durable consumer products. They tested whether the sequence that a product has passed through conformed to a PLC pattern. For instance, if a product was judged to be in a mature phase, they tested whether this was preceded by growth or maturity and followed by maturity or decline. If this test were positive then any sequence of these either/ors would be consistent with the PLC concept.

May be preceded by:	*Period*	*May be followed by:*
Introduction, growth	Growth	Growth, maturity, decline
Growth, maturity	Maturity	Maturity, decline
Growth, maturity, decline	Decline	Decline

(*Note*. The model was further subdivided into 'sustained maturity', 'maturity' and 'decaying maturity'.)

The results

Non-durable product class	*Number of product categories*	*% sequences significantly different from chance at: 5% confidence*	*1% confidence*
Health and personal care	51	60.8	31.3
Food	56	19.6	7.1
Cigarettes	33	60.6	51.5
ALL PRODUCTS	140	44.0	34.0

Source: 'The validity of the product life cycle', Polli and Cook, *Journal of Business*, October 1969.

Polli and Cook tested whether the results were significantly different from random events. They concluded that 44% of the total of all products were significantly different from chance at the 95% level of significance and 34% at the 99% level. Within the sample there was a considerable range of results when classified into non-durable product groups. 61% of 'cigarettes' and 'health and personal care' product groups were significantly different from chance at the 95% confidence level. This contrasts with only 20% of 'food'.

Polli and Cook concluded that the PLC was most likely to be relevant for products where consumer demand is high. From these results Polli and Cook concluded that 'for given categories of goods the product life cycle can be a useful model for marketing planning.'

A contradictory paper by Dhalla and Yuspeh attempts to expose what they term the myth of the PLC. They point out that 'in the absence of the technological breakthroughs many product classes appear to be almost impervious to normal life cycle pressures, provided they satisfy some basic need, be it transportation, entertainment, health, nourishment or the desire to be attractive'.

Notes

Whilst accepting the possibility of the existence of a *product* life cycle, the paper denies the existence of *brand* life cycles. They consider that any underlying PLC is a dependent variable which is determined by marketing actions; it is not the independent variable to which companies should adapt. In other words, if a brand appears to be in decline, this is not happening by Act of God, but as a result of market changes: either reduced or inappropriate marketing by the producer, or better marketing by competitors.

Dhalla and Yuspeh consider that treatment of the PLC as a binding constraint has led to many marketing errors. They sight the example of Ipana, an American toothpaste, that was marketed by a leading packaged goods company until 1968 when it was abandoned after entering a 'decline'. Two Minnesota businessmen then acquired the brand name and with hardly any promotion generated 250,000 dollars sales in the first seven months of operations. They point to how intelligent marketing has kept such brands as Budweiser Beer, Colgate toothpaste and Maxwell House around for a long time after competitive brands have been allowed to extinguish.

They cite conclusions reached by the Marketing Science Institute who examined over 100 product categories using Polli and Cook's test. 'After completing the initial test of the life cycle expressed as a verifiable model of sales behaviour, we must register strong reservations about its general validity, even stated in its weakest, most flexible form. In our tests of the model against real sales data, it has not performed equally well at different levels of product sales aggregation .... Our results suggest strongly that the life cycle concept, when used without careful formulation and testing as an explicit model, is more likely to be misleading than useful.'

Dhalla and Yuspeh come to the general conclusion that managers adhering to the sequences of marketing strategies recommended for succeeding stages of the cycle are likely to do more harm than good. In particular they cite the potential neglect of existing brands and wasteful expenditures on replacement 'me-too' products.

There are some legitimate criticisms of the product life cycle concept as a practical tool in strategic planning.

(a) The traditional S-shaped curve of a product life cycle

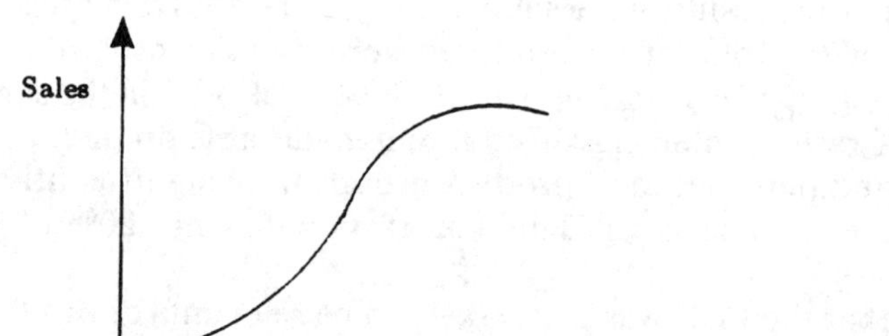

does not always occur in practice. Some products have no maturity phase, and go straight from growth to decline. Others have a second growth period after an initial decline. Some have virtually no introductory period and go straight into a rapid growth phase.

(b) Strategic decisions can change a product's life cycle: for example, by repositioning a product in the market, its life can be extended. If strategic planners 'decide' what a product's life is going to be, opportunities to extend the life cycle might be ignored.

Notes

(c) Competition varies in different industries, and the strategic implications of the product life cycle will vary according to the nature of the competition. The 'traditional' life cycle presupposes increasing competition and falling prices during the growth phase of the market and also the gradual elimination of competitors in the decline phase. Strategic planning would be based on these presuppositions. But in practice, this pattern of events is not always found. The financial markets are an example of markets where there is a tendency for competitors to follow-my-leader very quickly, so that competition has built up well ahead of demand. The rapid development of various banking services is an example of this: for example, with bank cash dispenser cards, when one bank developed the product all the other major banks followed immediately.

Exercise 4

In any event, how can managers recognise where a particular product is in its life cycle? In practice, they can't, with any degree of certainty. But how might they begin to attack the problem?

The strategic implications of the product life cycle

Having made these reservations about product life cycle planning, the strategic implications of the product life cycle might be as follows.

	Phase			
	Introduction	*Growth*	*Maturity*	*Decline*
Product	Initially, poor quality Product design and development are a key to success No standard product and frequent design changes (eg microcomputers in the early 1980s)	Competitor's products have marked quality differences and technical differences Quality improves Product reliability may be important	Products become more standardised and differences between competing products less distinct	Products even less differentiated. Quality becomes more variable

Notes

	Phase			
	Introduction	*Growth*	*Maturity*	*Decline*
Customers	Initial customers willing to pay high prices Customers need to be convinced about buying	Customers increase in number	Mass market Market saturation Repeat-buying of products becomes significant. Brand image also important	Customers are 'sophisticated' buyers of a product they understand well
Marketing	High advertising and sales promotion costs High prices possible	High advertising costs still, but as a % of sales, costs are falling Prices falling	Markets become segmented Segmentation and extending the maturity phase of the life cycle can be key strategies	Less money spent on advertising and sales promotion
Competition	Few or no competitors	More competitors enter the market Barriers to entry can be important	Competition at its keenest: on prices, branding servicing customers, packaging etc	Competitors gradually exit from the market Exit barriers can be important
Profit margins	High prices but losses due to high fixed costs	High prices. High contribution margins, and increasing profit margins High P/E ratios for quoted companies in the growth market	Falling prices but good profit margins due to high sales volume High prices in some market segments	Still low prices but falling profits as sales volume falls, since total contribution falls towards the level of fixed costs Some increases in prices may occur in the late decline stage

Notes

	Phase			
	Introduction	*Growth*	*Maturity*	*Decline*
Manufacturing and distribution	Overcapacity High production costs Few distribution channels High labour skill content in manufacture	Undercapacity Move towards mass production and less reliance on skilled labour Distribution channels flourish and getting adequate distribution is a key to marketing success	Optimum Low labour skills Distribution channels fully developed, but less successful channels might be cut	Overcapacity capacity because mass production techniques still used Distribution channels dwindling

Exercise 5

Referring back to the pioneering work of Everett Rogers, what proportion of the total market for a new product would you guess that each of his categories constitutes?

	Proportion
Innovators	
Early adopters	
Early majority	
Late majority	
Late adopters and laggards	
	100%

Product-market matrices

The product-market matrix refers to a simple technique which can be used to classify a product or even a business according to the features of the market and the features of the product. Such a technique is often used at the level of corporate strategy to determine the relative positions of businesses and identify strategies for resource allocation between them. Thus, for example, a bank might apply such a technique to evaluate the relative position and profitability of its corporate division vis a vis that of its personal division, its international division, its merchant banking division etc. However, the same techniques are equally valuable when considering products and the management of the product portfolio. The two most widely used approaches are the *Boston Consulting Group (BCG) growth-share matrix* and the *General Electric (GE) Business Screen.*

Notes

The BCG Matrix

The BCG matrix, which is illustrated below, works by classifying products (or businesses) on the basis of their market share relative to that of their competitors and according to the rate of growth in the market as a whole. The split on the horizontal axis is based on a market share identical to that of the firm's nearest competitor, while the precise location of the split on the vertical axis will depend on the rate of growth in the market. Products are positioned in the matrix as circles with a diameter proportional to their sales revenue. The underlying assumption in the growth-share matrix is that a larger market share will enable the business to benefit from economies of scale, lower per unit costs and thus higher margins.

The Boston Consulting Group Growth/Share Matrix

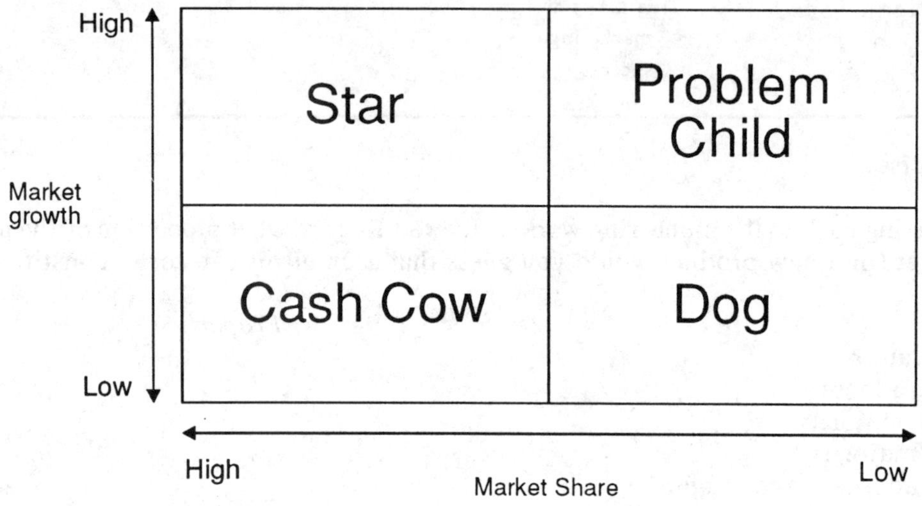

Each product can then fall into one of four broad categories.

(a) *Problem Child* (or question mark): a small market share but in a high growth industry. The generic product is clearly popular, but customer support for the specific company version is limited. A small market share implies that competitors are apparently in a strong position and that if the product is to be successful it will require a substantial injection of funds, particularly on the marketing side. If the market looks good and the product is viable, then the company should consider a *'build'* strategy to increase market share. This would essentially involve increasing the resources available for that product to permit more active marketing. If the future looks less promising then the company should consider the possibility of withdrawing the product. At this stage it is important to take decisive action to ensure that the product moves to a less ambiguous situation.

(b) *The Star:* this is a product with a high market share in a high growth industry. By implication, the star has potential for generating significant earnings currently and in the future. However, at this stage it may still require substantial marketing expenditures to 'maintain' this position, but would be regarded as a good investment for the future.

Notes

(c) *The Cash Cow:* a high market share but in a comparatively mature and slower growing market. Typically, a well established product with a high degree of consumer loyalty. Product development costs are typically low and the marketing campaign is well established. The cash cow will normally make a substantial contribution to overall profitability. The appropriate strategy will vary according to the precise position of the cash cow. If market growth is reasonably strong then a 'holding' strategy will be appropriate, but if growth and/or share are weakening, then a *harvesting* strategy may be more sensible - cut back on marketing expenditure and maximise short-term cash flow.

(d) *The Dog:* a product characterised by low market share and low growth - again, typically a well established product, but one which is apparently losing consumer support and may have cost disadvantages. The usual strategy would be to consider *divestment* unless cash flow position is strong, in which case the product would be harvested in the short term prior to deletion from the product range.

We should note that implicit in the matrix is the notion that markets are dynamic. The typical new product is likely to appear in the 'problem child' category to begin with; if it looks promising and with effective marketing it might be expected to become a 'star', then, as markets mature, a 'cash cow' and finally a 'dog'.

Exercise 6

If products are going to develop through these stages anyway, then what is the purpose of spending money on marketing?

The framework provided by the matrix can offer guidance in terms of developing appropriate strategies for products and in maintaining a balanced product portfolio - ensuring that there are enough cash-generating products to match the cash-using products.

However, there are a number of criticisms.

(a) The BCG matrix oversimplifies product analysis. It concentrates only on two dimensions of product markets, size and market share, and therefore may encourage marketing management to pay too little attention to other market features.

(b) It is not always clear what is meant by the terms 'relative market share' and 'rate of market growth'. Not all companies and not all products will be designed for market leadership, in which case describing performance in terms of relative market share may be of limited relevance. Many firms undertaking this approach have found that all their products were technically 'dogs' and yet were still very profitable, so saw no need to divest. Firms following market nicheing strategy will commonly find this occurring since they are looking to appeal only to a limited segment of the market.

(c) The validity of the matrix depends on the notion of a relationship between profitability and market share. There is empirical evidence for this in many industries, but it may not always be the case, particularly in situations were there is demand for more customised products.

(d) The basic approach may oversimplify the nature of products in large diversified firms with many divisions. In these cases, each division may contain products which fit into several of the categories. Despite these criticisms, the BCG matrix can offer

Notes

guidance in achieving a balanced portfolio. However, given the difficulty of generalising such an approach to deal with all product and market situations, its recommendations should be interpreted with care.

The General Electric Business Screen

The basic approach of the GE business screen is similar to that of the BCG matrix. The key difference is that it attempts to avoid the criticism of using a highly restrictive classification system and instead attempts to include a broader range of company and market factors in assessing the position of a particular product or product group. A typical example of the GE matrix is given below. This matrix classifies products (or businesses) according to industry attractiveness and company strengths. Obviously, there is no single number which can be used to measure industry attractiveness or company (product) strength; rather, the approach is to consider a variety of factors which will contribute to both these variables and sectionalise the matrix based on simple ordinal measures - namely high, medium and low. Typical examples of the factors which determine industry attractiveness and company strength are the following.

(a) *Industry attractiveness:* market size, market growth, competitive climate, stability of demand, ease of market entry, industry capacity, levels of investment, nature of regulation, profitability.

(b) *Company strengths:* relative market share, company image, production capacity, production costs, financial strengths, product quality, distribution systems, control over prices/margins, benefits of patent protection.

Although a broader range of factors are used in the classification of products, the manager should be aware that this is a much more subjective assessment. Products are positioned on the grid with circles representing market size and segments representing market shares. The strategy for an individual product is then determined according to that position. The possible options are shown below and it is interesting to note the apparent similarity in recommendations between the BCG matrix and the GE matrix; the basic difference arises simply from the method of classification.

The General Electric Business Screen

COMPETITIVE POSITION
- ie. business strengths of the firm

Strength of product attraction	Strong	Average	Weak
High	Invest for growth	Invest selectively for growth	?
Medium	Invest selectively for growth	?	Harvesting strategy
Low	?	Harvesting strategy	Harvesting strategy

? means that the choice of strategy is uncertain, and should be made selectively for each product and market.

Notes

The GE matrix, because of its broader approach, places emphasis on the notion of trying to match distinctive competences within the company to conditions within the market place. However, the difficulties associated with measurement and classification mean that again the results of such an exercise should be interpreted with care and not seen as an immediate prescription for expanding or divesting particular products.

Adding and deleting products

Innovation is the life blood of a successful organisation and the management of innovation is central to this success. New products can be developed following a major technical breakthrough in the field, or changes in society; or simply to copy existing products. Within the organisation itself management can adopt a proactive response to product development. Organisations can set up research and development departments to look into new product development. Ideas for new products do not have to come through this formal departmentalised system. Management, sales people, customers and competitors can all generate new product ideas. It is the task of marketing management to 'tap' these ideas and select some for further development.

What is a new product?

(a) One that opens up an entirely new market.
(b) One that replaces an existing product.
(c) One that broadens significantly the market for an existing product.

An old product can be new if:

(a) it is introduced to a new market;
(b) it is packaged in a different way;
(c) a different marketing approach is used.

Any new product must be perceived in terms of customer needs and wants.

Exercise 7

Can you think of examples of new products and 'new' old products to fit into each of the above categories? The notes below should point you in the right direction if you are struggling.

There are several degrees of newness.

(a) *The unquestionably new product*, such as the electronic pocket calculator. Marks of such a new product: high price - performance problems - patchy distribution.

(b) *The partially new product*, such as the cassette tape recorder. Marks of such a product: it performs better than the old ones did.

(c) *Major product change*, such as the Mini car. Marks of such a product: radical technological change altering the accepted concept of the order of things.

Notes

(d) *Minor product change,* such as styling changes. Marks of such a product: extras which give a boost to a product.

There are several sources of new products, including the following.

(a) Licensing.
(b) Acquisition: buy the organisation making it.
(c) Internal product development: your own research and development team.
(d) Customers: listen to and observe them, analyse and research.
(e) External inventors: both Kodak and IBM rejected Xerox.
(f) Competition: for example Kodak instant cameras, following the Polaroid concept.
(g) Patent agents.
(h) Academic institutions: for example the pharmaceutical industry.

Screening new product ideas

The mortality rate of new products is very high.

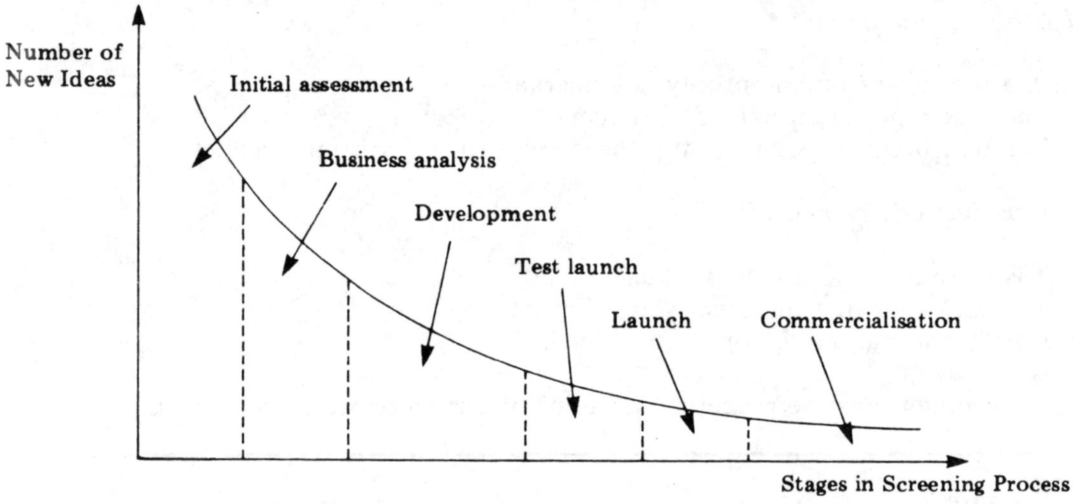

To reduce the risk of failure new product ideas should be screened. There is some evidence that the screening process for new products is becoming more effective. A study by Booz, Allen and Hamilton in 1968 concluded that it took fifty-eight ideas to yield one successful product that achieved commercial success. A repeat study by Booz, Allen and Hamilton in 1981 showed a dramatic improvement. This study of 700 companies in the USA found that on average only seven ideas were needed for every successful product. An eightfold increase in success rate!

New product development plan

New products should only be taken to an advanced development stage if they fit the criteria of:

(a) adequate demand;
(b) compatibility with existing marketing ability;
(c) compatibility with existing production ability.

Initial concept testing

Before investing money in making prototypes the concept for the new product could be tested on potential customers to obtain their reactions. It is common to use the company staff as guinea pigs for a new product idea although their reaction is unlikely to be typical. But it is difficult to get sensible reactions from customers. For example:

(a) New designs for wallpaper. When innovative new designs are tested on potential customers it is often found that they are conditioned by traditional designs and are dismissive of new design ideas.

(b) New ideas for chocolate confectionery have the opposite problem. Potential customers typically say they like the new concept (because everyone likes chocolate bars) but when the new product is launched it is not successful because people continue to buy old favourites.

Product testing

Here, money is invested to produce a working prototype of the product which can be tried by customers. This stage is also very useful to ensure that the product could be produced in sufficient quantities at the right price if it were to be launched. The form which the product test takes will depend very much on the type of product concerned. The best advice seems to be that to get realistic responses the test should replicate reality as clearly as possible. Thus, for example:

(a) if the product is used in the home, a sample of respondents should be given the product to use at home;

(b) if the product is chosen from amongst competitors in a retail outlet (as with chocolate bars) then the product test needs to rate response against competitive products;

(c) if inherent product quality is an important attribute of the product then a 'blind' test could be used in which customers are not told who is producing the new product;

(d) an industrial product could be used for a trial period by a customer in a realistic setting.

Quality policy

This is an important policy consideration. Customers do not necessarily want the best quality of goods, and there may be a market potential for a lower quality as well as a higher quality article. When a market is dominated by established brand names, a means of getting into a market might be to tap the potential demand for a lower quality (cheaper, or fashion) item.

Customers do not always know properly what they are buying, and tend to judge the quality of an article by its price. One aspect of quality policy may therefore be to decide a price and then manufacture a product to the best quality standard that can be achieved for the price, rather than making a product of a certain quality and then deciding what its price should be.

Notes

Quality should also be determined by the expected physical, technological and social life of the product because:

(a) there is no value in making one part of a product good enough to have a physical life of five years, when the rest of the product will wear out and be irreplaceable within two years (unless the part with the longer life has an emotional or irrational appeal to customers, so that, for example, a leather covering may be preferred to plastic);

(b) if technological advances will make a product obsolescent within a certain number of years, there is little value in producing an article which will last for a longer time;

(c) if social tastes determine the life of a product, the quality required need only be sufficient to cover the period of demand; the quality of fashion clothes, for example, is usually governed by their fashion life.

Quality policy must be carefully integrated with sales promotion, which will have poor success if a product is branded and advertised as having a certain quality which customers then find is not actually true. The quality of a product (involving its design, production standards, quality control and after-sales service) must be properly established and maintained before a sales promotion campaign can use it as a selling feature.

Test marketing

The purpose of test marketing is to obtain information about how consumers react to the product - will they buy it, and if so, will they buy it again? Will they adopt the product as a regular feature of their buying habits, and if so, how frequently will they buy it? With this information an estimate of the total market demand for the product can be made.

A test market involves testing a new consumer product in selected areas which are thought to be 'representative' of the total market. This avoids a blind commitment to the costs of a full-scale launch while permitting the collection of market data. In the selected areas, the firm will attempt to distribute the product through the same types of sales outlets it plans to use in the full market launch, and also to use the advertising and promotion plans it intends to use in the full market. A test marketing exercise can be expensive, but it enables the company to 'test the water' before launching the product nationally. Not only does it help to make sales forecasts, it can also be used to identify flaws in the product or promotional plans which can then be dealt with before the product is launched nationally.

Notes

In short, then, the stages of new product development are as follows.

CONCEPTION OF IDEAS

↓

SCREENING OF IDEAS

↓

ANALYSE (IN BUSINESS SENSE)

↓

TESTING - Concept and Use

↓

PRODUCT DEVELOPMENT

↓

MARKETING MIX ISSUES

↓

MARKET TESTING

↓

PRODUCT LAUNCH

The diffusion of the new product is the spread of information about the product in the market place. Adoption is the process by which consumers adopt the product. The diffusion process usually is assumed to follow a similar shape to the PLC curve. Adoption is thought to usually follow a 'normal' bell shaped curve. The classification of adopters is shown below.

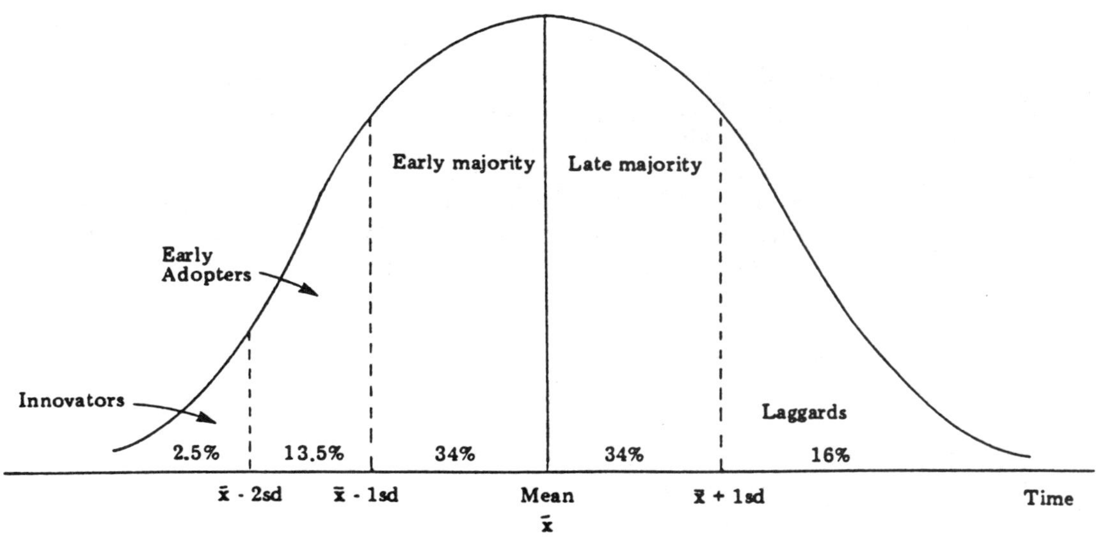

Notes

Early adopters and innovators are often considered to be 'opinion leaders' and are therefore targeted by companies to promote their product to their friends by word of mouth means.

3 Branding

Branding is a very general term covering brand names, designs, trademarks, symbols, jingles and the like. A *brand name* refers strictly to letters, words or groups of words which can be spoken. A *brand image* distinguishes a company's product from competing products in the eyes of the user.

A brand identity may begin with a name, such as 'Kleenex' or 'Ariel', but extends to a range of visual features which should assist in stimulating demand for the particular product. The additional features include typography, colour, package design and slogans.

Often brand names suggest desired product characteristics. For example, 'Fairy' gives impressions of gentleness and hence mildness.

Exercise 8

What characteristics do the following brand names suggest to you?

(a) Brillo (scouring pads)
(b) Pampers (baby nappies)
(c) Cussons Imperial Leather (soap)
(d) Kerrygold (butter)
(e) Hush Puppies (shoes)

The reasons for branding are as follows.

(a) It is a form of product differentiation, conveying a lot of information very quickly and concisely. This helps customers readily to identify the goods or services and thereby helps to create a customer loyalty to the brand. It is therefore a means of increasing or maintaining sales.

(b) Advertising needs a brand name to sell to customers and advertising and branding are very closely related aspects of promotion; the more similar a product (whether an industrial good or consumer good) is to competing goods, the more branding is necessary to create a separate product identity.

(c) Branding leads to a readier acceptance of a manufacturer's goods by wholesalers and retailers.

(d) It facilitates self-selection of goods in self-service stores and also makes it easier for a manufacturer to obtain display space in shops and stores.

(e) It reduces the importance of price differentials between goods.

(f) Brand loyalty in customers gives a manufacturer more control over marketing strategy and his choice of channels of distribution.

(g) Other products can be introduced into brand range to 'piggy back' on the articles already known to the customer (but ill-will as well as goodwill for one product in a branded range will be transferred to all other products in the range). Adding products to an existing brand range is known as *brand extension strategy*.

(h) It eases the task of personal selling (face-to-face selling by sales representatives).

(i) Branding makes market segmentation easier. Different brands of similar products may be developed to meet specific needs of categories of users.

The relevance of branding does not apply equally to all products. The cost of intensive brand advertising to project a brand image nationally may be prohibitively high. Goods which are sold in large numbers, on the other hand, promote a brand name by their existence and circulation.

Where a brand image promotes an idea of quality, a customer will be disappointed if his experience of a product fails to live up to his expectations. Quality control is therefore an important element in branding policy. It is especially a problem for service industries such as hotels, airlines and retail stores, where there is less possibility than in a manufacturing industry of detecting and rejecting the work of an operator before it reaches the customer. Bad behaviour by an employee in a face-to-face encounter with a customer will reflect on the entire company and possibly deter the customer from using any of the company's services again.

The decision as to whether a brand name should be given to a range of products or whether products should be branded individually depends on quality factors.

(a) If the brand name is associated with quality, all goods in the range must be of that standard. An example of a successful promotion of a brand name to a wide product range is the St Michael brand of Marks and Spencer; and Kelloggs use their family brand name to promote their (quality) cereal products.

(b) If a company produces different quality (and price) goods for different market segments, it would be unwise to give the same brand name to the higher and the lower quality goods because this would deter buyers in the high quality/price market segment.

Notes

Branding strategies

BRANDING STRATEGY	DESCRIPTION	IMPLIES
Family branding	The power of the family name to help products	Image of family brand applicable across a range of goods
Brand extension	New flavours, sizes etc	High consumer loyalty to existing brand
Multi-branding	Different names for similar goods serving similar consumer tastes	Consumers make random purchases across brands

Family brandings: the power of the 'family' name to assist all products is often debatable. In the early 1970s, United Biscuits and the Cadbury Group experimented with the joint distribution and manufacture of a range of cakes under the Cadbury brand. The Cadbury name was found to be a potent brand but *only* for chocolate cakes within the range.

Brand extension denotes the introduction of new flavours, sizes etc. New additions to the product range are beneficial for two main reasons.

(a) They require a lower level of marketing investment (part of the 'image' already being known).

(b) The extension of the brand presents less risk to consumers who might be worried about trying something new. (Particularly important in consumer durables with relatively large 'investment' in a car, stereo system or the like.) Recent examples include the introduction of Persil washing up liquid and Mars ice cream.

Multi-branding: the introduction of a number of brands that all satisfy very similar product characteristics.

(a) This can be used where little or no brand loyalty is noted, the rationale being to run a large number of brands to pick up buyers who are constantly changing brands.

(b) The best example is washing detergents. The two majors, Lever Brothers and Proctor & Gamble, have created a barrier to fresh competition as a new company would have to launch several brands at once in order to compete.

Trademarks

A trademark is a legal term covering words and symbols. A legally protected mark can be a very valuable asset because:

(a) the legal protection can continue after patent protection runs out;

Notes

(b) competitors will be prevented from using a market leader's branding as a generic term for a class of products (as has happened with aspirin and cellophane).

However, even with trademark protection the impact of a market leader's branding may be weakened by consumers who perceive the brand name as a generic term.

(a) How many people 'hoover' with an Electrolux machine?
(b) Have you ever 'xeroxed' on a photocopier not made by Rank?
(c) Hence the message 'It's the real thing' from Coca Cola.

Exercise 9

Think of some more examples on the same lines as Hoover and Xerox.

Brands and packaging

A manufacturer might produce goods under his own brand name and at the same time (or perhaps exclusively) supply large retailers with goods under their own brand name, 'own label' brands or dealer brands. The major examples are the own brand of supermarkets and major chain stores (eg. Tesco, Sainsbury, St Michael for Marks & Spencer and Winfield for Woolworths). The advantages of dealer brands to a manufacturer are:

(a) a high level of sales may be necessary to cover fixed costs of production and supplying dealer branded goods to a large retail organisation may be a necessary way of achieving a profitable sales level;

(b) large retailers with a high sales turnover and considerable control over the retail trade may insist on having their own brand, and supplying dealer branded goods may be essential to retain their business;

(c) it may be a well established and common practice in the industry;

(d) a manufacturer may wish to concentrate on production only, leaving the problem of design, quality and distribution to a multiple retailer.

The attraction of dealer brands to dealers are:

(a) the use of a brand helps to create customer loyalty to the store;

(b) the buying-in price is lower and cost of sales promotion (if any) negligible; therefore the price of dealer branded goods to customers can be lower. Price consciousness is a notable feature of dealer brands.

Packaging

Packaging has four functions:

(a) protection of the contents of the package;

(b) distribution - ie helping to transfer products from the manufacturer to the customer;

Notes

(c) production - ie the design of the package and the words printed on it should help to attract buyers to the product

(d) to conform to government regulations (eg by printing the contents of the package, as required by law)

The qualities required of a pack

(a) It should be reduced to a small range of size and variety in order to keep down purchasing, production and distribution costs, but the range should be sufficiently wide to improve sales with different, distinctive packs.

(b) In industries where distribution is a large part of total costs, packaging should be an important consideration.

   (i) Package should be designed so that they convey the product to its destination in the desired condition.

   (ii) They should assist in the maximum utilisation of space in the transport vehicles.

   (iii) They should help the mechanisation of distribution where mechanical handling is cheaper than labour.

   (iv) They should make optimum use of space in warehouses and retail stores, and lend themselves to display.

   (v) They should be informative so that assistants in self-service stores are not asked about the product by customers.

   (vi) They should keep the product in good condition throughout its shelf life in a retail store.

(c) Packaging is an important aid to selling. Where a product cannot be differentiated by design techniques, the pack takes over the design selling function. This is crucial where there are no real product differences between rival brands, or in the case of commodities such as flour.

   (i) A pack should help to promote the advertising/brand image, eg the brand should be clearly identifiable on the package, in order to take advantage of customer brand loyalty to a range of products.

   (ii) It should be the correct shape, colour and size to exploit customer motivation.

   (iii) It should be the correct size for the expected user of the product (eg family size packets of food).

   (iv) It should be designed so as to exploit impulse buying.

   (v) Where labour-saving convenience is important, it should be a convenience pack (eg tubes, aerosols).

   (vi) It should maintain the product at its expected quality standard.

(vii) In self-service stores, it should attract the eye of potential customers.

It should be apparent that packaging must appeal not only to customers, but also to resellers who must stock the product. A reseller wants a package design that will help sell the product, but also one which minimise the likelihood of broken packs and wasted goods, or which adds to the product's shelf life, or which makes more economic use of shelf space.

Exercise 10

The list above does not by any means exhaust the uses to which packs are put by producers. Try to think of some more.

The packaging of industrial goods is primarily a matter of conveyance in good condition to the point of use and this in itself is a selling aid in future dealings with the customer. The packaging of large pieces of equipment is only as good as the weakest point.

Brand images

Self-image

Each individual perceives himself to be a certain type of person, with certain qualities and circumstances: this is his self image. It is partly developed by reflection from other people, through the interpersonal contacts made in life: the way others respond to the individual teaches him about himself (which is why, for example, people who are constantly criticised develop a very low self image, with very low expectations of themselves).

In fact, the self image is not a single 'snap shot' of what the individual is like, but consists of:

(a) *actual self-concept:* how the individual perceives himself - what he is;

(b) *ideal self-concept:* how the individual would like to perceive himself - what he wishes to be; and

(c) *expected self-concept:* how the individual expects to perceive himself in future - what he aspires to be.

Self image affects product and brand choice because:

(a) products have a symbolic value for consumers: they 'say' something which may or may not be consistent with an individual's actual or aspirational self-image;

(b) consumers need to support or enhance their self images, and can do this by buying products that 'fit' the desired image, and avoiding those that do not;

(c) consumers may also identify with the image of a marketing campaign or retail outlet;

Notes

(d) consumers want to achieve their expected self-concept. Apart from a thriving 'personal image consultancy' industry (advice on wardrobe, presentation etc), there is a general vogue for aspirational products, such as mobile phones, Porsches, or membership of a health club.

Exercise 11

(a) Are you a 'boutique' person or a Marks & Spencer person? Does this image hold true across all product ranges (does M&S food have a different image to M&S clothes, say)?

(b) What kind of shop-window mannequins do you identify with (or not)?

(c) What kind of car do you drive? What kind of car would you like to drive? What is the most desirable kind of car you can really *see* yourself driving?

Brand image

The creation of an image of a product or brand in the market's perception is also known as *product positioning*. It is a very important marketing technique and is discussed in the final section of this chapter. It is important that consumers *perceive* that product to possess the attributes that will fulfil their particular needs better than any competing product.

One technique used by marketers to determine how their products are perceived by consumers, in relation to competing products, is *perceptual mapping*. A grid or cruciform chart is drawn up, indicating key features or benefits. Consumer respondents' perceptions of the products, with reference to those features, are then plotted.

The perceptual map can then be used:

(a) to identify areas where consumers do not feel their needs are being met (for example if no-one perceived products to possess a given benefit or attribute). This would enable you to reposition your product in this area, by an appropriate promotional message stressing the product's unique ability to meet the need (and perhaps also product modification to make it so!);

(b) to identify which competing brands are perceived to be similar to your brand - which may therefore need to be differentiated more clearly; and

(c) to assess the strengths and weaknesses of your product in relation to others, as the basis of your marketing strategy.

Notes

Perceptual map for brands of toilet tissue

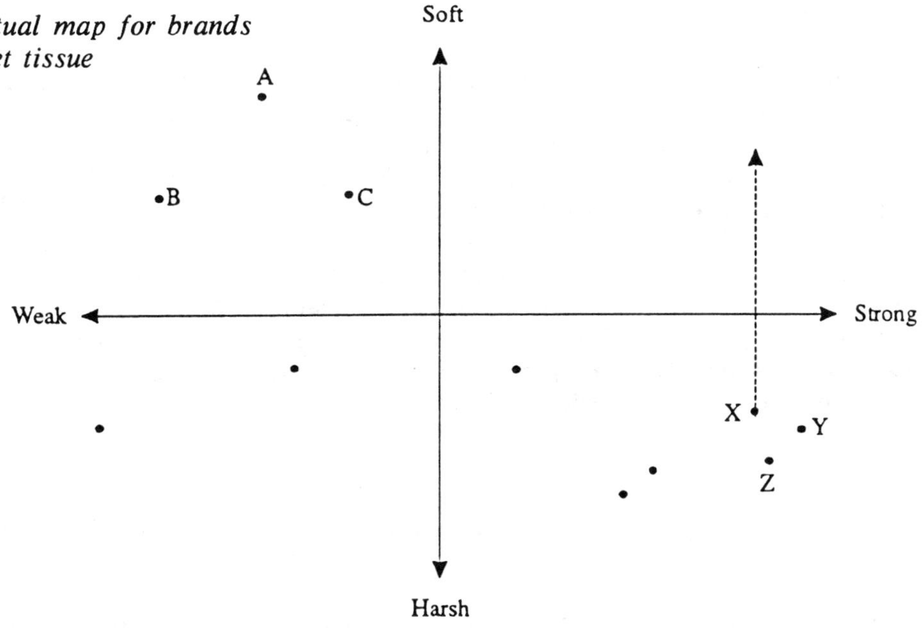

If you were the manufacturer of Brand X, you would be fairly pleased that your brand was perceived as one of the strongest available. You would, however, worry slightly that people found it harsh to the touch: people who want a soft tissue, and are less worried about strength, are presumably buying Brands A, B or C. You would also be a bit concerned that people see little to choose between your Brand X and competing Brands Y and Z: it may come down to price on the supermarket shelves. However, you would be delighted to see that a great opportunity exists for a soft *and* strong toilet tissue: there is no competition there at the moment, and if people are buying Brand A for its softness, how much more eagerly they will buy Brand X if it were sold on 'softness - with strength'!

Organisational image

It is worth noting that organisations also have images in people's minds.

(a) Retailers have their own image, reinforced by own-brand products and labels, in-store design and marketing 'style'. A consumer's perception of a product may be enhanced by the knowledge of its origin: even a loaf of bread looks good in a Harrods bag.

(b) Manufacturers and service providers have their own image, distinct from the brand names they produce. Large corporations with a variety of subsidiary companies and brands may be at pains to establish a unifying ('The name behind all these great brands') corporate image: Rowntree, Hanson Group and Allied Lyons are three recent examples. Corporate image may be based on community and environmental responsibility, sponsorship of sporting or artistic events, or sound managerial/financial performance.

(c) Organisations have an image as employers, both internally and in the external labour market. IBM, Hewlett-Packard and Sainsburys are examples of companies with a very high general reputation as 'enlightened' employers of talented people. Meanwhile, the corporate culture at companies like McDonald's and Walt Disney present a very strong image to and through all their employees.

Notes

The perception of quality

As we mentioned above, people evaluate products on the basis of certain informational 'cues' or indicators. Some of these cues are characteristics of the products themselves *(intrinsic cues)*, but some *(extrinsic cues)* are external factors associated with the product - price, brand name, promotion, display etc. A combination of these cues goes into the perception of a product's quality or value.

Intrinsic cues include the size, colour, smell, taste, feel and functional effectiveness of the product itself. Consumers tend to believe that their evaluations of product quality are based on these objective, physical cues. Indeed, they tend to *want* to believe it, because the buying decision is more readily justifiable on such a basis. However, the physical characteristics chosen as an indicator of quality may actually have little direct relevance.

(a) People claim to prefer the taste of certain brands (of cola-flavoured drink, or margarine, say) to that of others - yet blind tastings show that this discernment is not reliable.

(b) People associate the attributes of quality with irrelevant intrinsic cues - like the colour of biscuits or toothpaste, or the feel of the packaging.

Exercise 12

You will certainly have read of the efforts manufacturers take to ensure that the 'intrinsic cues' give the right message. Can you think of examples?

Extrinsic cues are brought to bear on quality evaluations, especially if the consumer has no direct experience of the product.

Price is a particularly interesting extrinsic cue. People perceive price to be related to quality, and it has even been shown that consumers may evaluate differently identical products with different price tags! In the absence of other more influential cues such as brand or shop image, price acts as a surrogate indicator of quality: there is a positive price/quality perception. Some products are therefore priced deliberately highly to position them as 'premium' or 'quality' brands: consumers may be suspicious of brands that are 'cheap'.

(a) Stella Artois beer has recently been marketed as 'reassuringly expensive'.

(b) Various brands (of beer, coffee, dishwashing liquid) have been positioned as 'costing a bit more', but 'worth the difference' because of their superior quality.

(c) However, given experience with a product, or familiarity with a brand name, price is a less important indicator of quality, and highly-priced brands which do not bear out expectations of quality difference can be negatively perceived: 'I'm not paying more for Brand X - it doesn't taste any different to this cheaper/own brand one!'

Notes

Perceived risk

Perceived risk is 'the uncertainty that consumers face when they cannot foresee the consequences of their purchase decisions'. Any purchase decision involves some risk, and to the extent that risk is *perceived* by the consumer, it will influence his decision.

Perceived risks may be:

(a) *functional* - will the product do what 'they' say it will, and what I want it to do? Is there a better one?

(b) *financial* - will it be worth its cost? Am I getting a good deal on it? Ought I to spend this money?

(c) *physical* - is it difficult or dangerous to use, or environmentally unfriendly?

(d) *social/psychological* - will the family/friends/Joneses approve of it? Will I be embarrassed if it fails, or is the 'wrong' one? Will I feel good about it?

The extent to which an individual *perceives* any of these risks to be present depends on:

(a) *personality and post experience.* Some people are high risk perceivers, risk-averse and wanting to 'play safe', while others are low risk perceivers, preferring to 'live dangerously' in the choices they make. People learn about risk from experience: 'once bitten, twice shy';

(b) *the product.* Buying a car or microwave oven is more high-risk than, say, buying a book or a set of cookware;

(c) *the situation.* Ordering by mail or telephone is riskier than buying something in a shop. Choosing something in your own time is perceived as less risky than having to make up your mind in front of a door-to-door salesman;

(d) *culture.* Some cultures are more risk-sensitive than others, because of attitudes to money, status, the environment or whatever. Marketers cannot take for granted the effectiveness of their risk-reduction strategies in one country, if they want to apply them to another.

Consumers handle risk in various ways, according to the type and degree of risk they perceive. Typical strategies - which marketers may support with their own efforts - include:

(a) gathering more information from product users and trusted others. Marketers can help this process by encouraging word-of-mouth reports (or simulating them in a promotional message: 'I always buy...', 'I wouldn't swap my ... for anything else'). Endorsements and consumer reports are perceivedly 'unbiased' sources of reassuring information, but advertisements and sales force presentations may also be directed at overcoming specific doubts;

(b) loyalty to a tried and trusted brand, avoiding the risky situation of trying something new and unknown. This is most common for products like shampoos and detergents;

Notes

(c) trust in a well-known, established and/or 'best selling' brand name/image. Such a brand has been positioned as dependable, high-quality or whatever, and appears as a 'safer bet': 'x is well-known for its quality', or 'two million people can't be wrong' (yes they can, but few people perceive the logical flaw);

(d) trust in the price/quality relationship. The expensive brand is often assumed to be the best;

(e) trust in the image/reputation of the retail outlet. If they have no experience of the product, but have positive experience of the shop in which it is being sold, consumers may trust the judgement of the shop - especially if it also gives them the option of returning the product, or getting after-sales service.

Marketing organisations can also offer reassurance in the form of: guarantees and warranties, offering money-back for fault or dissatisfaction; free trials, samples or periods of 'home approval'; publicity for awards and official approvals gained; certificates of laboratory testing; qualification for British Standard or similar quality 'marks'.

Exercise 13

Can you think of some examples of these reassurances.

A 'brand' is a name, term, sign, symbol or design intended to identify the product of a seller and to differentiate it from those of competitors.

Not long ago, and this is still the case in many less developed countries, most products were sold unbranded from barrels and bins etc. Today in developed and even developing countries hardly anything goes unbranded. Even salt, oranges, nuts and screws are often branded. There has however been a limited return recently in some developed countries to 'generics'. These are cheap, unbranded products, packaged plainly and not heavily advertised.

To brand or not to brand?

The advantages of branding include the following.

(a) Branding facilitates memory recall, thus contributing to self-selection and improving customer loyalty.

(b) In many cultures branding is preferred, particularly in the distribution channel.

(c) Branding is a way of obtaining legal protection for product features.

(d) It helps with market segmentation. (Take toothpaste for example: Crest is marketed to a health conscious segment, Ultrabrite is marketed for its cosmetic qualities).

(e) It helps build a strong and positive corporate image, especially if the brand name used is the company name (eg Kelloggs, Heinz). It is not so important if the company name is not used (eg Procter & Gamble).

(f) Branding makes it easier to link advertising to other marketing communications programmes.

(g) Display space is more easily obtained and point-of-sale promotions are more practicable.

(h) If branding is successful, other associated products can be introduced.

(i) The need for expensive personal selling/persuasion may be reduced.

Branding is not relevant to all products, only those:

(a) that can achieve mass sales because of the high cost of branding and the subsequent advertising. This is particularly important if global branding is sought; and

(b) whose attributes can be evaluated by consumers.

Thus chocolate bars can be branded, but not concrete slabs; whisky can be branded, but not coal.

The most successful examples of worldwide branding occur where the brand has become synonymous with the generic product: Hoover, Cellophane, Sellotape, Aspirin, Kleenex, Filofax, Xerox. This can eventually, however, carry its own dangers. When the brand name has been adopted as the description of the generic product (such as Thermos for a vacuum flask) the manufacturer of the brand can find it difficult to convey the specific product advantages of the brand.

Types of brand

There are four choices of brand.

(a) *Individual brand name*. This is the option chosen by Procter & Gamble for example, who even have different brand names within the same product line, eg Bold, Tide. The main advantage of individual product branding is that an unsuccessful brand (eg Strand cigarettes) does not adversely affect the firm's other products, nor the firm's reputation generally.

(b) *Blanket family brand name* for all products, eg Hoover, Heinz (originally 'Heinz 57 varieties'). This has the advantage of enabling the global organisation to introduce new products quickly and successfully. Also the cost of introducing the new product in terms of name research and awareness advertising will be reduced (eg Honda lawn mowers).

(c) *Separate family names* for different product divisions, eg the US-based company Sears sells electrical appliances under the name Kenmore, and women's clothing under the Kerrybrook brand.

This is obviously the option for the global organisation with 'inconsistent' product lines where the family brand name above is not appropriate. But within each 'family' the advantages identified in (b) still apply.

Notes

(d) *The company trade name combined with an individual product name,* eg Kelloggs - Corn Flakes, Rice Crispies etc). This option both legitimises (because of the company name) and individualises (the individual product name). As in (b) above it allows new 'names' to be introduced quickly and relatively cheaply.

Success criteria for branding

Branding should be a central and strategic part of both product and promotional planning. It should not be a casual afterthought. It therefore requires research in all the markets in which the brand is planned to be marketed. For international companies name research can avoid possible faux pas because of cultural and language differences.

Worldwide research suggests that the beneficial qualities of a brand name are that they should:

(a) suggest benefits, eg Ultrabrite toothpaste, Slimline tonic;

(b) suggest qualities such as action or colour, (eg Shake 'n Vac);

(c) be easy to pronounce, recognise and remember (ie short and punchy);

(d) be acceptable in all markets both linguistically and culturally;

(e) be distinctive, eg Kodak;

(f) be meaningful. When Procter & Gamble wished to launch 'Crest Tartar Control' into South American countries, research found that there was no recognised Spanish translation for dental tartar. A similar word implied 'sorrow'. The brand name was successfully changed to 'Crest Anti-Sorro'.

Global brand decisions

For the international company marketing products which can be branded there are two further policy decisions to be made. These are:

(a) the problem of deciding if and how to protect the company's brands (and associated trademarks); and

(b) whether there should be one global brand or many different national brands for a given product.

The major argument in favour of a single global brand is the economies of scale that it produces, both in production and promotion. But whether a global brand is the best policy or even possible depends on a number of factors, which address the two basic policy decisions above.

Legal considerations for branding

(a) Legal constraints may limit the possibilities for a global brand, for instance where the brand name has already been registered in a foreign country

Notes

(b) Protection of the brand name will often be needed, but internationally is hard to achieve because:

(i) in some countries registration is difficult;
(ii) brand imitation and piracy are rife in certain parts of the world.

There are many examples of imitation in international branding, with products such as cigarettes (USA), and denim jeans.

Worse still is the problem of piracy where a well known brand name is counterfeited. It is illegal in most parts of the world but in many countries there is little if any enforcement of the law. (Levis is one of the most pirated brand names).

Cultural aspects of branding

Even if a firm has no legal difficulties with branding globally, there may be cultural problems, eg unpronounceable names, names with other meanings (undesirable or even obscene).

There are many examples of problems in global branding, for example Maxwell House is Maxwell Kaffee in Germany, Legal in France and Monky in Spain. But sometimes a minor spelling change is all that is needed, such as Wrigley Speermint in Germany.

Other marketing considerations

Many other influences affect the global branding decision, including:

(a) differences between the firm's major brand and its secondary brands. The major brand is more likely to be branded globally than secondary brands;

(b) the importance of brand to the product sale. Where price, for example, is a more important factor, then it may not be worth the heavy expenditure needed to establish and maintain a global brand in each country. A series of national brands may be more effective;

(c) the problem of how to brand a product arising from acquisition or joint venture. Should the multinational company keep the name it has acquired?

Exercise 14

In the 1950s, the BBC ran an experiment in its live In Town Tonight programme. A journalist stood at Piccadilly Circus offering passers-by the opportunity to buy £1 notes for 10 shillings (50p). What do you think was the reaction of the passers-by?

Positioning

Brands can be positioned against competitive brands on product maps that are defined in terms of how buyers perceive key characteristics.

Yoram Wind identifies a comprehensive list of these characteristics.

Notes

(a) *Positioning by specific product features.* This is the most common approach to positioning, especially for industrial products. Price and specific product features are used as the basis for positioning. Most car advertisements stress the combination of product features available and may also stress what good value for money this represents.

(b) *Positioning by benefits, problems, solutions, or needs.* The emphasis is on benefits, which is generally more effective than positioning on product features without referring to the benefits. Pharmaceutical companies position their products to doctors by stressing effectiveness and side effects. Other examples include Crest, which positions its toothpaste as a cavity fighter, and DHL, which uses its worldwide network of offices as a basis for its positioning.

(c) *Positioning for specific usage occasions.* This approach is related to benefit positioning but uses the specific occasion as the major basis for the positioning. Johnson's Baby Shampoo is, thus, positioned as a product to use if you shampoo your hair every day, and Hennessy Cognac is for special occasions.

(d) *Positioning for user category.* Examples here include 7-Up's use of the Fido Dido character to target urban adolescents. Age has been used as a basis for positioning by Saga Holidays, by many breakfast cereal producers (compare the target markets for Kellogg's Rice Krispies and Special K) and by Affinity shampoo for women over 40.

(e) *Positioning against another product.* Although Avis never mentions Hertz explicitly in its advertising, its positioning as Number 2 in the rent-a-car market is an example of positioning against a leader.

(f) *Product class disassociation.* This is a less common basis for positioning, but it can be effective when introducing a new product that is different from standard products in an established product category. Lead-free petrol is positioned against leaded petrol.

(g) *Hybrid basis.* Often, a positioning strategy will be based on several of these alternatives, incorporating elements from more than one positioning base. The Porsche positioning, for example, is based on the product benefits as well as on a certain type of user.

A basic perceptual map is to plot brands in perceived price and perceived quality terms.

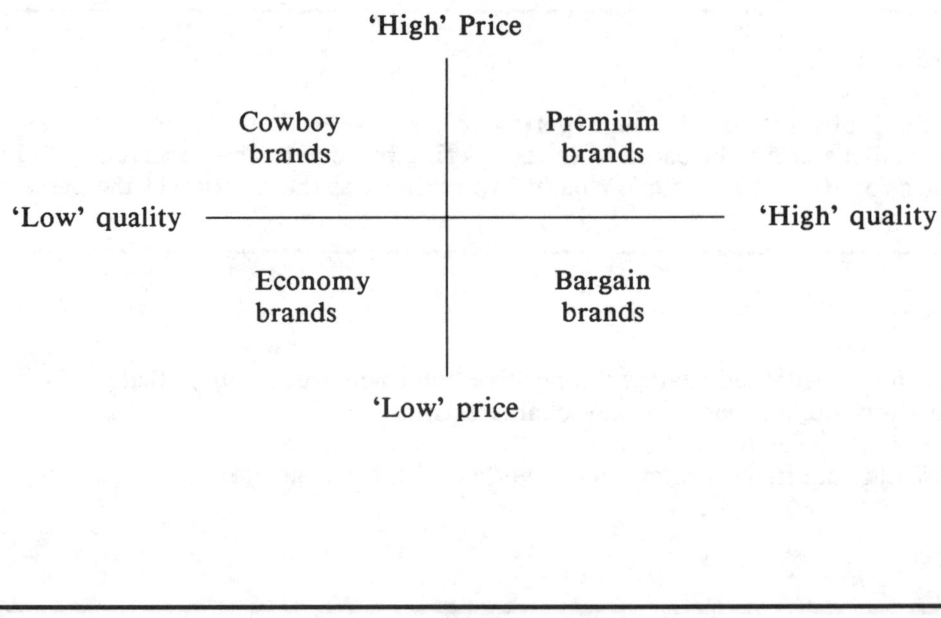

Notes

Price and quality are important elements in the marketing mix, but they will not, in the customer's opinion, be considered independent variables. A 'high' price will usually be associated with high quality and equally low price with low quality. Thus, while everybody would like to buy a bargain brand, there is a problem to overcome. This is a question of belief: will customers accept that a high quality product can be offered at a low price?

Where would you place MFI in quality/price space? MFI would claim to be in the 'bargain' quadrant. Many potential customers think that they are at the lower end of the economy segment. MFI's practice of frequent sales and discounts has the effect of overcoming at least some of the difficulties resulting from individuals using price as a surrogate for assessment of quality. Thus the price label shows the higher pre-discounted price and the low sale price. The assumption is that customers will use the pre-sale price to confirm promotional claims about quality.

Public concern about the use of such promotional pricing has led to the introduction of restrictions on the use of these techniques. Stores now have to provide evidence that the promotion is part of a genuine 'sale'.

Identifying a gap in the market

Market research can determine where customers think that competitive brands are located.

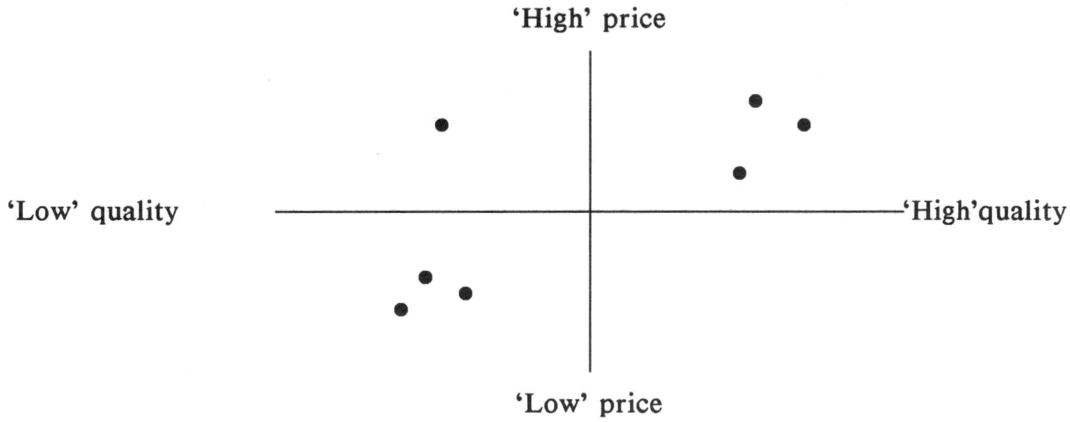

Restaurants in Anytown

In the hypothetical model above, there appears to be a gap in the market for a moderately priced reasonable quality eating place. This is shown between clusters in the high price/high quality and the low price/low quality segments.

However, it would be necessary to sound a note of caution before rushing off to set up such an establishment. Why does the gap exist? Is it that no entrepreneurial restaurateur has noticed the opportunity? Or is it that, while there is sufficient demand for gourmet eating and cheap cafes, there are insufficient customers to justify a restaurant in the middle range segment? More research would be needed to determine which of these conditions apply.

Perceptual maps can also be drafted to plot how customers perceive competitive brands performing on key product user benefits. Kotler provides the following hypothetical examples. He starts by considering the various products that serve the US breakfast market.

Notes

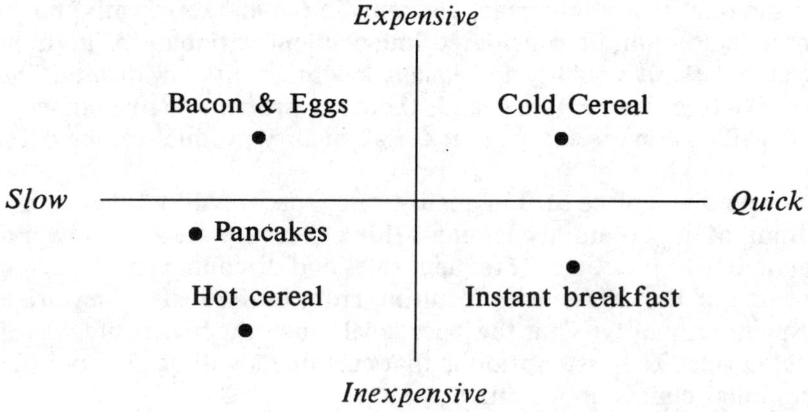

Product-positioning map: Breakfast market

Within the breakfast market, a producer might be interested in entering the instant breakfast market. It would then be advisable to plot the position of the various instant breakfast brands.

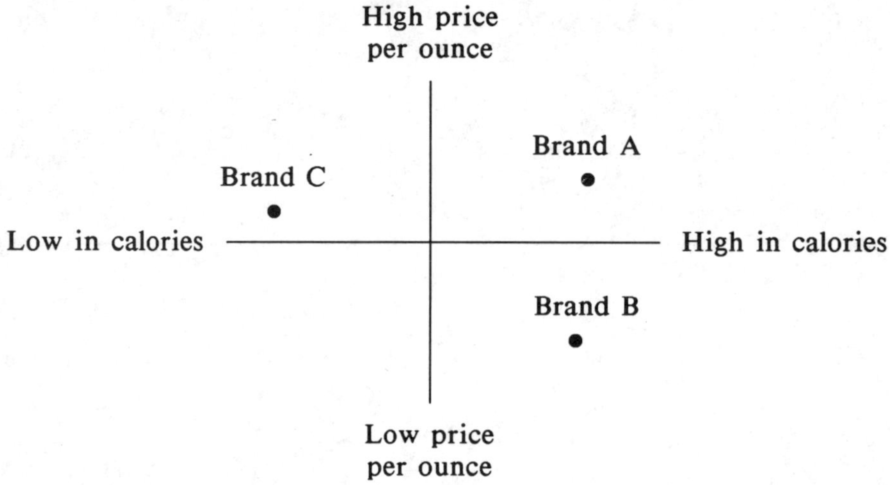

Brand-positioning map (Instant breakfast market)

(Kotler, *Marketing Management)*

The above analysis now shows an apparent gap for a modest priced slimmers brand. Once again, it would be necessary to establish whether or not there exists sufficient demand for such a product to ensure that its production would be profitable.

When Ford launched the Fiesta, market research showed that whilst potential customers thought highly of the new car's performance and considered it economical, there were problems with perceptions of safety. This was inevitable given that its small size was seen as a minus point with regard to safety in the event of collision. Ford knew their product to be safe and so, when the Fiesta was relaunched, targeted the advertising copy line to change people's perception. One such advertisement showed the Fiesta braking in wet conditions. Another showed an expectant mother being delivered to hospital on time in spite of having to make an emergency stop when some idiot stepped out onto a zebra crossing.

Competitive positioning

Competitive positioning concerns 'a general idea of what kind of offer to make to the target market in relation to competitors' offers' (Kotler). Important considerations in competitive positioning are product quality and price, and Kotler identified a 3 × 3 matrix of nine different competitive positioning strategies.

Product quality	*High price*	*Medium price*	*Low price*
High	Premium strategy	Penetration strategy	Superbargain strategy
Medium	Overpricing strategy	Average quality strategy	Bargain strategy
Low	Hit and run strategy	Shoddy goods strategy	Cheap goods strategy

Chapter roundup

(a) The growth strategy adopted by a firm will reflect a choice between various options relating to the firm's products (existing and new) and markets (existing and new).

(b) The classification of products (and markets) has been the subject of research for many years. Well known models include the product life cycle, the Boston matrix and the General Electric business screen.

(c) Product innovation is a key factor in the success of many organisations. We looked at different features of a product which may enable it to be classified as 'new', and also at the process by which new product ideas are screened and, if successful, developed.

(d) Branding is a powerful marketing tool, and is adopted almost universally by firms in developed economies. But the use of branding gives rise to complex strategic decisions.

Notes

Quick quiz

1 What is 'cannibalisation'?

2 What are the four stages in the product life cycle?

3 Everett Rogers classified the people adopting a new product into five groups. List them.

4 Summarise the results of Polli and Cook's research into the product life cycle. For what category of products did they conclude that the plc would be relevant?

5 In the Boston matrix, what is signified by the position of the split on the vertical axis?

6 Describe what is meant by a 'cash cow'.

7 List five possible sources of ideas for new products.

8 List six reasons why companies brand their products.

9 What is meant by brand extension?

Solutions to exercises

1 Everyone's answer will differ, but here is one possibility.

Market penetration. Technological developments, combined with a rise in the general level of real incomes, have enabled manufacturers of 'consumer durables' (fridges, washing machines etc) to push their products into the vast majority of UK homes.

Market development. Think of how East European motor manufacturers have gradually won acceptance for their products in the UK.

Product development. You are reading an example of this. BPP Publishing at one time produced books only for students of professional examinations. More recently the list has developed to include books for undergraduates.

Diversification. This is the hardest to find examples for. You will certainly have thought of diverse groups (such as Hanson Group, Lonrho etc), but they exemplify acquisition more than diversification. Perhaps you thought of Richard Branson (from records to airlines, though he divested himself of the records business). A more mundane example might be Marks & Spencer introducing its food business (which more recently has spanned an up-market City sandwich bar).

2 The key is the phrase 'wide social connections'. Communication is often by word of mouth.

Notes

3 Every one of these is open to debate, but here is the author's opinion for what it's worth! You may find it worthwhile to think further about the ones you disagree with.

(a) Mobile telephones. Growth
(b) Baked bean. Maturity
(c) Satellite television. Introduction (possibly growth).
(d) Cigarettes. Probably decline in the Western hemisphere, though for Third World countries this is a growth product.
(e) Carbon paper. Decline.
(f) Mortgages. Maturity
(g) Writing implements. Maturity
(h) Car alarms. Maturity
(i) Organically grown fruit and vegetables. Introduction.

4 For one thing, they can look at the product's sales history. They can also attempt to extrapolate past sales into forecasts of future sales. Finally, their experience of earlier products may provide indications relevant to later products.

5 The figures produced by Rogers himself, though somewhat arbitrary, make interesting reading.

	Proportion
Innovators	2.5%
Early adopters	12.5%
Early majority	34.0%
Late majority	34.0%
Late adopters and laggards	17.0%
	100.0%

6 This argument has been suggested as a weakening of the case in favour of marketing. But looked at another way, it is the reverse of that. Poor marketing may mean that a product moves from being a problem child to being a dog without making much contribution to profits in the meantime. Equally, good marketing may prolong the 'star' and 'cash cow' phases.

9 Not all personal organisers are made by Filofax. Another example is Sellotape.

10 Two possibilities are:

(a) as a vehicle for carrying sales promotions (eg collecting labels to earn a prize);

(b) as a toy (at the time of writing, Kelloggs Cornflakes packets are carrying a dinosaur feature. Once you've finished eating the cornflakes you can fold the packet to make a model pteranodon, euoplocephalus and so on).

Notes

12 One example is the use of colouring agents, for example in frozen vegetables. The fact that such agents are entirely tasteless does not affect their value from a marketing point of view. On the same theme, people appear to prefer eggs with brown shells to those with white, and many farmers adjust their hen feed to produce the desired colour.

13 (a) Most electrical appliances carry a guarantee.
(b) Cars - and even computers - can be 'test driven' at the showrooms.
(c) Sample packs of shampoos, perfumes, instant drinks etc are widely circulated.
(d) Most product packaging carries a sticker with the British Standards kitemark, or 'No animal testing' or 'Voted best ... of 19XX', or 'x million copies sold'.

14 To begin with, passers-by spurned the offer, apparently concerned by the risk of losing money. Then the journalist reported, over the live broadcast, that nobody so far had taken up the offer. Almost immediately, he was swamped by people eager to trade. All they had needed was reassurance that a genuine bargain was on offer.

7 DISTRIBUTION

Your objectives

After completing this chapter you should:

(a) understand the nature and the main types of distribution channel;
(b) understand the factors involved in the selection of distribution channels;
(c) be aware of the additional factors relevant to distribution elsewhere in Europe and in the international markets.

1 What are distribution channels?

The fourth 'P' in the marketing mix is place and this component is essentially concerned with the processes by which the product is made available to the consumer. Other more commonly used terms for 'place' include distribution, delivery systems and marketing channels. The terms are often used interchangeably since they all concern themselves with making products available to the market. Although place is normally the last element in the list of marketing mix variables, its importance should not be underestimated, especially in provision of services. After all, a considerable amount of marketing effort will be wasted if the product is not actually in the right place at the right time to enable a purchase to be made. Furthermore, it is beneficial to any organisation to give thorough consideration to the place component of the marketing mix since effective and efficient distribution can be an important source of competitive advantage.

Distribution is often seen as the Cinderella of the marketing mix. In companies where distribution involves the physical transport of goods and stores, the marketing executive may have insufficient control over the distribution function, resulting in a lack of real co-ordination within the marketing mix. However, the choice of a particular distribution policy, such as whether or not to use wholesalers, may result in the company delegating to intermediaries much of its marketing function, such as selling to the end user.

Exercise 1

For many type of goods, producers invariably use retailers as middlemen in getting the product to the customer. Try to think of some of the disadvantages of doing this, from the producer's point of view.

It is important to recognise that independently owned and operated distributors have their own objectives, strategies and plans which, in their decision making processes, are likely to take precedence over those of the manufacturer or supplier with whom they are dealing. This fact can lead to conflict and in some cases suppliers solve the problem by buying their own distribution route or by distributing direct to their customers. Direct distribution is common for many industrial and/or customised systems suppliers. In some consumer markets direct distribution is also in evidence, for instance for insurance ('the man from the Pru'), double glazing and Avon cosmetics.

Notes

However a product is distributed a number of basic distributive functions usually need to be fulfilled.

(a) *Transport*

This function can be provided by the supplier or by the distributor or indeed can be sub-contracted to a specialist. For some products, such as perishable goods, transport planning is vital. The 'rent or buy' decision on transport is important and has both financial and operational consequences.

(b) *Stockholding and storage*

For production planning purposes a smooth flow of production is often essential, so stocks of raw materials and components accumulate and need to be stored. Significant costs and risks can be involved in holding stock.

For consumer goods, the costs of holding stock at the point of sale is very expensive; the cost of city centre retail locations is prohibitive and a good stock control system must be used, designed to avoid stockouts whilst keeping stockholding costs low.

(c) *Local knowledge*

As production has tended to become centralised to obtain maximum economies of scale, the need to understand local markets has grown. This point applies particularly when international marketing takes place. To understand the intricacies and idiosyncrasies of local markets is a key marketing input. Whilst it is possible to buy specialist market research help, the local distributor with day-to-day customer contact has a vital role.

(d) *Promotion*

Whilst major promotional campaigns for national products are likely to be carried out by the supplier, the translation of the campaign to local level is usually the responsibility of the local distributor, often as a joint venture. Hence the advertising agency of the supplier will produce local advertising material which leaves space for the local distributor's name to be added. National press campaigns can feature lists of local stockists.

(e) *Display*

Presentation of the product at the local level is often a function of the local distributor. Again, specialist help from merchandisers can be bought in but decisions on layout and display need to be taken by local distributors, often following patterns produced centrally.

Types of distribution channel

Channels of distribution include the following.

(a) *Retailers*. These are traders operating outlets which sell directly to households. They may be classified by:

(i) type of goods sold (eg hardware, furniture);
(ii) type of service (self-service, counter service);

(iii) size;
(iv) location (rural, city-centre, suburban shopping mall, out-of-town shopping centre).

Another classification, overlapping with the first, is:

(i) independent retailers (including the local corner shop, although independents are not always as small as this);

(ii) multiple chains. Some of these are associated with one class of product; others are 'variety' chains, holding a wide range of different stocks; still others are voluntary groups of independents, usually grocers.

Exercise 2

Think of at least one example of each of these catagories of multiple chains.

(b) *Wholesalers.* These are intermediaries who stock a range of products from competing manufacturers to sell on to other organisations such as retailers. Many wholesalers specialise in particular products. Most deal in consumer goods, but some specialise in industrial goods (eg steel stockholders and builders' merchants).

(c) *Distributors and dealers.* These are organisations which contract to buy a manufacturer's goods and sell them to customers. Their function is similar to that of wholesalers, but they usually offer a narrower product range, sometimes (as in the case of most car dealers) the products of a single manufacturer. In addition to selling on the manufacturer's product, distributors often promote the products and provide after-sales service.

(d) *Agents.* Agents differ from distributors in the following ways.

(i) Distributors buy the manufacturer's goods and re-sell them at a profit.
(ii) Agents do not purchase the manufacturer's goods, but earn a commission on whatever sales they make.

(e) *Franchisees.* These are independent organisations which in exchange for an initial fee and (usually) a share of sales revenue are allowed to trade under the name of a parent organisation. For example few of the Kall Kwik chain of High Street print shops are actually owned by Kall Kwik - most are run by franchisees.

Exercise 3

Some very well known businesses are run partly or wholly on a franchise basis. Can you think of any? What are the advantages of such an arrangement to the franchisor?

(f) *Multiple stores* (eg supermarkets) which buy goods for retailing direct from the producer, many of them under their 'own label' brand name.

(g) *Direct selling.* This can take place by various means:

Notes

(i) mail order;
(ii) telephone selling;
(iii) door-to-door selling;
(iv) personal selling in the sale of industrial goods;
(v) a vertically-integrated organisation which includes both manufacturing and retail outlets;
(vi) computer-shopping or TV shopping.

2 The choice of distribution channels

The choice of distribution channels is an important one for any organisation, not least because once a set of channels has been established, subsequent changes can be costly and are likely to be slow to implement. In very broad terms we can consider distribution channels as falling into one of two categories: *direct* and *indirect channels*. The distinction is fairly crude, but nevertheless useful.

Direct distribution concerns itself with ways in which the product can be supplied directly from producer to consumer without the use of a specific intermediary. These methods are often described as active since they typically involve the supplier making the first approach to a potential customer. Direct distribution methods generally fall into two categories: those using *media* such as the press, leaflets and telephones to invite response and purchase by the consumer, and those using a *sales force* to contact consumers face to face.

The alternative type of distribution system is *indirect distribution* which typically refers to systems of distribution, common among manufactured goods, which make use of an intermediary; usually a wholesaler, retailer or both. In contrast to direct distribution, these methods are often thought of as being passive in the sense that they rely on consumers to make the first approach by entering the relevant retail outlet.

Exercise 4

One factor influencing the choice between direct and indirect methods is the average order size for a product. State what you think the relationship might be between average order size and the occurrence (or non-occurence) of direct distribution.

General principles in the choice of distribution channel

Marketing involves certain basic processes.

(a) Bringing buyers and sellers into contact.
(b) Offering a sufficient choice of goods to meet the needs of buyers.
(c) Persuading customers to develop a favourable opinion of a particular product.
(d) Distributing goods from the manufacturing point to retail outlets.
(e) Maintaining an adequate level of sales.
(f) Providing appropriate services (eg credit, after-sales service).
(g) Maintaining an acceptable price.

The choice of channels of distribution will depend on how far a manufacturing company wishes to carry out these processes itself, and how far it decides to delegate them to other organisations - ie there is a range of choice between direct selling and selling through independent outlets.

In building up efficient channels of distribution, a manufacturer must consider several factors.

(a) How many intermediate stages should be used? There could be zero, one, two or three intermediate stages of selling. In addition, it will be necessary to decide how many dealers at each stage should be used - ie how many agents should be used, or how many wholesalers should be asked to sell the manufacturer's products, and even then 'what should the size of the direct sales force be?'

(b) The support that the manufacturer should give to the dealers. It may be necessary to provide an efficient after-sales and repair service, or to agree to an immediate exchange of faulty products returned by a retailer's customers, and to regularly weekly, bi-weekly or monthly visits to retailers' stores. To help selling, the manufacturer might need to consider advertising or sales promotion support, including merchandising.

(c) The extent to which the manufacturer wishes to 'dominate' a channel of distribution. A market leader, for example, might wish to ensure that its market share of sales is maintained, so that it might, for example, wish to offer exclusive distribution contracts to major retailers.

(d) The extent to which the manufacturer wishes to integrate its marketing effort up to the point of sale with the consumer. Combined promotions with retailers, for example, would only be possible if the manufacturer dealt directly with the retailer (and did not sell to the retailer through a wholesaler).

Exercise 5

The use of intermediaries has a dramatic effect on the number of distribution channels. Suppose a product is available from 30 suppliers and purchased for re-sale by 200 retailers. How many channels of distribution does this represent? Now suppose that all sales/purchases are transmitted through a single wholesaler, taking product from all 30 suppliers and selling to all 200 retailers. How many channels are there now?

We will now examine the choice of distribution channels in more details. To give focus to the discussion, we will adopt the following headings: customers, product characteristics, distributor characteristics, the channel chosen by competitors and the supplier's own characteristics.

Customers

The number of potential customers, their buying habits and their geographical locations are key influences. The use of mail order for those with limited mobility (rural location, illness) is an example of the influence of customers on channel design. Marketing industrial components to the car industry needs to take account of location of

Notes

the car industry in the UK. Selling to supermarket chains in the UK is now very difficult as the concentration of grocery retailing into a few large chains has increased the power of the buyers: specialist centralised buyers can extract highly favourable terms from suppliers. Unless the supplier is successful in selling to the big chains, the product will only be available to small numbers of shoppers each week.

Product characteristics

Some product characteristics have an important effect on design of the channel of distribution

(a) *Perishability*
Fresh fruit and newspapers are examples of perishable products which must be distributed very quickly or they become worthless. Speed is therefore a key factor in the design of the distribution system.

(b) *Customisation*
Customised products tend to be distributed direct. Where a wide range of options are available, such as fitted kitchens, sales are made from demonstration units with customised delivery to follow.

(c) *After-sales service/technical advice*
When these are to be offered, the extent and cost must be considered, training given and quality control systems set up. Training programmes are often provided for distributors by suppliers. Exclusive area franchises can be allocated to ensure distributor co-operation; the disadvantage of this is that a poor distributor may cost a supplier dearly in a particular area.

(d) *Franchising*
Franchising has become a popular means of growth both for suppliers like Body Shop and for franchisees who carry the set-up costs and licence fees and are clearly controlled by the supplier. The supplier gains more outlets more quickly and exerts more control than is usual in distribution.

Exercise 6

This is not an exhaustive list of the ways in which product characteristics influence channel choices. Try to add to it.

Distributor characteristics

The capability of the distributor to take on the distributive functions already discussed above is obviously an important choice influence for the supplier.

Competitors' channel choice

For many consumer goods, a supplier's brand will sit side by side with its competitors' products and there is little the supplier can do about it. For other products it is common for distributors to stock one name brand only (for example, in car distribution) and in return to be given an exclusive area. In this case new suppliers can face difficulties in breaking into a market if all the best distribution outlets have been taken up.

Supplier characteristics

A strong financial base offers the supplier the option of buying and operating a distribution channel: Boots the Chemist is a prime example. The market position of the supplier is also important: distributors are keen to be associated with the market leader but the third, fourth or fifth brand in a market is likely to find more distribution problems.

Making the channel decision

The above considerations can be translated into a number of decision options.

(a) What types of distributor are to be used (wholesalers, retailers, agents)?

(b) How many of each type will be used? The answer to this depends on what degree of market exposure will be sought:

  (i) intensive - blanket coverage;
  (ii) exclusive - appointed agents for exclusive areas;
  (iii) selective - some but not all in each area;

(c) Who will carry out specific marketing tasks such as:

  (i) credit provision;
  (ii) delivery;
  (iii) after-sales service;
  (iv) training (sales and product);
  (v) display?

(d) How will the performance of distributors be evaluated?

  (i) In terms of cost?
  (ii) In terms of sales levels?
  (iii) According to the degree of control achieved?
  (iv) By the amount of conflict that arises?

To sum up, to develop an integrated system of distribution, the supplier must consider all the factors influencing distribution combined with a knowledge of the relative merits of the different types of channel available.

Notes

Factors favouring the use of direct selling

(a) There may be a need for an expert sales force to demonstrate the product, explain product characteristics and provide after sales service. Publishers, for example, use sales reps to keep booksellers up to date with new titles, to arrange for the return of unsold books and so on.

(b) Intermediaries may be unwilling or unable to sell the product. For example, the ill fated Sinclair C5 eventually had to be sold by direct mail.

(c) Existing channels may be tied to other producers or reluctant to carry new product lines.

(d) The intermediaries willing to sell the product may be too expensive. After all, they make their profits from selling goods for more than they pay for them. Alternatively, they may not be maximising potential sales. This is the problem which caused Nissan to terminate its contract with its sole UK distributor in 1991: Nissan believed that the distributor's pricing strategy was inappropriate.

(e) If specialised transport requirements are required intermediaries may not be able to deliver goods to the final customer.

(f) Where potential buyers are geographically concentrated it is easy for the supplier's own sales force to reach them (typically an industrial market). One example is the financial services market centred on the City of London.

Exercise 7

Again, the list is far from complete. Try to add to it.

Factors favouring the use of intermediaries

Although middlemen take a share of the profit from a product, it might be commercially profitable for a manufacturer to use them for the following reasons.

(a) Middlemen might (depending on individual circumstances) bear the costs of:

  (i) stockholding;
  (ii) transportation;
  (iii) consolidation of small orders into larger ones;
  (iv) providing display facilities.

(b) Manufacturers might receive payment more quickly from middlemen than if they tried to sell direct to the customer.

(c) *Consolidation of small orders into large ones.* A manufacturer produces goods in large quantities and the final customer buys in small quantities. There is, therefore, the need for a consolidation function in the distribution network which can convert large volumes of output into smaller selling units. Because of the cost of processing individual customers' orders, there is a higher cost involved in selling in small units than in large units, and another factor in distribution policy is the consideration of the extent to which a manufacturer wishes to take on this task and how far it will be delegated.

(d) *Display space and distribution.* Selling involves display, and a manufacturer's problem in obtaining sufficient display for his goods concerns distribution policy as well as sales promotion.

(e) There may be insufficient financial resources to finance the extra overhead of a large sales force.

(f) It may be a policy decision to invest in increased productive capacity rather than extra marketing effort.

(g) The supplier may not have sufficient in-house marketing 'knowhow' in selling to retail stores, such as lack of shelf-space allocation skills.

(h) The assortment of products may be insufficient for a sales force to carry. A wholesaler can complement a limited range and make more efficient use of his sales force.

(i) There may be large numbers of potential buyers over a wide geographical spread (typically consumer markets).

A producer serving both industrial and consumer markets may decide to use intermediaries for his consumer division and direct selling for his industrial division. For example, a detergent manufacturer might employ salesmen to sell to wholesalers and large retail groups in their consumer division. It would not be efficient for the sales force to approach small retailers directly.

Industrial and consumer distribution channels

The distribution channels appropriate for industrial markets may not be suitable for consumer markets. The common channels for each sector will now be outlined.

Industrial markets may be characterised by having fewer, larger customers often purchasing expensive products that may be custom-built. It is due to these characteristics that industrial distribution channels tend to be more direct and shorter than for consumer markets. It has to be remembered, however, that the most appropriate distribution channels will depend specifically on the objectives of the company regarding market exposure. There are specialist distributors in the industrial sector, which may be used as well as, or instead of, selling directly to the companies within this sector.

Exercise 8

Given the obvious advantages of direct selling in industrial markets, why might the use of distributors sometimes be preferable?

Notes

There are fewer direct distribution channels, from the manufacturer to the consumer in the *consumer market*. Examples can be found in small 'cottage' industries or mail order companies. It is more usual for companies in consumer markets to use wholesalers and retailers to move their product to the final consumer.

(a) *Wholesalers* break down the bulk from manufacturers and pass products on to retailers. In doing so they take on some of the supplier's risks by funding stock. Recently in the UK there has been a reduction in importance of this type of intermediary.

(b) *Retailers* sell to the final consumers. In so doing they may give consumers added satisfaction by providing services such as credit, delivery and a wide variety of goods. In the UK, retailers have increased in power whilst wholesalers have decreased. Retailing has also become more concentrated with increased dominance of large multiples.

Distribution strategy

There are three main strategies.

(a) *Intensive distribution* involves maximum sales exposure, through the maximum number of outlets.

(b) Using *selective distribution*, the producer selects a group of retail outlets from amongst all retail outlets. The choice may be on grounds of the brand image ('quality' outlets), or the choice may be related to the retailers' capacity to provide after - sales service. Rolls Royce's image is safe in the hands of H R Owen but would be damaged if sold by an 'Arthur Daley'.

(c) *Exclusive distribution* is an extension of selective distribution. Particular outlets are granted exclusive handling rights within a prescribed geographical area. Sometimes exclusive distribution or franchise rights are coupled with making special financial arrangements for land, buildings or equipment, such as petrol station agreements.

Selective and *exclusive distribution* have been criticised by the European Commission as being restraints on competition (Articles 65 and 66 Treaty of Rome). Grundigs, who had earlier refused to sell through the Comet electrical discount stores, could have run foul of this ruling. In the UK the Monopolies and Mergers Commission has criticised the brewers' 'tied house' system, a form of exclusive distribution.

Exercise 9

In comparison with exclusive and selective distribution, the intensive strategy involves high costs for the producer. List some of the reasons for this.

Logistics management

Logistics management includes physical distribution and materials management. It therefore encompasses the inflow of raw materials and goods together with the outflow of finished products. Logistics management has developed because of an increased awareness of:

(a) customer benefits that can be incorporated into the overall product offering because of efficient logistics management;

(b) the cost savings that can be made when a logistics approach is undertaken;

(c) trends in industrial purchasing that necessarily mean closer links between buyers and sellers, for example Just in Time purchasing and computerised purchasing.

Logistics managers organise inventories, warehouses, purchasing and packaging to produce an efficient and effective overall system. There are benefits to consumers of products that are produced by companies with good logistic management. There is less likelihood of goods being out of stock, delivery should be efficient and overall service quality should be higher.

Examples

Contracted-out distribution services require enormous trust, especially in the food business. Sensitive information must be exchanged between the retailer or manufacturer and the distribution company and responsibility for food safety and hygiene must be shared. However, contracting out offers great benefits in terms of flexibility and the elimination of the need for costly capital investment: hence the success of specialist distribution companies such as NFC, Christian Salvesen and Hays. Hays, for example, runs a distribution centre which delivers short-life food products to 97 Waitrose supermarkets. It receives goods from 200 suppliers and handles 2,500 chilled product lines and 440,000 cases of products a week.

Distribution is now a critical factor in Europe's paper industry. Logistics is seen as a means of reducing costs and increasing efficiency, to counteract declining demand and 'dumping' of cut-price products from overseas. The *buyer* dominates the market and manufacturers therefore expect their distribution specialists to develop supply systems that result in zero damage and allow customers to minimise stockholding costs. One of the leading UK producers of paper for packaging has customers in the Benelux countries and northern France who expect orders to be delivered within 24 hours. The supplier is therefore having to set up warehouses to hold stock closer to the customers and speed up the delivery reaction time.

3 International distribution

The cost of physically transporting goods between countries has been estimated to be as high as 25% of the landed price of an item (more typically 15%), and thus represents a significant part of the cost structure of the item involved. But international logistics provide services to the customer in terms of availability, speed of delivery and convenience, which provide significant added value to the goods themselves.

In international marketing the longer distances involved and the problem of dealing with alien cultures, means that the time between placing an order and its delivery can be quite considerable when compared to locally sourced supplies, and the cost significantly higher.

Notes

A key concept in the management of international logistics is that of customer service. Customer service involves defining adequate levels of performance for:

(a) order cycle time (order to delivery);
(b) accuracy of order processing; and
(c) delivered quality of goods.

It is thus concerned with getting the right goods (and all of them with a mixed order), to the right person, at the right time, at a reasonable cost.

Transportation

Transport between markets is often the easier part of the problem, with good transport systems and infrastructure (roads, ports, airports, railheads etc) between nations. Within a particular country however both the transport systems and the infrastructure may vary in quality considerably. Generally the more developed nations have reasonably efficient transport facilities internally, but as we look to the lesser developed countries, the quality of communications, availability of transport facilities, and the physical infrastructure may pose significant problems to the international marketeer.

Modes of transport

The international marketeer has not only to take into account the cost of transport between countries, but also the cost within the country. This applies regardless of the nature of the contract (ie who pays for it) as it affects the competitive nature of the offer.

Temporary storage and handling form a significant part of the overall cost of transport. Thus methods of transport which minimise them tend to be more competitive. The development of container systems for road, rail, sea and air has reduced the amount of labour involved in transferring goods between types of transport. The preference is therefore to use a mode of transport which, wherever possible, provides a 'through delivery' to the customer.

Road transport has a major advantage in its ability to deliver directly to the customer's premises, thus minimising both delay and handling. Since other forms of transport (rail, air, water) normally use road transport at the beginning and end of the journey, they require handling on the transfer from one form of transport to another. Per tonne-mile road transport is more expensive than rail due to the upper size limit on vehicle loads in most countries, and is generally slower on long journeys than air, even taking handling transfer into account. Nevertheless, where good land borders, or short sea ferry services exist, the use of road transport for loads up to, say, 40 tones, and distances of up to, say, 1500 km, allied with the flexibility and lack of intermode transfer, gives it the advantage.

Where physical conditions permit, the use of *rail transport* has significant advantages over its main inland rival, road, in that it can carry much larger quantities over long distances. Per tonne-mile, rail is far superior to road in cost over distances exceeding 1500 km. Over shorter distances the advantages of the load capacity are outweighed by the transfer costs on and off the rail network. Rail is not economical for short journeys. Bulky, low unit value items such as raw materials are more economically moved by rail where circumstances permit.

For bulk transfer of items, *water transport* has similar advantages to rail, and is widely used where geography allows. Where a suitable network of rivers and canals exists, inland waterways can bring the load nearer to the customer. Again the problem of transfer and handling may make this approach expensive. But its bulk carrying capacity does provide significant cost advantages over long distances.

Air transport is probably the most expensive of all four options for short journeys. The economics of air transport, together with handling costs, make air uncompetitive both in time and cost over short distances. The advantage of air transport lies in speed rather than cost, and this can be most effective over longer distances. The load carrying capacity and fuel costs do not make sense for bulky, low unit value loads, but where high value, small unit size loads are being considered, air transport may be viable.

In particular, where early speedy delivery to a market can give significant price advantages (for example early flowers and vegetables can command a 10-fold price advantage over maincrop in many cases) air transport costs can be justified because of the high unit value of the goods. Similarly where the customer is willing to pay a premium for speedy delivery, for example a spare part for a manufacturing plant, air transport can be justified. It is of course widely used for high value, low volume, perishable items such as pharmaceutical drugs.

The advantage of air transport, speed, can however be lost where delays at the airport in forwarding to the customer erode the time saving.

Exercise 10

In respect of the criteria listed below, try to decide which method of transport (rail, water, road or air) is best and which is worst.

(a) Speed of delivery from door to door
(b) Cost of delivery
(c) Reliability in meeting schedules
(d) Variety of goods carried
(e) Number of locations served

Chapter roundup

(a) Distribution is an important element (the fourth 'P') in the marketing mix. There are many possible channels of distribution, including retailers, wholesalers, distributors/dealers, agents, franchisees, and direct selling.

(b) Firms need to choose their preferred distribution channels by reference to factors such as the number and location of their customers, the characteristics of their products, the characteristics of available intermediaries, the channels chosen by competitors and the characteristics of their own organisation.

(c) Distribution abroad gives rise to additional problems, especially in relation to the choice of transportation method.

Notes

Quick quiz

1 List five key functions included under the heading of distribution.

2 Explain the differences between wholesalers, distributors and agents.

3 Explain what is meant by direct and indirect distribution.

4 How do product characteristics influence the choice of distribution channels?

5 List as many factors as you can which favour:

(a) direct selling;
(b) the use of intermediaries.

6 How does the choice of distribution channels differ between industrial markets on the one hand and consumer markets on the other?

7 What is meant by logistics management?

8 Briefly compare the merits of sea transport and air transport in overseas distribution.

Solutions to exercises

1 Your answers might include some of the following points.

(a) The middleman of course has to take his 'cut', reducing the revenue available to the producer.

(b) The producer needs an infrastruture for looking after the retailers - keeping them informed, keeping them well stocked - which might not be necessary in, say, a mail order business.

(c) The producer loses some part of his control over the marketing of his product. The power of some retailers (for example W H Smith in the world of book publishing) is so great that they are able to dictate marketing policy to their suppliers.

2 Stores associated with one class of product: Boots, Sainsbury's etc (though you may have noted a trend towards diversification in both of these).

'Variety' chains: Littlewoods, Woolworths
Voluntary groups of independents: Spar, VG.

3 Apart from the example quoted (Kall Kwik - its competitor PDC Copyright also operate this way), you might have thought of Wimpy, McDonalds, Body Shop, Ryman (the stationers) and Allied Breweries.

From the franchisor's point of view, the arrangement is excellent in terms of cash flow. The franchisee pays in a substantial amount up front, finances his own working capital and pays a regular revenue share to the franchisor.

Notes

4 Other things being equal, if the order pattern is a small number of high-value orders, then direct distribution is more likely to occur. If there are numerous low-value orders, then the cost of fulfilling them promptly will be high and the use of intermediaries is likely.

5 To begin with, there are 6,000 channels (30 × 200). The introduction of a wholesaler reduces this to 230 (30 into the wholesaler and 200 out).

6 (a) Some types of groceries can only be sold to outlets having a freeze room
(b) Many specialised products (such as motor cars) can only be sold through dealers with the requisite specialised skills and knowledge.
(c) Bulky products (such as fridges or lawnmowers) can only be sold through outlets with ample display and storage space.

7 (a) The producer gets closer to his ultimate consumer, which improves his market knowledge.

(b) Order sizes from retailers will be few and large (which means they can be serviced relatively cheaply), particularly where the product is one that consumers are accustomed to buying through large stores.

(c) Selling direct to retailers may give producers some say in how their products are displayed and sold.

8 One important factor is the stockholding cost. If the product is large and expensive, or again if a wide variety of brands must be produced (for example in the case of small machine tools), the producer may prefer to shift the stockholding cost to the distributor.

9 (a) It is more costly to fulfil a large number of small orders than a small number of large orders.

(b) The wide geographical dispersion of potential outlets will add to costs.

(c) The whole of the advertising/promotional costs fall on the producer, because outlets will be reluctant to share such costs if the benefit (of attracting a sale) may go to some other outlet nearby.

10 (a) Water is usually slowest. Fastest over long distances is air travel, but for shorter distances rail or road may be quicker door to door.

(b) Water is usually cheapest, air the most expensive.

(c) Air and rail tend to be more reliable than roads and water.

(d) The widest range of goods is probably carried by rail and water, with roads and air next (in that order).

Road transport can penetrate just about everywhere. Rail is probably next best. Water and air transport are severely restricted by the need for port or airport facilities.

8 PRICE

> *Your objectives*
>
> After completing this chapter you should:
>
> (a) understand the objectives of pricing policy;
> (b) be aware of the main methods used by businesses to price their products and services;
> (c) be aware of the main influences on the price of a product or service;
> (d) understand how different marketing objectives can affect pricing policy.

1 The objectives of pricing

All profit organisations and many non-profit organisations face the task of setting a price on their products or services. Historically price was the single most important decision made by the sales department. Over time, the importance of the interrelated elements of the marketing mix has been realised. To the modern marketing executive, price, whilst important, is not necessarily the predominant factor. As an example, marketing managers may now seek to interpret and satisfy consumer wants and needs by modifying existing products or introducing new products to the range. This contrasts with earlier production oriented times when the typical reaction was to cut prices in order to sell the firm's product.

In fact, it is often suggested that one of the functions performed by marketing is to make price relatively unimportant to the consumers' decision making process. There is certainly some truth in this view, in that the other elements of the marketing mix are ultimately concerned with adding value to the product and tailoring it to the consumers' needs, to ensure that the choice between two products is not simply based on their different prices. However, this devalues the role of pricing as an element of the marketing mix. Price can be defined as a measure of the value exchanged by the buyer for the value offered by the seller. As such it might be expected that the price should reflect the costs to the seller of producing the product and the benefit to the buyer of consuming it.

Unlike the other marketing mix elements, pricing decisions affect profits through their impact on revenues rather than costs. Pricing is the only element of the mix which generates revenue rather than creating costs. In addition, it also has an important role to play as a competitive tool which can be used to differentiate a product and an organisation and thus exploit market opportunities. It is also important that pricing is consistent with other elements of the marketing mix since it contributes to the overall image created for the product. No organisation can hope successfully to offer an exclusive high quality product to the market with a low price - the price must be consistent with the overall product offer.

Exercise 1

In what circumstances would you expect price to be the main factor influencing a consumer's choice?

Pricing can be thought of as fulfilling a number of roles within a marketing context. However, in overall terms a price must produce the desired level of sales in order to meet the objectives of the overall business strategy. Pricing must be systematic and it must take into full consideration the internal needs and the external constraints of the organisation.

Ultimately, the objective of pricing, as with other elements of the marketing mix, is to ensure that the required level of sales is generated to enable the organisation to achieve its specified objectives. Two broad categories of objectives may be specified for pricing decisions; they may not be mutually exclusive, but they are different.

(a) *Maximising profits*
This approach to pricing will be one that concerns itself with maximising the returns on assets or investments. This may be realised with a comparatively small market share depending on the patterns of cost and demand.

(b) *Maintaining or increasing market share*
The alternative approach which is concerned with increasing or maintaining the customer base may require a different and possibly more competitive approach to pricing, and the company with the largest market share may not necessarily be the company which earns the best profits.

Either of these approaches may be used in specifying pricing objectives, and as was mentioned earlier, they may appear in some combination based on a specified rate of return and a specified market share. It is important that the stated objectives are consistent with overall corporate objectives and corporate strategies.

2 Methods of price determination

Price setting in theory

In classical economic theory, price is the major determinant of demand and brings together supply and demand to form an equilibrium market price. More recently, emphasis has been placed, especially in marketing, on the importance of non-profit factors in demand. Thus the roles of product quality, promotion, personal selling and distribution and, in overall terms, brands, have grown. Whilst it can be relatively easy for a competitor to copy a price cut, at least in the short term, it is much more difficult to copy a successful brand image based on a *unique selling proposition*. Successful branding can even imply premium pricing.

Economic theory can only determine the optimal price structure under the two extreme market conditions.

Notes

(a) *Perfect competition:* many buyers, many sellers all dealing in an identical product. Neither producer nor user has any market power and both must accept the prevailing market price.

(b) *Monopoly:* one seller who dominates many buyers. The monopolist can use his market power to set a profit maximising price.

However, in practice most of British industry can be described as an *oligopoly:* where relatively few competitive companies dominate the market. Whilst each large firm has the ability to influence market prices the unpredictable reaction from the other giants makes the final industry price indeterminate. Economists in the field of oligopoly pricing think that price competition is dangerous, given that there are no clear market forces to support a given price level.

The airline industry provides an example of this. When Sir Freddie Laker introduced his cut price Skytrain service on the transatlantic air routes he challenged the legally protected cartel of IATA (the International Air Traffic Association). IATA fixed air fares on many international routes. The fares were typically priced at a relatively high level that allowed the least efficient, marginal carrier to remain in business. IATA has international blessing as its rules allow every small (and therefore high cost) national airline carrier to remain in business. As having an airline is a mark of national prestige this approach is much favoured in the United Nations.

Initially, British Airways, TWA and Pan Am ignored Laker. But when the service started picking up significant market share, the major airlines reacted by introducing their own cut-price transatlantic fares. The result was that every major carrier recorded losses on its transatlantic business. These losses were only alleviated when Laker himself went out of business.

Exercise 2

Try to think of another industry in which this kind of 'price war' periodically takes place.

It is also difficult in economic theory terms to identify precisely what is market power. Many small producers enjoy some market power because they are producing distinctly different products and have a degree of local monopoly.

The agricultural sector comes closest to perfect competition with farmers having to accept market prices that they cannot directly influence.

To summarise, economic theory, whilst giving an insight into price decisions, may be of little practical help.

However, the concept of *price elasticity* is important. If you have studied economics, you may already know that price elasticity is measured as

$$\frac{\%\text{ change in sales demand}}{\%\text{ change in sales price}}$$

(a) When elasticity is greater than 1 *(elastic)*, a change in price will lead to a change in total revenue so that, if the price is:

  (i) lowered, total sales revenue would rise, because of the large increase in demand;
  (ii) raised, total sales revenue would fall because of the large fall in demand.

(b) When elasticity is less than 1 *(inelastic)*, if the price is:

  (i) lowered, total sales revenue would fall, because the increase in sales volume would be too small to compensate for the price reductions;

  (ii) raised, total sales revenue would go up in spite of the small drop in sales quantities.

Marketing management needs to be able to estimate the likely effects of price changes on total revenue and profits. 'Price elasticity of demand gives precision to the question of whether the firm's price is too high or too low. From the point of view of maximising revenue, price is too high if demand is elastic and too low if demand is inelastic. Whether this is also true for maximising profits depends on the behaviour of costs'. (Kotler)

Exercise 3

What are the limitations of price elasticity as a factor in determining prices?

Price setting in practice

There are three main types of influence on price setting in practice: costs, competition and demand.

Costs

In practice cost is the most important influence on price. For many firms the influence is very direct: they actually set prices by estimating total costs and then adding a margin for profit.

There are two types of cost-based pricing: full cost pricing and cost-plus pricing.

Full cost pricing takes account of the full average cost of production of a brand, including an allocation for overheads. A conventional profit margin is then added to determine the selling price. This method is often used for non-routine jobs which are difficult to cost in advance, such as the work of solicitors and accountants where the price is often determined after the work has been performed.

Although the full cost pricing method is basically straightforward in principle, the allocation or apportionment of overheads between brands in a multibrand company can be difficult, especially when joint or by-products are involved.

Notes

Superficially, it would appear that demand factors are ignored in this analysis; in practice, however, especially in the longer term, demand can be reflected through the level of the profit margin which is added (the margin is not going to be high if demand is being squeezed). The profit margin is also likely to reflect the level of actual or potential competition from firms already in the industry or capable of entering it.

Using *cost-plus pricing* only the more easily measurable direct cost components such as labour and raw material inputs are calculated in the unit cost, whilst an additional margin incorporates an overhead charge and a residual profit element. This method is used where overhead allocation to unit costs is too complex or too time consuming to be worthwhile.

A common example occurs with the use of mark-up pricing by retailers in which a fixed margin is added to the buying-in price of goods for resale. This fixed margin tends to be conventional within product classes. In the UK, for example, fast moving items such as cigarettes carry a low 5-8% margin (also because of tax factors), fast moving but perishable items such as newspapers carry a 25% margin, while slow moving items which involve retailers in high stockholding costs (such as furniture or books) carry 33%, 50% or even higher mark-up margins.

The percentage margin may vary to reflect changes in demand or competition, while the cost basis for calculations may be actual costs, expected costs or standard costs. If all the firms in the industry use the same pricing basis then prices will reflect efficiency, the lowest price firm being the most efficient.

Exercise 4

Cost-based pricing is quite common in practice, even though it is not necessarily a profit maximising policy. What do you think are the reasons for its popularity?

The problems with cost-plus pricing arise out of difficulties in defining direct costs and allocating overheads, and with over- or underestimation of attainable production levels (particularly where standard costs are used). Also price adjustments may cause high administrative costs because of the cost-based price-setting process used.

Because the cost-plus approach leads to price stability, with price changing only to reflect cost changes, it can lead to a marketing strategy which is *reactive* rather then *proactive*.

There is very limited consideration of demand in cost-based pricing strategies. From a marketing perspective, cost-based pricing can reflect missed opportunities as little or no account is taken, particularly in the short run, of the price consumers are willing to pay for the brand, which may prove to be higher than the cost-based price.

The use of cost-based pricing for a new brand can cause particular problems as initial low production levels in the introduction stage could lead to a very high average unit cost and hence a high price. It may thus be necessary to take a longer term view which accepts short-term losses until full production levels are attained. Finally, if the firm is using a product line promotion strategy then there is likely to be added complexity in the pricing process.

Notes

Competition

Prices may be set on the basis of what competitors are charging rather than on the basis of cost or demand. A theoretical justification of the phenomenon was presented by Sweezy as the kinked demand curve theory. This is shown below.

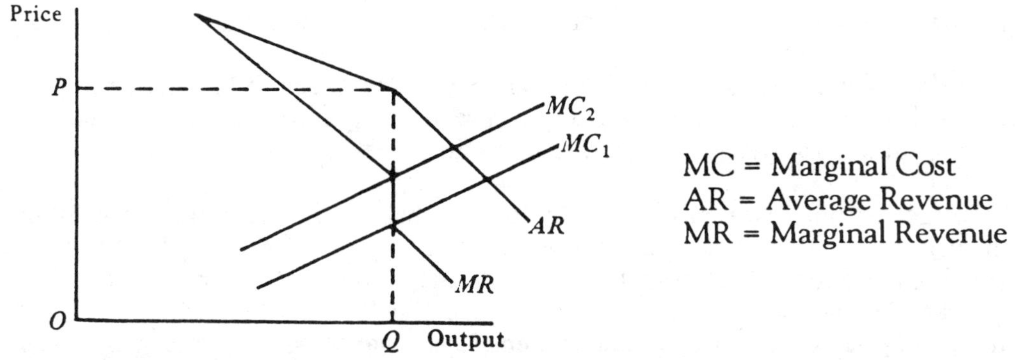

It is argued that price remains at OP even if marginal costs increase from MC_1 to MC_2. The justification is that firms assume that competitors will all follow a price decrease but that none will follow a price increase. Thus they assume that demand is elastic for a price rise, but is inelastic for a price fall. In each case a price change would reduce sales revenue. But note that this approach does not explain how the price is arrived at in the first place!

In practice the kinked demand curve theory would lead to *going rate pricing* in which some form of average level of price becomes the norm, perhaps, in the case of a high level of branding in the market, including standard price differentials between brands.

In certain market structures price competition may be avoided by tacit agreement leading to concentration on non-price competition; the markets for cigarettes and petrol are examples of this. In such cases price-setting is influenced by a need to avoid retaliatory responses by competitors which would lead to a breakdown in the tacit agreement and so to price competition. Often price changes based on real cost changes are led by a 'representative' firm in the industry and followed by other firms.

Exercise 5

There is at least one service industry in which this practice is the norm and which is regularly reported in the headlines. Can you think of it?

From time to time tacit agreements break down leading to a period of price competition which may then be followed by a resumption of the tacit agreement. Often such actions are the result of external factors affecting the industry. Industry level agreements do not necessarily preclude short-term price competition for specific brands, especially where sales promotion devices, such as special offers, are used.

A special case of competition-based pricing is *competitive bidding*. Many supply contracts, especially concerning local and national government purchases, involve would be suppliers submitting a *sealed bid tender*. In such circumstances, the firm's submitted price needs to take account of expected competitor bid prices. Frequently the firms involved will not

Notes

even know the identity of their rivals for the bid. However, often past successful bids are published by purchasers and, if this is the case, it is possible to use this data to formulate a current bid price.

If the firm has the particular problem of bidding for a number of contracts before the result of any one bid is known, the production (or supply) capacity may be important. The firm may need to win some contracts only: not too few nor too many.

If past bid data is not published then there is very little objective basis for bid price setting. The firm may have to rely on trade gossip, on conjecture or on an estimate of likely competitors' cost and profit requirements in price-setting.

If the contract is not awarded purely on price (that is, if the lowest bid is not automatically accepted) the problem is exacerbated. In the case of the supply of branded goods, the relative value of each brand must be considered on a value for money basis by the purchaser. The bidder may have to rely on subjective 'feel of the market' analysis in determining bid prices. There are, of course, numerous instances where cases of actual and attempted bribery of officials have been uncovered in attempts by firms to use underhand means of winning contracts.

Demand

Rather than use cost or competition as the prime determinants of price a firm can base pricing strategy for a product or service on the intensity of demand, although, of course, cost and competition factors remain influences or constraints on its freedom to set price.

A strong intensity of demand may lead to a high price, and a weak intensity to a low price: much depends on the ability of the firm to segment the market price by elasticity.

In practice, measurement of price elasticity and hence implementing price discrimination can be very difficult. There are a number of bases on which discriminating prices can be set.

(a) *By market segment*
A cross-channel ferry company would market its services at different prices in England, Belgium and France, for example. Services such as cinemas and hairdressers are often available at lower prices to old age pensioners and/or juveniles.

(b) *By product version*
Many car models have 'add on' extras which enable one brand to appeal to a wider cross-section of customers. The final price need not reflect the cost price of the add on extras directly: usually the top of the range model would carry a price much in excess of the cost of provision of the extras, as a prestige appeal.

(c) *By place*
Theatre seats are usually sold according to their location so that patrons pay different prices for the same performance according to the seat type they occupy.

(d) *By time*
Perhaps the most popular type of price discrimination. Off-peak hotel prices, telephone and electricity charges are all attempts to increase sales revenue by covering variable but not necessarily the average cost of provision.

Exercise 6

Think of another common example in which price discrimination is practised based on the time at which services are consumed.

In each of these cases, some customers pay more than others for essentially the same product or service, reflecting different intensities of demand. There is an ethical dimension to this practice and firms need to consider their objectives carefully before using this approach. For instance, by taking advantage of a short-term shortage of a product and increasing price, a firm may harm long-term profit prospects because customers resent what they interpret as exploitation. This is particularly the case as *consumerism* develops, since vociferous groups of consumers can create widespread publicity which can be damaging for the product supplier in the short and/or longer term.

Price discrimination can only be effective if a number of conditions hold.

(a) The market must be segmentable in price terms, and different sectors must show different intensities of demand. Each of the sectors must be identifiable, distinct and separate from the others, and be accessible to the firm's marketing communications.

(b) There must be little or no chance of a black market developing so that those in the lower priced segment can resell to those in the higher priced segment.

(c) There must be little chance that competitors can and will undercut the firm's prices in the higher priced (and/or most profitable) market segments.

(d) The cost of segmenting and administering the arrangements should not exceed the extra revenue derived from the price discrimination strategy.

The firm could use a *market test* to estimate the demand effect of a price change. This would involve a change of price in one region and a comparison of demand for the brand with past sales in that region and with sales in similar regions at the old prices. This is a high risk strategy: special circumstances may affect the test area (such as a competitor's advertising campaign) which could affect the results. Also customers may change allegiance from the test brand if a price rise is being considered and become loyal to a competitive brand; they may not switch back even if the price is subsequently lowered again.

The other alternative is to attempt a *direct attitude survey* with respondents. *Pricing research* is notoriously difficult, especially if respondents try to appear rational to the interviewer or do not wish to offend him or her. Usually there is a lack of realism in such research; the respondent is not in an actual 'choice' situation faced with having to pay out hard earned income and therefore may give a hypothetical answer which is not then translated into actual purchasing behaviour. Nevertheless, pricing research is increasingly common in practice as firms attempt to assess the perceived value customers give to a brand as an input to their pricing decisions.

Notes

3 Influences on price

Price sensitivity will vary amongst purchasers. Those that can pass on the cost of purchases will be the least sensitive and will therefore respond more to other elements of the marketing mix.

(a) The business traveller will be more concerned about the level of service and quality of food in looking for a hotel than price, provided that it fits the corporate budget. In contrast, the family on holiday are likely to be very price sensitive when choosing an overnight stay.

(b) In petrol retailing, the largest take up of trading stamps and other promotional offerings has been from the company sales representative, looking for perks whilst charging what might be relatively expensive petrol to the company.

(c) In industrial marketing the purchasing manager is likely to be more price sensitive than the engineer who might be the actual user of new equipment that is being sourced. The engineer and purchasing manager are using different criteria in making the choice with the engineer placing product characteristics as the most important element within the marketing mix.

Finding out about price sensitivity

Research on price sensitivity of customers has shown that:

(a) customers have a good concept of a 'just price' - a feel for what is about the right price to pay for a commodity;

(b) customers search for price information before buying, becoming price aware when wanting to buy but forgetting soon afterwards unless a regular purchase is involved;

(c) customers will buy at what they consider to be a bargain price without full regard for need and actual price;

(d) for consumer durables it is the down payment and instalment price rather than total price which is important;

(e) in times of rising prices the price image tends to lag behind the current price, which indicates a resentment of the price increase. It is thus very important to relate customers' image of price to the actual price as this image will determine reactions to a price change. For instance, Bell Telephones in the US were concerned about the lack of sales of extension telephones. When, as part of a market research survey, customers were asked to name the actual price of an extension telephone, most overestimated it. By keeping the existing price but running an advertising campaign featuring it, Bell were able to increase sales as customers became aware of the lower than anticipated price.

Exercise 7

You ask a friend to empty his wallet of receipts and lay them on the table. You find receipts from different shops for the following.

Notes

(a)	A pint of milk	£0.47
(b)	A man's suit	£149.99
(c)	A bottle of wine	£6.50
(d)	A book of 10 first class stamps	£2.40

In each case the *price* tells you something about one or more of the following:

(a) the product purchased;
(b) the place where it was purchased;
(c) the circumstances in which it was purchased;
(d) the purpose for which it was purchased;
(e) the person making the purchase.

Explain each of the purchases in these terms.

Finding out about price perception

Price perception is an important factor in the ways customers react to prices. The economist's downward sloping demand curve may not in fact hold, at least in the short term. For example, customers may react to a price increase by buying more because:

(a) they expect further price increases to follow (they are 'stocking up');
(b) they assume the quality has increased;
(c) the brand takes on a 'snob appeal' because of the high price.

Several factors complicate the pricing decisions which an organisation has to make.

Intermediaries' objectives

If an organisation distributes products or services to the market through independent intermediaries, the objectives of these intermediaries complicate the pricing decision. Such intermediaries are likely to deal with a range of suppliers and their aims concern their own profits rather than those of suppliers. Also, the intermediary will take into account the needs of its customers. Thus conflict over price can arise between suppliers and intermediaries which may be difficult to resolve.

Many industries have traditional margins for intermediaries and to deviate from these might cause problems for suppliers. In some industries, notably grocery retailing, the power of intermediaries allows them to dictate terms to suppliers. The relationship between intermediaries and suppliers is therefore complex, and price and the price discount structure is an important element.

Exercise 8

Are you familiar with the relationship between Marks & Spencer and its suppliers? If not, try to find out about it and analyse its effects in the light of the discussion above.

Notes

Competitors' actions and reactions

An organisation, in setting prices, sends out signals to rivals. These rivals are likely to react to these signals in some way. In some industries (such as building societies, mentioned earlier) pricing moves in unison; in others, price changes by one supplier may initiate a price war, with each supplier undercutting the others.

Suppliers

If an organisation's suppliers notice a price rise for the organisation's products, they may seek a rise in the price for their supplies to the organisation on the grounds that it is now more able to pay a higher price. This argument is especially likely to be used by the trade unions in the organisation when negotiating the 'price' for the supply of labour.

Inflation

In periods of inflation the organisation may need to change prices to reflect increases in the prices of supplies, labour, rent and so on. Such changes may be needed to keep relative (real) prices unchanged (this is what is meant by saying that prices are adjusted for the rate of inflation).

Quality connotations

In the absence of other information, customers tend to judge quality by price. Thus a price change may send signals to customers concerning the quality of the product. A price rise may indicate improvements in quality, a price reduction may signal reduced quality, for example through the use of inferior components. Thus any change in price needs to take such factors into account.

Income effects

In times of rising incomes, price may become a less important marketing variable compared with product quality and convenience of access (distribution). When income levels are falling and/or unemployment levels rising, price will become a much more important marketing variable. This has been particularly noticeable in the recession of the early 1990s. The major grocery multiples such as Tesco, Sainsbury, Safeway and Waitrose steadily moved up market in the 1980s with great success, leaving the 'pile it high, sell it cheap' philosophy behind. However, bargain stores are now becoming a serious threat.

New product pricing

Most pricing decisions for existing products concern price changes for one reason or another: in other words, such changes have a reference point from which to move (the existing price). But when a new product is introduced for the first time there may be no such reference points; pricing decisions are most difficult to make in such circumstances. It may be possible to seek alternative reference points, such as the price in another market where the new product has already been launched, or the price set by a competitor.

Notes

Multiple products

Most organisations market not just one product but a range of products. These products are commonly interrelated, being complements or substitutes for example. The management of the pricing function is likely to focus on the profit from the whole range rather than that on each single product. Take, for example, the use of *loss leaders:* a very low price for one product is intended to make consumers buy other products in the range which carry higher profit margins. People will buy many of the high profit items but only one of the low profit items - yet they are 'locked in' to the former by the latter. Loss leaders also attract customers into retail stores where they will usually buy normally priced products as well as the loss leaders.

Exercise 9

Try to think of some examples of a low-priced product 'locking in' a consumer to higher-priced products.

Sensitivity

Price decisions are often seen as highly sensitive and as such involve top management more clearly than do other marketing decisions. As already noted, price has a direct relationship with profit. Ethical considerations are a further factor, for example whether or not to exploit short-term shortages through higher prices. The outcry surrounding the series of petrol price rises following the outbreak of the Gulf Crisis in 1990 was a good example of public sensitivity to pricing decisions.

4 Price setting objectives

Market penetration objective: here the organisation sets a relatively low price for the product or service in order to stimulate growth of the market and/or to obtain a large share of it. This strategy was used by Japanese motor cycle manufacturers when entering the UK market. It worked famously: UK productive capacity was virtually eliminated and the imported Japanese machines could then be sold at a much higher price and still dominate the market.

Sales maximising objectives are favoured when:

(a) unit costs fall with output (economies of scale);
(b) the market is price sensitive and relatively low prices will attract additional sales;
(c) low prices will discpurage any new competitors.

Market skimming objective: in many ways an opposite objective to market penetration, market skimming involves setting a high initial price for a new product. The intention is to take advantage of those buyers who are ready to pay a much higher price than others for a product because it has a high price value to them. The strategy is initially to command a premium price and then gradually to reduce the price to obtain more price sensitive segments of the market. This strategy is really an example of price discrimination over time.

Notes

This strategy is favoured when:

(a) there is insufficient market capacity and competitors cannot increase capacity;
(b) buyers are relatively insensitive to price increases;
(c) high price perceived as high quality (interaction in marketing mix);
(d) *but* there is the danger of encouraging firms to enter market.

Early cash recovery objective: an alternative pricing objective is to recover the investment in a new product or service as quickly as possible, that is to achieve a minimum payback period. The price is set so as to facilitate this objective. Such an objective would tend to be used in conditions where:

(a) the business is high risk;
(b) rapid changes in fashion or technology are expected;
(c) the innovator is short of cash.

Product line promotion objective: as noted above, management of the pricing function is likely to focus on profit from the range of products which the organisation produces rather than to treat each product as a separate entity. The product line promotion objective will take account of the constitution of the whole range in terms of:

(a) the interaction of the marketing mix;
(b) monitoring returns to ensure that net contribution is worthwhile.

Intermediate customers: some companies set a price to distributors and allow them to set whatever final price they wish. A variation is to publish an inflated *recommended retail price* so that retailers can give large promotional discounts.

Cost-plus pricing: a firm may set its initial price by marking up its unit costs by a certain percentage or fixed amount, as already discussed.

(a) This conforms to internal rules laid down by the company for 'satisfactory' return on investment

(b) This takes no account of risk: riskier product lines should make higher returns

(c) This cannot ultimately avoid market pressures: if 'overpriced' stocks will build up, or if 'underpriced' excess demand will be created that exceeds the firm's capacity and encourages market entrants.

Target pricing: a variant on cost-plus where the company tries to determine the price that gives a specified rate of return for a given output. This is widely used by large USA manufacturers, such as General Motors and Boeing.

Price discrimination: offering different prices to different classes of buyer. The danger is that price cuts to one buyer may be used as a lever when another buyer is negotiating. To avoid such leverage:

(a) buyers must be in clearly defined segments, such as overseas and home (Rover cars have at times been cheaper in the USA), or students' concessionary fares;

(b) own branding where packaging is changed for supermarkets is a variation on this;

(c) bulk buying discounts and aggregated rebate schemes can favour large buyers.

Going rate pricing: try to keep in line with industry norm for prices. Don't 'rock the boat' if everybody is charging relatively high near-monopolistic prices.

(a) This is typical behaviour of a mature oligopoly, akin to a cartel.

(b) Suppliers engage in less damaging competition than price cutting, such as advertising campaigns and post-sales service.

(c) This is often technically illegal but this does not stop individual firms accepting the role of price leaders in an industry.

Quantum price: in retail selling the concept of a 'quantum point' is often referred to. When the price of an item is increased from, say, £9.65 to £9.95, sales may not be affected because the consumers do not notice the price change. However, if the price is increased from £9.95 to £10.05 a major fall in sales may occur, £10 acting as a *quantum point* which can be approached but not passed if the price is not to deter would be purchasers.

Odd number pricing: as an interesting aside, the phenomenon of odd number pricing (pricing at £1.99, £2.99 etc rather than £2, £3 etc) is said to have originated not as a marketing concept but in department stores in order to ensure the honesty of sales assistants. The customer has to wait for change from £1.95 when, as is usual, they offer, say, £2 in payment, so the assistant has to use the till. If the price was £2 and the customer need not wait for the change, there was thought to be a greater temptation to shop assistants to pocket the money and not to enter it into the till!

One coin purchase: confectionery firms have used the psychologically based concept of a 'one coin purchase' in pricing tactics. Rather than change price to reflect cost changes, such firms often alter the quantity in the unit of the product and keep the same price. This is a case of 'price-minus' pricing in which the firm determines what the market will bear and works backwards, planning to produce and market a brand which will be profitable to them, selling at the nominated retail price.

Gift purchases: gift purchasing is often based on price where it is taken to reflect quality. Thus if a gift is to be purchased in an unfamiliar product category a price level is often fixed by the buyer and a choice made from the brands available at that price. Cosmetics are often priced at £4.99 and £9.99 to appeal to gift purchasers at the £5 and £10 price level. Importantly, packaging is a major part of the appeal and must reflect a quality brand image, an important part of the psychology of gift choice.

Product line pricing

When a firm sells a range of related products, or a product line, its theoretical pricing policy should be to set prices for each product which maximise the profitability of the line as a whole. A firm may therefore have a pricing policy for an entire product line.

(a) There may be a *brand name* which the manufacturer wishes to associate with high quality but high price, or reasonable quality and low price etc. All items in the line will be priced accordingly. For example, all major supermarket chains have an 'own brand' label which is used to sell goods at a slightly lower price than the major named brands.

(b) If two or more products in the line are *complementary,* one may be priced as a *loss leader* in order to attract more demand for all of the related products.

Notes

(c) If two or more products in the line share joint production costs *(joint products)* the prices of the products must be considered as a single decision. For example, if a common production process makes one unit of joint product A for each one unit of joint product B, a price for A which achieves a demand of, say, 17,000 units, will be inappropriate if associated with a price for product B which would only sell, say, 10,000 units. 7,000 units of B would be unsold and wasted.

Price changes caused by cost changes in the firm

In the prolonged period of inflation since the 1970s, price increases caused by increased costs to the manufacturer became a common experience. The effect of inflation on price decisions was very noticeable and different organisations reacted in different ways.

(a) Some firms raised their prices regularly, eg car manufacturers often raised their prices every three or six months.

(b) Other firms gave advance warning of price rises, especially in an industrial market. Customers might then be persuaded to advance their purchases in order to avoid paying the higher price at a later date.

(c) A firm which did not raise its prices was in effect reducing its prices in real terms.

Competitive pricing

It is in the field of competition that price is the most potent element in the marketing mix. Professor Corey of the Harvard Business School summarised the role of price in competitive game-playing: 'The struggle for market share focuses critically on price. Pricing strategies of competing firms are highly interdependent. The price one competitor sets is a function not only of what the market will pay but also of what other firms charge. Prices set by individual firms respond to those of competitors; they also are intended often to influence competitors' pricing behaviour. Pricing is an art, a game played for high stakes; and for marketing strategists it is the 'moment of truth'. All of marketing comes to focus in the pricing decision.'

Competitive price changes

A firm may lower its prices to try to increase its market share; on the other hand, a firm may raise its prices in the hope that competitors will quickly do the same (that is, in the expectation of tacit price collusion). The purpose of such competitive initiatives will presumably be to raise profits or the firm's market share; however, in established industries dominated by a few major firms, it is generally accepted that a price initiative by one firm will be countered by a price reaction by competitors. In these circumstances, prices tend to be fairly stable, unless pushed upwards by inflation or strong growth in demand. Thus in industries such as breakfast cereals (dominated in Britain by Kelloggs, Nabisco and Quaker) or canned soups (Heinz, Crosse & Blackwell and Campbells) a certain price stability might be expected without too many competitive price initiatives, except when cost inflation pushes up the price of one firm's products with other firms soon following.

Exercise 10

If your competitor cuts his prices in the expectation of increasing market share, what are your possible responses?

Price leadership

Given that price competition can have disastrous consequences in conditions of oligopoly, it is not unusual to find that large corporations emerge as price leaders. The operation of such price leadership brings about relative price stability in otherwise unstable price dynamic oligopolies.

A price leader will have the dominant influence on price levels for a class of products. Price increases or decreases by the price leader provides a direction to market price patterns. The price dominant firm may lead without moving at all. This would be the case if other firms sought to raise prices and the leader did not follow, then the upward move in prices will be halted. The price leader generally has a large, if not necessarily largest, market share. The company will usually be an efficient low-cost producer that has a reputation for technical competence.

The role of price leader is also earned by a track record of having initiated price moves that have been accepted by both competitors and customers. This is frequently associated with a mature well established management group.

Any dramatic changes in industry competition, such as a new entrant, or changes in the board room can endanger the price leadership role. In the UK petrol retailing sector Shell is frequently identified as fulfilling the role of price leadership.

Chapter roundup

(a) Two broad categories of objectives in pricing are maximising profit and maintaining/increasing market share.

(b) Methods of pricing stem from considerations of cost, competition and market demand.

(c) Influences on the level of prices include the price sensitivity of consumers, the actions of intermediaries, competitors and suppliers, quality considerations, income levels, and the particular problems of new products and multiple products.

(d) Pricing policy may be shaped by a wide variety of marketing objectives.

Notes

Quick quiz

1 Why do economists believe that price competition in an oligopoly market is dangerous?

2 Define price elasticity.

3 Why is cost plus pricing popular?

4 List four bases for price discrimination.

5 Why might a price rise lead to a temporary increase in sales?

6 When are sales maximising objectives favoured?

7 What is a quantum point?

8 Why are gift packaged items often sold at £4.99 or £9.99?

Solutions to exercises

1 You might have identified a number of different factors here. Perhaps the most important general point to make is that price is particularly important if the other elements in the marketing mix are relatively similar across a range of competing products. For example, there is a very wide variety of toothpastes on the market, most of them not much differentiated from the others. The price of a particular toothpaste may be a crucial factor in its sales success.

2 There are plenty of possibilities. You might have mentioned the oil/petrol industry where 'forecourt price wars' hit the headlines from time to time. Another example in recent years has been the High Street banks' attempts to attract customers by offering free banking, subject to certain conditions. The effect of this on the banking industry has been painful, and at the time of writing (June 1993) the policy appears likely to be abandoned very soon.

3 The main problem is that unless very detailed research has been carried out the price elasticity of a particular product or service is likely to be unknown. As a theoretical concept, it is useful in gaining an understanding of the *effects* of price changes; but it is of little use as a practical tool in *determining* prices.

4 Many possible reasons could be given; the ones below are identified in a study by Lanzilotti.

(a) Planning and use of scarce capital resources are easier
(b) Easier assessment of divisional performance
(c) Emulation of successful large companies
(d) Belief by management in a 'fair return' policy
(e) Fear of government action against 'excessive' profits

Notes

(f) Tradition of production orientation rather than marketing orientation in many organisations
(g) Tacit collusion in industry to avoid competition
(h) Adequate profits for shareholders are already made, giving no incentive to maximise profits
(i) Easier administration of cost-based pricing strategies based on internal data
(j) Stability of pricing, production and employment produced by cost-based pricing over time
(k) Social equability

5 The industry referred to is the building societies industry. When economic factors cause alterations in interest rates (one of the main 'costs' borne by building societies, because of their interest payments to investors), the societies reduce or increase their lending rates (the 'price' of their mortgage products). It is usual to see one of the larger societies leading the way, after which the others fall into line.

6 The obvious example is off-peak travel bargains. British Rail is a successful price discriminator, charging more to rush hour rail commuters whose demand for the service is inelastic at certain times of the day.

8 One distinctive feature of many Marks & Spencer suppliers is that they are 'tied', in the sense that Marks & Spencer are able, by virtue of their immense purchasing power, to dictate the prices charged. If the supplier is not happy with the price, and tries to raise it, he runs the risk of losing a potentially enormous volume of business.

9 A simple example might be a low-priced razor, with a high price charged on the corresponding razor blades. Another might be a low-priced compact disc player - the price of compact discs themselves is often criticised as being unfairly high relative to the prices of records or audio tapes.

10 (a) You might *maintain your existing prices* if the expectation is that only a small market share would be lost, so that it is more profitable to keep prices at their existing level. Eventually, the rival firm may drop out of the market or be forced to raise its prices.

(b) You might *maintain your prices* but *respond with a non-price counter-attack*. This is a more positive response, because you will be securing or justifying your current prices with a product change, advertising, or better back-up services etc.

(c) You might *reduce your prices*. This should protect your market share so that the main beneficiary from the price reduction will be the consumer.

(d) You might *raise your prices* and *respond with a non-price counter-attack*. The extra revenue from the higher prices might be used to finance an advertising campaign or product design changes. A price increase would be based on a campaign to emphasise the quality difference between your own product and the rival's product.

9 COMMUNICATING WITH THE TARGET MARKET

Your objectives

After completing this chapter you should:

(a) understand the role of communication in marketing;
(b) be aware of the main elements in the communications mix;
(c) understand the considerations involved in selecting the ingredients in the mix.

1 The role of communication

In the context of marketing, communication refers to the process by which a seller informs potential buyers of his products and persuades them to purchase. It embraces advertising, promotion, publicity and public relations, direct marketing techniques and personal selling.

Before going on to discuss these elements in detail, a brief analysis of the communication process, in general terms, will be helpful

As a process, communication has elements and interrelationships that can be modelled and examined in a structured way. The need to establish a commonness of thought between a sender and a receiver implies that a sharing relationship must exist between them. It is incorrect to view the sender as active and the receiver as passive. Both must be active if communication is to pass.

Try speaking to a friend who is daydreaming. It may appear that communication is taking place, she may even answer, but her mind is engaged elsewhere and the responses are automatic and meaningless.

Communication begins when a message is encoded. Encoding is the process of putting thought into symbolic form. Decoding is the process of transforming the message symbols back into thought. It is obviously important that the sender selects a code that is understood (and welcomed if possible) by the intended receiver. It follows that the sender must know something about the receiver in order to make judgements about the message transmission.

Exercise 1

You write a letter, you put it in an envelope, you address it correctly, you post it, you check that it has been received. Can you be sure that you have communicated?

Notes

A general model of the communications process is as follows.

Figure 6.1

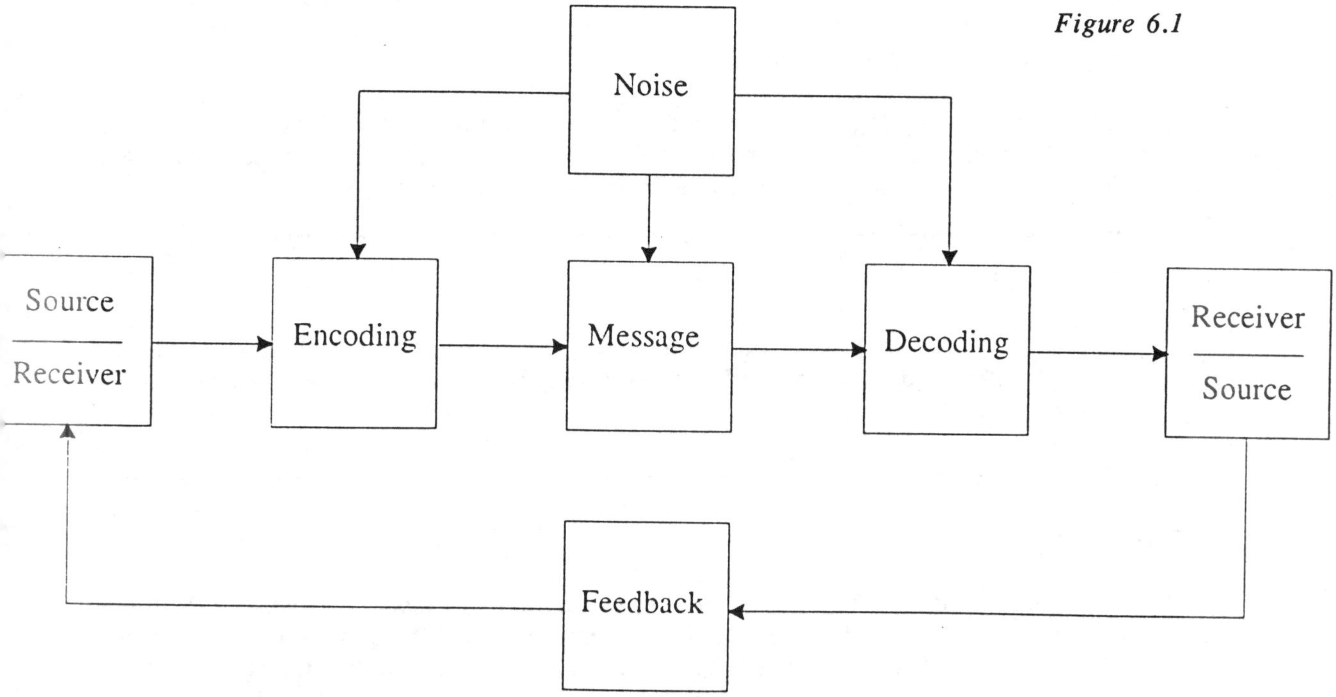

(a) The sender encodes the message so that the receiver should be able to decode it and then selects a channel, a path along which to transmit the message. If the channel selection is good the receiver will be exposed to the message. If it impacts sufficiently the receiver will attempt to decode it.

(b) There must be a feedback loop so that the sender can monitor how well the message has survived the journey along the channel, whether it has impacted upon the receiver, whether it has been decoded accurately and whether any intended action has been instigated. This demonstrates the two-way nature of communication. Both parties are senders as well as receivers and the process is active and dynamic.

(c) With feedback a message can be refined and re-transmitted. Advertisers are well advised to test their proposed advertisements on a sample of their intended audience before launching the actual campaign.

There will always be noise along a channel. A message will have to contend with extraneous distracting stimuli. These stimuli interfere with the reception of the message in its pure and original form and are always present to some degree. They may be explicit, such as a faulty telephone line, or implicit, for example a receiver who has other things on his mind or who does not comprehend the subtlety of the message.

A transceiver is a middleman in the process, for example a newspaper that carries an editorial based upon a press release. The transceiver will decode, perhaps filter, re-code and re-transmit. It is unlikely that the original message will survive in its pure form. The more transceivers there are the more the message will be altered. Therefore the wise communicator knows that clarity of image and brevity of message are essential if the communication is to be effective.

Notes

Consider these examples which show how effective a promotional tag can be.

(a) The slogan 'Persil washes whiter' is not permissible under current regulations relating to advertisements, and in fact has not been used for more than 20 years. Yet it has so infiltrated itself into the psyche of the British public that it is still regarded by many as current.

(b) 'Probably the best lager in the world' has been adopted as a cliche for general use. Did Carlsberg intend that? Intended or not it is very powerful since it acts as a free ad for the product every time it is used, in whatever context.

Exercise 2

You are probably aware of other slogans that have stood the test of time. Try to list a few. You may question how well some of them communicate - do you still remember which products they advertised?

Perception

Effective communication depends on an area of shared experience. A field of experience depends upon *perception* and is made up of the sum total of all the experience a person has had during their lifetime. Thus basic aural and written language(s), cultural understandings and expectations, body language, mathematical symbols and professional jargon all contribute to an individual's perceptual field.

The larger the overlap or commonness of the perceptual fields the greater the chances of accurate decoding. If the sender uses signs that are not common to both fields the receiver will be unable to decode the message.

Notes

Figure 6.2

Cymru Lan

Gardez propre la Grande Bretagne

Haltet Grossbritannien sauber

Mantenga limpia Gran Bretana

Tenete pulita la Gran Bretagna

حافظوا على نظافة بريطانيا

イギリスをきれいに

Keep Britain Tidy

This Keep Britain Tidy leaflet demonstrates how the visual image transcends the written language. Not only does it communicate with clarity and brevity, it also has an impact that a written request lacks.

Marketing communications mix

We will now go on to relate this general discussion of communication more directly to the specific problems of marketing. We will consider in turn each element in the marketing communications mix: advertising, sales promotions, publicity, direct marketing techniques and personal selling.

Firms will use a combination of these methods and the optimal *communications mix* will depend on the nature of the product, the market and the customer. For example, a manufacturer of industrial goods will rely more heavily on direct selling and sales literature, whereas a consumer goods manufacturer will use more advertising and sales promotion devices.

Notes

'Push' and 'pull' effects

The promotional mix is often described in terms of 'push' and 'pull' effects.

(a) A 'pull' effect is when customers ask for the brand by name, inducing retailers or distributors to stock up with the company's goods. Thus, an advertisement that persuades customers to go to a retailer to make a purchase has a clear pulling effect in drawing products through the distribution channels.

(b) A 'push' effect is targeted on getting the company's goods into the distribution network. This could be a special discount on volume to ensure that wholesalers stock up with products that the company is promoting. The analogy is that of pushing the company's products into shops and distributors so that they are available to the end user.

Note that some promotional activities can have both 'push' and 'pull' effects. For example dealers could be given advance screenings of an advertising campaign that is to run. If the dealers are subsequently convinced that the campaign will generate customer enquiries (the 'pull' effect) they are likely to stock up in advance (the 'push' effect).

2 Advertising

Advertising is defined by the American Marketing Association as 'any paid form of non-personal presentation and promotion of ideas, goods or services by an identifiable sponsor'.

There are three important elements in this definition.

(a) Advertising is non-personal communication, and so the seller does not come face to face with potential customers.
(b) It is paid for.
(c) There is a clear, identifiable sponsor of the advertisements.

This definition clearly distinguishes advertising from personal selling and publicity (which is often not paid for, and if it is, the sponsor does not openly present ideas or products).

There is a grey area between advertising and publicity which might be called *sponsorship*. This is now a common feature in sporting competitions and events which bear the name of the sponsor.

Advertising should be distinguished from *sales promotions* which are defined as 'those marketing activities other than personal selling, advertising and publicity, that stimulate consumer purchasing and dealer effectiveness, such as displays, shows and exhibitions, demonstrations and various non-recurrent selling efforts not in the ordinary routine'. They are also called 'below-the-line' activities, distinguishing them from advertising, personal selling and publicity, which are 'above-the-line' activities.

Exercise 3

List a few sales promotions techniques that you have encountered.

Advertising can be seen as attempting to move consumers along a continuum stretching from complete unawareness of the product to regular usage (brand loyalty). The AIDA model postulated by Strong in 1925 is a simple example of this approach known as the 'hierarchy of effects' model.

Awareness → Interest → Desire → Action

Strong's AIDA model has been extended by many writers, notably Engel Blackwell and Kollat in 1978, as follows:

Perceived Information → Problem Recognition → Search → Evaluation of Alternatives → Beliefs → Attitudes → Intentions → Choice.

Both these models assume that customers formulate a behavioural intention which then leads to actual purchasing behaviour.

The purpose of advertising

Advertising is 'purposive communication' to a target market. It assists in selling by drawing attention to the characteristics of a product which will appeal to the buying motives (conscious or subconscious) of customers in the target segment of the market. It does not necessarily instruct or inform about all the characteristics of a product; its function is to identify an exploitable characteristic (that is, one which distinguishes it from other products) and to suggest that this characteristic gives it a special value for potential customers. If the product does not have a distinguishing characteristic, uniqueness is promoted by brand image.

Exercise 4

Some advertising appears to be almost the reverse of informative, in that it attempts to stimulate interest by causing the viewer to wonder what the ad can be referring to. Think of examples of this technique that you have seen.

Advertising does not sell a product by itself. 'The purpose of advertising is to enhance potential buyers' responses to the organisation and its offerings. It seeks to do this by providing information, by trying to channelise desires and by supplying reasons for preferring the particular organisation's offerings.' (Kotler).

Notes

Advertising is often classed under one of three headings.

(a) *Informative advertising:* the advertising is concerned primarily with conveying information and raising consumer awareness of the product or the organisation. This form of advertising is common when a product is in the early stages of its lifecycle, or if it has been modified in some significant way.

(b) *Persuasive advertising:* this type of advertising is much more concerned with creating a desire for the product and stimulating actual purchase. It will tend to be more common for well established products, often in the growth/maturity stages of the product life cycle. This is probably the most competitive form of advertising.

(c) *Reminding advertising:* this approach is also often used for well established products and it is concerned with reminding consumers about the product or organisation, reinforcing the knowledge held by potential consumers and reminding existing consumers of the benefits they are receiving from their purchase of a particular good.

Brand vs generic advertising

All advertising has some generic content as it stimulates demand for all similar products in the market whilst attempting to promote the brand against competitive products.

It will only be worthwhile for an individual firm to advertise if it can differentiate its products from other competitive products in the eyes of the consumer. In the absence of *product differentiation* all advertising purchased by an individual firm would be generic benefiting all producers equally at the firm's expense.

It is difficult to differentiate agricultural produce. This has led to the evolution of the Milk and Egg Marketing Boards to advertise on behalf of UK farmers. Product differentiation can be strengthened by the creation of a unique brand image using advertising, eg the famous message 'Guinness is Good for You' that made an accumulative impact over some three decades of advertising. Campaigns using this slogan were the major factor in Guinness' growth from being just another stout brewery to the predominant producer of this particular brew. So successful have Guinness been that the term 'stout' has virtually disappeared from common usage.

The objectives of advertising

The objectives of advertising may be any of the following:

(a) to ensure a certain exposure for the advertised product or service;

(b) to create awareness of new products, or developments to existing products;

(c) to improve customer attitudes towards the product or the firm;

(d) to increase sales (although it is difficult to relate advertising to sales volumes) and profits. For a non-profit making organisation, the equivalent purpose will be to increase response to the product or service;

(e) to generate enquiries from potential customers. (Advertisements in magazines might include a coupon or card, to be filled in and returned if the reader would like further information. Similarly, TV advertisements sometimes give a telephone number to call for further information);

(f) to change the attitudes and habits of people at whom the advertisement is directed. Government advertisements often have this objective - eg campaigns against drinking and driving, against smoking, warnings about burglaries and fire hazards and appeals to save energy.

Unlike sales promotion activities, advertising can have a long-term as well as a short-term effect. For example, 'Fly the Flag' for British Airways or 'This is the age of the train' or 'Clunk-click' for seat belt advertisements have created a lasting impression.

Advertising is also a means of protecting the longer-term position of a company. A manufacturer of a speciality good, for instance, may advertise the quality image of his product so that if at any time in the future a competitor provides a rival product, the longstanding image of the speciality good might be invaluable in protecting its market.

The objectives of advertising which were listed above are rather general. The more specific targets of an advertising campaign might be as follows.

(a) To communicate certain information about a product. This is perhaps the most important objective.

(b) To highlight specific features of a product which make it different from the competitors. The concept of the *unique selling proposition* (or USP) is that by emphasising a unique feature which appeals to a customer need, customers will be influenced to buy the product.

(c) To build up a 'brand image' or a 'company image' (*corporate advertising* - for example, oil firms like Esso and BP and the conglomerate Hanson Trust have all used television advertising in recent years to promote a company image).

(d) To reinforce customer behaviour. It would appear that advertising can reinforce brand loyalty or customer loyalty and 'remind' customers to buy again.

(e) Influencing dealers and resellers to stock the items (on as much shelf-space as possible). Resellers will probably prefer to sell items which are widely advertised.

(f) In the case of government advertising, to achieve a policy objective, such as increasing the takeup of benefits, publicising government unemployment initiatives, increasing recruitment to the teaching and nursing professions and eating more healthily.

Exercise 5

You have seen the long-running series of coffee advertisements - you may even have read the book! - in which a couple are drawn together by their shared love of the finest things in life, including a particular brand of coffee. Try to analyse this form of advertising. And by the way, can you remember which brand it was?

Notes

The role of advertising in industrial marketing

Looking specifically at advertising aimed at industrial rather than consumer markets, the following are the principal aims of advertising.

(a) *Awareness building*. If the prospect is not aware of the company or product, he may refuse to see the salesman, or the salesman may have to use up a lot of time in introducing himself and his company.

(b) *Comprehension building*. If the product represents a new concept, some of the burden of explaining it can be effectively carried on by advertising.

(c) *Efficient reminding*. If the prospect knows about the product but is not ready to buy, an advertisement reminding him of the product would be much cheaper than a sales call.

(d) *Lead generation*. Advertisements carrying return coupons are an effective way to generate sales leads for salesmen.

(e) *Legitimisation*. Company salesmen can use tear sheets of the company's advertisements to show prospects in order to demonstrate that their company and products are not fly by night but respectable and sufficiently financially sound to run an advertising campaign.

(f) *Reassurance*. Advertising can remind customers how to use the product and reassure them about their purchase.

The theoretical optimal level of advertising

It is generally undisputed that it is necessary to advertise. The problem facing management is just how much advertising maximises profits.

It is possible to construct a theoretical model showing an idealised solution. Such a model is shown below.

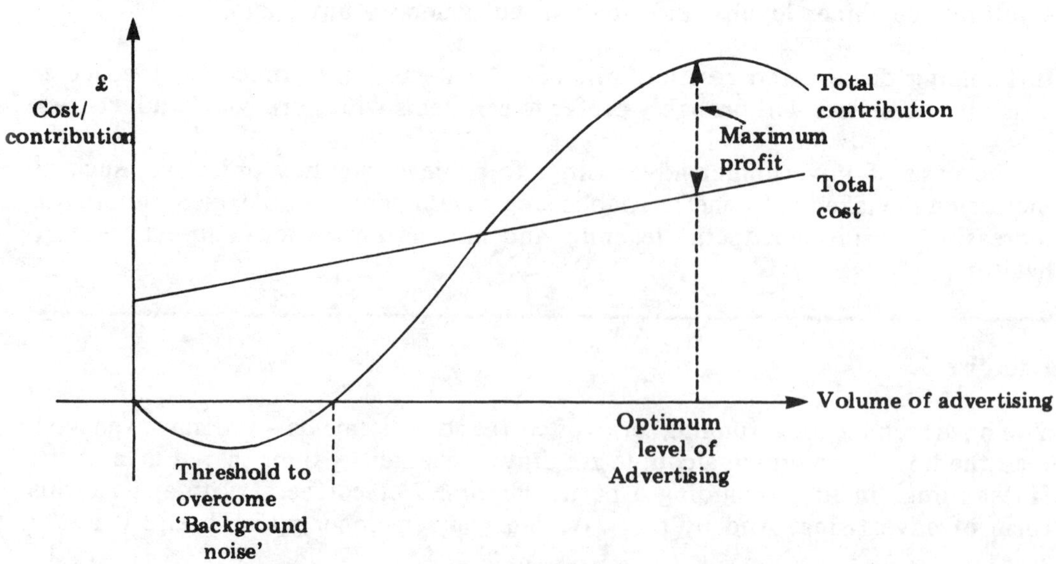

Assumptions: no scale discounts for volume of advertising
S shaped total contribution curve

Market research and advertising agencies attempted with little success to produce computer simulations of models similar to the above in the mid 1960s. These attempts failed because economists always make the proviso *ceteris paribus* (all other things being equal) which in practice renders many theories impossible to prove or disprove. All other things rarely are equal - they change unexpectedly.

In reality exogenous influences such as the marketing activities of competitors mask any underlying relationship between advertising spend and profits. The above model shows a threshold effect where more money is being spent on advertising but where consumers do not yet notice the campaign, perhaps because of the background noise effect of all the other, perhaps larger scale, campaigns. Once past this threshold consumers start taking notice and the contribution of advertising spend shows increasing returns to scale. This effect cannot be maintained indefinitely and whilst contribution still increases the effect moves into an area of diminishing returns. Where the slope of the total advertising cost is tangential to the total advertising contribution curve, the theoretical maximum benefit is achieved.

The advertising campaign

Large organisations spend very large sums of money on advertising, and to use the money to the best effect, it is obviously essential to produce an advertising plan. Although organisations usually try to maintain a continual exposure of consumers/customers to their products, there are often periods of intensive advertising, involving perhaps TV advertising in one or more regions. This intensive activity is called an *advertising campaign.*

An advertising campaign will be planned and executed with reference to the following factors.

(a) What is the aim of the campaign: to increase awareness and/or increase sales?

(b) The advertising message - what does the organisation want to tell its customers?

(c) Media selection.

(d) The frequency of displaying the message (for example, the number of TV commercial slots).

(e) The style of the message: is it a factual campaign or a humorous campaign?

(f) The budget. How much money will be needed to achieve the desired campaign, or what budget constraints limit what the campaign will do?

(g) Evaluation of the campaign. The organisation and its advertising agency will want to know how effective the advertising might be/has been. Plans should be developed for:

    (i) testing reactions to planned advertising during the development of the campaign;
    (ii) testing reactions after the campaign has been launched.

An organisation might hope that sales will increase because of an advertising campaign. This is probably what does happen, but the link between advertising and higher sales has not yet been conclusively or scientifically proved.

Notes

Exercise 6

Try a little self-analysis for a moment. Think of an occasion when you bought something as a result of an advertisement. Why did you do so? Was is just that you had not known about the product until you saw the ad? Or did the ad improve your perception of the product? Or what?

Planning an advertising campaign

A successful advertising campaign must be well planned. There are six distinct steps:

Step 1: Identify the target audience
Step 2: Specify the message
Step 3: Select media
Step 4: Schedule media
Step 5: Set the budget
Step 6: Evaluate effectiveness

Step 1: identifying the target audience

A list of dimensions which could be of use in identifying the target audience, depending on the type of product, is given below.

(a) Sex
(b) Age group
(c) Marital status
(d) Number and ages of children
(e) Social group
(f) ACORN group
(g) Location
(h) Income levels
(i) Social group membership (sports, hobbies, professional)
(j) Stage in life cycle
(k) Buying roles within the family (purchaser, user, influencer)
(l) Ownership of particular consumer durables.

In addition to these basic factors, personality and attitudinal variables can be added to give a more detailed insight into the lifestyle of the audience. The *psychographics* approach enables campaigns to be planned which emphasise how the brand has relevance for the style of living of the target audience. Creativity is used to emphasise mood, atmosphere and environment for brand usage, usually relying on non-verbal communication such as background setting for an advertisement (indoor/outdoor, relaxed or tense environment, type of music, style of furniture, use of colour schemes, appearance of models etc).

These factors are particularly relevant when the aim of the campaign involves persuasion of the audience. Various research projects have been conducted which have attempted to identify relevant correlates of persuasibility. On balance the evidence is not conclusive. However, Karlins and Abelson conclude their studies by stating that 'In our society, women are more persuasible than men'. Other studies, summarised by Delozier, have shown that 'in general a person of low self-esteem is more persuasible than someone high in self esteem, especially when social approval is involved' and that 'no consistent relationship exists between general intelligence and persuasibility'.

For industrial goods the social and socio-psychological variables are still valid but are perhaps not as important as are economic factors in the audience dimension process. Factors affecting behaviour include:

(a) size of company (turnover, number of employees, profit levels);
(b) production process;
(c) type of business activity;
(d) location;
(e) centralisation of buying;
(f) buying process;
(g) interdepartmental rivalries.

Step 2: specifying the message

People are very specific about the advertisements to which they pay attention. Most of us have the opportunity to see many hundreds of advertisements in many media each day, and cannot give our attention to each and every one.

The nature and degree of selectivity reflect the needs, value systems and past experience of the audience. Unless a particular advertisement engages the recipient's attention, it will simply be ignored or forgotten.

Exercise 7

What broad approaches can an advertiser employ to engage the attention of his target audience?

Thinking of a suitable advertising message is not the spectacular creative process it is sometimes made out to be. It is usually a long and painstaking process. Potential messages need to be tested on a representative sample of the target audience. Commonly, this test is carried out using *qualitative marketing research methods* involving group discussions. In these discussions, the reaction to the proposed message is probed and refinements suggested. Given the competition between advertisements for attention by the target audience the need to maximise the initial impact of the proposed advertisement is vital. Care is also necessary that the correct psychological clues as to the nature of the product and the people to whom it is intended to appeal are incorporated into the advertisement.

The essence of specifying the promotional message lies in identifying the intended function of the campaign. This function could be:

Notes

(a) to convey information;
(b) to alter perceptions;
(c) to stimulate desires;
(d) to produce conviction;
(e) to direct action;
(f) to provide reassurance.

Each function can suggest an appropriate form for, and content of, the message.

Much research has been directed at how far the content of the message is likely to be influential in effecting attitude change. In particular, studies have been concerned with the varying effects of persuasive messages, some of which are assumed to have greater influence because they play upon the emotions of an audience, whilst others rely on a rational approach to intelligence and good sense. Both the rational and emotional appeal approaches have strong supporters - people tend to advocate one or the other as being the more potent.

In many early experiments the findings were quite contradictory. This is understandable if for no other reason than that clear-cut identification of messages and their effects is not easy. What might be regarded as an entirely rational appeal may arouse emotions and, conversely, emotional appeals may make a person think. Other problems were evident also; independent judges could not agree upon which of the two categories the message fell into, and many of the experiments failed to indicate how and why one or other form of appeal was effective.

A very common type of emotional appeal is the 'fear appeal', often conveyed through the mass media (TV, radio, national papers). Governments try to induce greater efforts on the part of individuals by indicating the likelihood of national bankruptcy if there is a failure to produce and export more. Medical organisations may emphasise how pain and disease will follow upon disregard for health and hygiene. Insurance companies may display posters of the 'this could happen to you' type when attempting to promote the sales of their varied policies: life, accident, fire, childrens' education and so on. Commercial advertisers play upon our need for acceptance and popularity by showing how these can be achieved if we use their toothpaste or deodorants.

The conclusion from various studies appears to be that a strong appeal induces considerable anxiety but is unlikely to change attitudes. A restrained appeal may well change attitudes (resulting, for example, in purchase of a new brand of toothpaste) and such attitudes are likely to last longer.

Step 3: select media

'Media advertising' means advertising through the media, which include national newspapers, regional newspapers, magazines and periodicals, trade and technical journals, directories, posters and transport advertising, cinema, television and radio.

Exercise 8

Try to analyse the main characteristics of the above media from the point of view of a potential advertiser.

The criterion governing the choice of medium for conveying a persuasive message for a potential market is that the medium used should be the one which will contact the optimum number of potential customers most efficiently at the lowest cost. The choice of medium will depend on who the advertiser wishes to reach with the advertising message. If the advertiser wishes to sell to a particular market segment, advertising through a national medium might not be cost effective.

The choice of medium begins with a study of the target audience's *media habits*. The audience for a particular medium may be analysed and the media which are most used by customers in the potential market will be chosen for advertising.

(a) *Television* is watched by viewers from all social groupings and is an ideal medium for advertising mass consumer goods.

(b) A particular medium may reach audiences with special characteristics; for example:

    (i) the cinema is visited mainly by young couples;
    (ii) many magazines and local newspapers are read predominantly by women;
    (iii) there are magazines for qualified accountants, magazines for student accountants, magazines for data processing managers and so on.

(c) The size of *circulation* or *audience* for a particular medium is important, but there is no value in reaching a wide audience if they are not potential customers for the product being advertised. Expensive cameras, for example, are more profitably advertised in photography magazines (with small, specialist readership) than in national newspapers (despite their larger circulation). A high street butcher or car dealer should advertise locally (for example in local newspapers or the cinema) rather than over a wider area. Industrial goods would be advertised in a trade magazine, should advertising be required.

(d) It may be too expensive to try and reach an entire potential market with an advertising campaign; too wide a choice of media will probably bring diminishing returns on the money spent.

The advertiser will want reliable information about the audiences for each medium in order to help in the choice of media for an advertising campaign. Research into audiences is provided by the following:

(a) for major newspapers and magazines - the National Readership Survey or JICNARS (the Joint Industry Committee for National Readership Surveys);

(b) for television - JICTAR (the Joint Industry Committee for Television Advertising Research);

(c) for radio - RAJAR (Radio Joint Audience Research);

(d) for poster audiences - JICPAS;

(e) for the cinema - the Screen Advertisers' Association.

Another important consideration is *cost*. Advertising costs consist of:

(a) the cost of producing the advertisements;
(b) the cost of exposure in the media.

Notes

The costs of exposure are perhaps ten times the cost of production in consumer goods advertising.

The cost of a medium is measured by the 'cost per thousand' criterion. If a full page advertisement in a national newspaper circulating to 2 million readers is £7,000, the cost per thousand is £3.50.

Cost per thousand is a very simple measure, which should be interpreted with caution.

(a) There is no value in advertising female fashions to male readers, although males might account for half the readership of a newspaper; in other words, the advertisement might be reaching many people who will not be affected by it.

(b) Not all users of the medium will see the advertisement. Many TV viewers will leave the room during a commercial break; magazine and newspaper readers will not look at every advertisement.

Other factors in the choice of media are as follows.

(a) How many competitors use the medium? A company is likely to use a medium which is used by the competition. Competing advertising (in a magazine, for example) is likely to result in diminishing returns from the advertisements.

(b) What is the 'environment' of the medium - that is, the circumstances in which an advertisement is shown to its audience? As mentioned above, one of the features of television advertising is that a large number of people leave the room during a commercial break, or during short programmes for a charity appeal. Radio commercials are often sandwiched between music, and the problem here is to ensure that an advertising message is memorable and registers with the listener.

    Posters are seen for brief moments, and are mainly useful as 'reminders' rather than as a medium for conveying an initial message. Newspaper and magazine advertisements are 'confined' by the static, limited space available to them, and they have to 'fight' with the news and features for the attention of the reader. Cinema audiences are largely 'captive' and are usually prepared to watch advertisements on the screen.

(c) What is the nature of the product? Some items are more suited to advertisements in a Sunday newspaper colour supplement and others to a trade journal.

(d) What is the message? The nature of the information might help to determine the choice of media, for example technical data would be suited to a technical journal. (Advertising copywriters will adjust the *wording* of a message to suit the medium, but they cannot change the nature of the information which the advertiser wishes to put across.)

Step 4: scheduling media

An advertiser will not restrict his campaign to one advertisement in a single newspaper or one appearance of an advertisement on television.

(a) An advertisement must be repeated because many of the target audiences will miss it the first time it appears.

(b) It has been found that a larger target audience is reached by advertising in several newspapers instead of just one, and in several media instead of just one.

Step 5: setting the advertising budget

In an ideal world the budget for a campaign should be determined by a consideration of the four steps discussed so far. The budget needed is that which meets the objectives using the chosen media to convey the required message. In reality the constraint of what the organisation can afford is commonly paramount. It is noteworthy that in an economic recession it is often the advertising budget that is first to be cut when one could argue that it should be increased. The 'value for money' from advertising is not always appreciated by senior management, often because it is very difficult to quantify.

The advertising budget is often linked to sales using:

(a) a percentage of last period sales;
(b) a percentage of expected (target) sales;
(c) a percentage of past (or target) profit.

Exercise 9

You may find this an illogical way to set an advertising budget. Can you put your finger on what is wrong with it?

By using these methods advertising is determined by sales quantity rather than by revenue (quantity × price). When sales (past or present) increase then advertising expenditure will increase - when one could argue that it should decrease. Another approach is to match the advertising expenditure levels of rivals; again, there is little theoretical justification for this approach.

Step 6: measuring the success of advertising

An advertising campaign can only be termed successful if it generates profit for the company. However, it is almost impossible to measure the effect on sales and profits by any direct means. The problem is that advertising never takes place in a vacuum and other events in the market place, such as competitors' actions, changing attitudes and relative price changes, swamp the advertising effect. It is therefore necessary to observe changes earlier on in the buying process. The assumption is that favourable changes in awareness and attitude will result in higher sales and profits.

There is a paradox involved in trying to measure the effectiveness of advertising. The early stages in the process by which advertising generates sales are easy to measure (for example exposure by readership and/or viewer surveys) but are of little direct importance. The real effect that is of interest is obviously the net increase in sales. However, the sales effect can at best be inferred.

Notes

Stage	*Relative*	*Ease of*	*Method of measurement*
		importance	*measurement*
Exposure	Low ↑	High ↑	Frequency & reach
Awareness			Consumer survey recall
Attitude			Consumer survey attitude test
Sales			Usually inferred from above
Profit	↓ High	↓ Low	Usually inferred from above

(a) *Exposure.* Exposure can be measured in terms of frequency (for example the number of times a TV advertisement is screened, the number of posters put up on hoardings) and the number of potential customers reached. One TV advertisement might reach 2 million people; by repeating the advertisement, the intention would be to reach people who missed the advertisement previously, but also to reinforce the message through repetition to people who have seen it before.

(b) *Awareness.* Awareness would have to be clearly defined as awareness of the existence of a product, or awareness of certain particular features of a product. Awareness could be measured by recall tests or recognition tests (see chapter 2).

(c) *Attitudes.* The aim of a campaign might be expressed in terms of 'x% of customers should show a preference for Product A over rival products'; or 'y% of customers should show a favourable attitude towards the product or service'. Market research can be used to discover whether targets appear to have been achieved.

(d) *Sales (volume and/or revenue).* Advertising is often intended to increase sales. In the case of mail order advertising, where there is direct dealing between the seller and the consumer, often on application forms issued by the seller, the effect of a new advertising campaign on sales should be fairly easy to measure. In other cases, however, the effect of advertising on sales is not easy to measure.

Exercise 10

Try to pick out some of the difficulties in measuring the effect of advertising on sales.

(e) *Profits.* The aim of an advertising campaign might be to increase profits, sales volume or revenue. The difficulties of measuring the effect of an advertising campaign on profits are therefore the same as those described in (c) above.

However, an advertising campaign must earn at least sufficient extra profits (contribution) to cover the costs of the campaign itself. Breakeven analysis can be used to calculate the volume of extra sales required to cover the (fixed) costs of the advertising. In monitoring the effects of a campaign, management might be able to judge whether this minimum increase in sales probably has, or probably has not, been achieved.

(f) *Enquiries*. Advertising might be aimed at generating extra enquiries from potential customers (for example mail order advertising, but also advertising for goods and services such as building services, double glazing, plumbing services and so on). Where possible, enquiries should be traced back to the advertisement. For example, a customer reply coupon in a magazine advertisement should be printed with an identification number or label, identifying the magazine and date of its issue.

Successful advertising

The *content* of an advertisement is determined largely by the objective of the advertising and the motivation of the potential customer. For example, it may be informative, or it may 'knock' competing products. Some advertising slogans succeed in becoming well known phrases. Emotions may be exploited (for consumer goods rather than industrial goods) to attract attention to the advertisement so that the message of the advertisement can be put across to a potential customer whose emotional interest has been aroused. An advertisement should present information which leads to a greater awareness of the product; using non-economic emotions (fear, humour) should be an attention-getter, but inciting these feelings should not be allowed to be the only effect of the advertisement.

The content of advertisements is regulated by the British Code of Advertising Practice and members of the public can make individual complaints to the Advertising Standards Authority (ASA). There are also many statutory controls, which for example, include the Trades Description Acts 1968, the Foods and Drugs Act 1965 and the Labelling of Food Regulations.

In certain classes of products that may be injurious to health it is virtually impossible to make any product claims in advertisements that are acceptable within the ASA's code of practice. Increasingly, therefore, advertisements for cigarettes and alcoholic drinks are designed to hold the viewer's attention, thus reinforcing the exposure to the brand image, without attempting to communicate any product benefits.

Advertising will be most successful if the following conditions apply.

(a) The product should have characteristics which lend themselves to advertising.

   (i) It should be distinctive and identifiable (if it is not, a distinctive brand may be created).

   (ii) It should stimulate emotional buying (emotive products such as medicine, insurance and cosmetics and products which can be made to arouse social instincts, such as cars, alcohol, cigarettes and household appliances, can be advertised with great effectiveness).

   (iii) If at the point of sale a customer can refute an advertising claim simply by inspecting the product, advertising will achieve no sales at all.

(b) There should be consistency throughout the sales operation. Advertising, the activities of salesmen and dealers, branding, packaging and pricing should all promote the same product image.

(c) There should be co-operation between advertising staff and all other activities in the company. Product design, production, distribution, selling and financial operations should all combine to achieve customer orientation and maximum selling efficiency.

Notes

Advertising agencies

Most large-scale advertising involves not just an advertiser and the media owners, but also an advertising agency. An advertising agency advises its client on the planning of a campaign and buys advertising 'space' in various media on behalf of its client. The success of advertising depends largely on the artistic skills of an agency's copywriters and artists but there is a 'scientific' approach to advertising which complements the artistic side.

An advertising agency is appointed by clients to conduct an advertising campaign on their behalf. In the UK they receive a commission (often 10%) from the owners of the media with whom they place the advertisements.

Large or medium sized agencies may be creative agencies (specialising in originating creative ideas, which are necessary for, say, TV advertising) or media buyers (whose specialist skills are in buying media space and air time). Advertising of industrial goods is usually handled by smaller 'industrial agencies' which have the accounts of chemical, transportation and engineering firms. Most of their work is in the sphere of sales promotions, such as direct mail, exhibitions and public relations.

Exercise 11

Analyse the advantages of using an advertising agency:

(a) from the point of view of the media owner; and
(b) from the point of view of the advertiser.

The advertiser and the agency

To take full advantage of the agency's services, the advertisement manager of the advertising company must:

(a) have a working knowledge of advertising;

(b) be able to negotiate with the agency so that the proposed campaign appears to achieve the marketing aims of the organisation;

(c) transmit whatever information is necessary to the agency which may be of value in furthering the advertising campaign in the best interests of the organisation (for example the annual report and accounts, copies of all the news releases and house journals, changes in products, packaging or distribution methods and news about R & D).

The advertisement manager may be supported by specialist staff within the firm (for example an exhibitions manager, brand manager or product manager or a public relations officer) but he should be involved in all dealings between in-house specialists and advertising agency staff, to ensure that advertising campaigns are fully co-ordinated. Before looking at other promotional activities we will discuss the role of 'branding' in the communications mix and product design.

Notes

3 Sales promotions

Non-media advertising and *below the line* advertising (or activities) are alternative terms which mean sales promotion activities. Sales promotions are used extensively, because there is often a direct link between the promotion and short-term sales volume. For example, the offer of a free gift or a reduced price 'bargain' will be made dependent on the purchase of the product. A promotion offer might be a free gift if the consumer sends in three packet tops of the product; or a competition entry form might be printed on the product's packaging.

Sales promotional techniques have a more direct effect on usage than does advertising. As such sales promotions can be particularly useful in inducing trials by consumers of rival products, the three for the price of two offer being a sufficient inducement to wean the consumer away from purchasing their usual brand.

Examples of sales promotion activities are as follows.

(a) *Consumer promotions:*

- (i) free samples;
- (ii) coupon offers (money-off offers);
- (iii) price reductions as sales promotions;
- (iv) competitions;
- (v) free gifts (in exchange for, say, packet tops. These are known as 'free sendaway premiums');
- (vi) combination pack offers (two for the price of one);
- (vii) off-price labels;
- (viii) trading stamps;
- (ix) samples;
- (x) exhibitions and demonstrations (eg the Motor Show or Ideal Home Exhibition);
- (xi) catalogues (notably the large mail order catalogues of mail order firms);
- (xii) on-pack offers (ie free gifts which come with the product. This is sometimes used for first editions of new magazines).

(b) *Retailer or middleman promotions as a 'push policy':*

- (i) extended credit;
- (ii) merchandising facilities;
- (iii) contests for retailers or shop assistants;
- (iv) consumer promotions and advertising act as a 'pull policy' to attract dealer attention by means of consumer demand.

(c) *Sales force promotions:*

- (i) bonuses;
- (ii) contests between salesmen (based on volumes of sale);
- (iii) sales motivators - ie gifts linked to sales.

(d) *Industrial promotions:*

- (i) sales literature and catalogues;
- (ii) special discounts;
- (iii) exhibitions and trade fairs;

Notes

(iv) events - eg invitations to customers to visit the Wimbledon Tennis Championships or the Open Golf Championship;
(v) trade-in allowances;
(vi) inducements (such as diaries and calendars).

Exercise 12

Think back on your own exposure to consumer promotions. Have you encountered all or most of the techniques listed in (a) above? Have any of them induced you to buy?

Sales promotions are essentially short-term sales measures and an advertiser planning a campaign should not be tempted to sacrifice long-term prospects (for example brand image built up through media advertising) in order to spend too much on short-term promotions. Although sales promotion is short-term in its effects, its objectives are broadly similar to those of above-the-line advertising:

(a) to increase sales revenue by generating extra interest;
(b) to attract new customers;
(c) to encourage resellers to stock the item or increase their stocks;
(d) to encourage slow moving lines;
(e) to clear out stocks;
(f) to counter the moves of a competitor;
(g) to launch a new product;
(h) to encourage the sales force to greater effort.

Sales promotion can also supplement media advertising. 'Although display advertising can be very effective in making consumers aware of the existence of a product, inertia frequently prevents consumer sampling and some additional incentive is required to persuade non-users to try it. Promotions are designed to provide this incentive.' (Baker)

At whom are sales promotion activities directed?

Sales promotion activities may be directed at any of the following.

(a) People who do not currently use the product or service. The sales promotion will attempt to persuade them to try out the item.

(b) Existing customers. The sales promotion will try to persuade them to use the product or service more frequently, or in larger quantities.

(c) People who currently use rival products. The sales promotion will try to weaken their current brand loyalty and persuade them to try out the promoter's own brand.

If the target for a sales promotion is a particular segment of a market (for example young girls, young boys, mothers with small children) the type of promotion (the type of free gift for example) will be specifically designed to appeal to a particular type of person.

A target for a sales promotion campaign might be to boost the morale of the sales force. By offering some incentive to customers or consumers to purchase their products, a manufacturer will then be indirectly trying to influence his sales force by making their task of selling easier - by giving them something extra to sell with.

Some types of sales promotion will now be considered in a little more detail.

Merchandising

A manufacturer of consumer goods usually relies on reseller organisations (rather than direct selling) to bring the goods to the point of sale with the consumer. This dependence on resellers for the sales volume of a product will be unsatisfactory to the manufacturer, who may therefore try to take on some of the job of selling to the consumers. Manufacturer involvement in selling to consumers is achieved by advertising, packaging design or sales promotion offers. Another way of extending manufacturer involvement in selling is by means of merchandising.

Merchandising is a method by which the manufacturer tries to ensure that a retailer sells as many of his products as quickly as possible. The manufacturer therefore gives advice to the retailer, either from the sales force or from full time merchandising specialists.

Merchandising is concerned with putting the manufacturer's goods in the *right place* at the *right time.*

(a) *In the right place.* The right place means not just the stores and shops with the highest turnover, but also the best locations within the store. In self service stores, some shelves are in 'strategic' positions which attract greater customer attention, and merchandising staff attempt to secure these strategic positions for the manufacturer's products. Owing to the costs of merchandising work, these efforts will usually be restricted to the larger, more profitable stores with a high turnover.

(b) *At the right time.* In most stores, there are some days when demand is at a peak. Merchandising staff should try to ensure that if a strategic location is only available for a limited time, then this time should include a period of peak demand. Similarly, it is important to ensure that seasonal goods (Christmas items or Easter eggs) receive prominent display at the right time of year.

In spite of the need to ensure that the costs of merchandising are justified by the benefits of greater sales volumes, a manufacturer might provide staff for a short period to exhibit, demonstrate and sell his products within a store on behalf of the retailer.

The term 'merchandising' may also be extended to include the special sales promotion devices such as premium offers, competitions, free samples, two for the price of one banded packs, free gifts, gift coupons, picture cards, children's contests, which are used by the manufacturer, not only to attract consumer interest, but also to persuade the retailer to give the product a prime location in the store.

As an aspect of sales promotion activity, merchandising is designed to give a short-term boost to sales. It is essentially short-term in its intended effect and the retailer will later move the product away from prime locations, or give it a reduced amount of shelf space.

Notes

Other items associated with merchandising activities are *point of sale material*. The point of sale is the shop where goods are sold, and point of sale material is used in sales promotion. It includes:

(a) posters (for example holiday posters in travel agents' offices);
(b) showcards (for example dispensers from which customers can take the product);
(c) mobiles (display items suspended from the ceiling of, say, a supermarket);
(d) dump bins or dumpers: a product is dumped into a bin, suggesting a bargain offer;
(e) dummy packs;
(f) metal or plastic stands (to display the birthday cards etc of one manufacturer, say);
(g) plastic shopping bags;
(h) 'crowners' - the price tags or slogans slipped over the neck of a bottle.

In the UK merchandising tactics have gained ground at the expense of traditional advertising media (especially the press) in the sales promotion of bulk-bought materials.

Exercise 13

Everything that you have read about advertising, branding and sales promotion will sound very familiar, but can you think of examples? Pick some products that you buy regularly or are interested in and make a point of tracking their advertising and promotion over a period of several months. Note how posters and shop displays back up TV campaigns, and see whether the campaign attracts any 'free' publicity in the form of press coverage, or references by public figures like TV comedians. Is the promotion talked about by your friends? Has the slogan caught on and fallen into general usage?

The more you look, the more you will see.

Sales literature

A further aspect of sales promotion is the provision of sales literature such as specification sheets, catalogues, price lists, leaflets or brochures, wall charts, calendars etc. These are particularly useful for industrial goods (although catalogues are an important feature of mail-order business and one used by some chain stores such as Habitat and Mothercare).

Exhibitions and trade fairs

Britain has been fairly backward in its use of exhibitions and trade fairs and even the new Birmingham centre does not rival the foreign exhibition centres of Hanover or Geneva.

Exhibitions as a form of sales promotion may be:

(a) public indoor exhibitions (the Ideal Home Exhibition);
(b) trade indoor exhibitions (Commercial Motor, Hotelympia);
(c) public and trade indoor exhibitions (the Boat Show, the Motor Show);
(d) private indoor exhibitions (arranged by a single firm, with guests invited to attend);

(e) agricultural shows;
(f) overseas trade fairs, where national pavilions exhibit goods from a particular overseas country.

The advantage of exhibitions to the visitor are that:

(a) the products can be viewed and demonstrated;
(b) a wide range of up to date products can be seen in one place and expert assistance is available for answering queries.

The advantages of exhibitions to the manufacturer are:

(a) they attract many visitors who are potential customers. Prospective customers are met quickly and cheaply;
(b) they are a valuable public relations exercise;
(c) they are useful for launching a new product, or testing a market;
(d) they sell the product.

Disadvantages of exhibitions are:

(a) they are costly to prepare and operate;
(b) they take salesmen away from normal selling duties because exhibition stands must be permanently staffed.

Exhibitions are more naturally suited to some products than to others. Where demonstrations are particularly valuable to the prospective customer (for agricultural equipment for example) or at least visual inspection and expert information are required (for example motor cars) exhibitions are a valuable means of sales promotion.

4 Publicity

Publicity is defined as being any form of non paid, non personal communication, and like advertising, it involves dealing with a mass audience. We can also include public relations under this general heading although some components are 'paid for', since it is concerned more generally with building and maintaining an understanding between the organisation and the general public.

Publicity offers a number of benefits to the organisation. It has no major time costs, it provides access to a large audience and the message is considered to have a high degree of credibility. The information is seen as coming from an independent or quasi-independent source as opposed to from the company itself. However, it is also one of the more difficult forms of promotion to implement and to control since the presentation and timing of information about the organisation will be in the hands of particular publicity channels such as television and newspapers.

Traditionally, publicity and public relations were seen as being centred around producing regular, informative press releases and building up good contacts with journalists. As a consequence, its importance has often been underestimated. However, with increasing pressure on advertising space, time and costs, the importance of publicity seems likely to increase.

Notes

Sponsorship

It is becoming increasingly difficult to undertake any sporting activity which is not sponsored. Sponsorship has grown very rapidly in the last ten years, and this growth rate shows no signs of falling off. Insurance companies and tobacco companies have been at the forefront of this booming industry covering cricket, swimming, table tennis, horse racing, snooker and a host of other sports, and indeed arts, events.

Exercise 14

It is not only at sporting events that sponsorship is evident. List some other examples of sponsorship you have come across.

In marketing terms, sponsorship can be seen as a form of marketing communication. It stands alongside media advertising, personal selling, public relations and other forms of sales promotion as a method by which companies can communicate with potential customers.

It seems unlikely that there is a direct link between sponsorship and increased sales. It can be argued that the objective of sponsorship should be communication and is therefore seen as one form of marketing communication. There are many other influences on sales, and it is extremely difficult to isolate the effects on them of specific marketing activity. There are, however, several other potential *advantages* of sponsorship, besides awareness creation in a wider audience than could be reached cost-effectively by other forms of advertising and the media coverage generated by the sponsored events.

(a) Distributor and customer relations. Hospitality facilities at sponsored events can be used with effect to create and maintain positive attitudes towards the company on the part of middlemen.

(b) The impact of sponsoring 'worthy' events can have a wide positive effect on the attitude of *potential customers* toward the company's services. It should then be easier for the company's salespeople to convert these prospects into sales.

(c) Sponsorship has wider implications in public relations terms. It demonstrates good *corporate citizenship* and it may also have a positive impact on the company's employees. This would seem to be more likely the more the sponsored event fits in with the desired image of the company. The image of 'solid dependability' and 'protectiveness' and 'traditional British values' which might be thought to be likely to appeal to those seeking insurance policies should fit with the types of event which insurance companies sponsor: cricket, tennis, golf and athletics, as well as national orchestras and other arts events, are likely to provide such image links. The images of 'youth', 'fun', 'creativity' and 'imagination' connected with pop concerts make them attractive sponsorship events for soft drinks manufacturers and other suppliers to young people.

5 Direct marketing techniques

The increasing volume of direct mail is often criticised by those who receive it. Those who are responsible for sending it out answer that results are very satisfactory and that the waste bin is readily available for people who strongly object. This is the same argument as was used in the early days of commercial television - 'they always have an "off" switch'. In the case of direct mail, however, the Data Protection Act provides both access to mail lists, and the right to be removed from them. Doubtless figures will be released in due course showing how many have taken advantage of the opportunity that the law provides.

Recently there has been concern that the UK's extremely well developed direct response marketing industry, estimated to be worth £2.25bn annually, will be destroyed by a data protection proposal that is under consideration by the EC. The proposed legislation would stop companies developing customer lists, doing mailings or instigating many kinds of joint marketing activities with non-European countries. It would allow contact through the telephone directory and/or electoral roll but, at best, it would severely restrict other common activities.

Intense lobbying in Brussels ahead of the European Parliament's decision is funded by a 'fighting fund' that has speedily been raised by the hastily formed Direct Marketing Association (DMA), which came into being on 1 April 1992.

New list-broking regulations from the ASA came into force on 1 January 1992, and the DMA intend to work under those and within self-regulation and explicit rules established by the Institute of Practitioners in Advertising (IPA). They say that the 'draconian rules' are evidence of 'excessive zeal' by the EC.

Direct mail is a media with unique characteristics. It already accounts for nearly 10% of all advertising spend, and as more marketers appreciate its value and learn its unique skills its importance is growing rapidly.

Databases to support mail lists are becoming every more accurate, and list brokers can provide lists for rent or sale that match target audience profiles. At the present time anybody can set up as a broker and so before signing a deal it is prudent to check the broker's background and credentials thoroughly.

The cost of rental varies from £90 to £130 per thousand for lists of proven responders, but this figure will increase for really hot lists. Again it is not cost per thousand that should interest the marketing communicator. In direct mail the measure is cost per response. Lists can be bought for as little as £50, but in general these are roughly compiled and the response rate is very low.

It is possible to earn a reasonable income by making one's own proven lists available for rental through a list broker. Security is not broken since the actual names and addresses need not be disclosed. The renter can supply the package contents to a fulfilment house who will stuff and despatch the envelopes. It is wise, however, to vet the proposed contents before despatch, and to seed lists with decoy names and addresses so that what is actually sent out can be verified and any theft of a list can be discovered. The presence of decoys should be made known, overtly.

Good lists do not become overworked. It seems that those who like direct mail respond to a range of offers, and welcome the arrival of the next envelope. As lists are revised these responders naturally provide the backbone, while proven non-responders are dropped.

Direct mail is totally flexible: virtually any message can be delivered. However, the techniques for creating an effective direct mailshot are specialised. Most advertising agencies do not possess the necessary skills, although they may think they do. A marketing communicator cannot afford to allow an agency to learn technique on his or her budget! This is an area where there is often a clear need to use à la carte techniques.

Notes

Reader's Digest have developed direct mail to a fine art. Although there is much criticism about the volume of paper they put in their envelopes, and the way in which they design the overall package, the fact is that their promotion works extremely effectively.

Exercise 15

(a) Open all your post very carefully until you have collected six mailshots.

(b) Examine each in close detail. Does the envelope encourage you to open it? Are the contents intriguing? Are the benefits spelled out in lengthy copy that is well written to catch and hold your attention? Is it clear what action is required? Is the response address easy to locate on the main part of the offer? Does the response slip repeat the key points and carry the full response address? What is your overall reaction?

(c) Rank the six in order of effectiveness, and say why.

Marketers in every field should be building and maintaining their databases. The post code is the key element and this should be solicited from every prospect and customer. Geo-demographic segmentation databases can only be accessed through the post code.

6. Personal selling

The sales force is an important part of the communication mix. It engages in 'personal' selling, as compared with the 'non-personal' selling of advertising and sales promotion activities.

Each individual probably has his own ideas of the 'typical' personal sales representative, but it is interesting to consider the wide range of face to face sales activities which exist. Types of selling personnel include:

(a) delivery staff who also sell (the classic example being a milkman);

(b) sales staff within the premises of the sales organisation (such as a shop assistant);

(c) travelling sales representatives, who require limited technical knowledge (for example soap, food and drink);

(d) sales staff who need technical expertise to sell their product, probably selling to a small number of potential industrial customers (for example salesmen of computer hardware or software systems);

(e) sales staff who need to create a sale through their selling methods where an established market does not exist (for example door-to-door selling of encyclopaedias and insurance policies).

To be an effective sales person, it is necessary to recognise problems of potential customers and to offer help in solving them. The buyer-seller relationship is critical, and it is the immediacy of this relationship of face to face selling that helps to 'make a sale'.

Given that the term 'sales person' covers a wide range of selling activities, it may be apparent that the desirable personality of the sales person is likely to vary from one type of selling to the next.

(a) Shop assistants are expected to conform to the shop's norms for appearance (so that, for example, Harrods staff should look smart and conventional), easily recognisable (for example, because they wear a uniform or stand behind a counter), and polite and pleasant.

(b) Travelling sales representatives must be able to strike up an instant rapport with potential customers. Shopkeepers welcome fast talkers and sales reps who bring news and gossip to accompany their sales 'patter'.

(c) A travelling sales representative dealing in consumer goods might also need to be able to convince shopkeepers and managers of the advantages of a sales promotion, in order to win more shelf space or a prominent display position in a store or supermarket. Sales promotion skills are therefore essential.

(d) A sales representative for industrial goods will expect to sell his product on its technical merits (or other comparative advantage). Persuading the customer by rational suggestions will require technical expertise, pamphlets and reference to other industrial users. Customers may be 'persuaded' over a business lunch. This style of selling, because of its special nature, is probably well suited to a more sober personality.

Recruitment and training programmes should operate to ensure that the right type of person is employed to do the job of selling.

The task of selling

The task of selling involves the following.

(a) *Communicating the advantages of a product* to the customer, to develop the target customer's 'product and market knowledge'.

(b) *Securing a sale.*

(c) *Prospecting* for additional customers. This involves searching for prospective customers, perhaps visiting them several times, and then making a sales 'pitch'.

(d) *After-sales service.* Queries and complaints will arise and must be dealt with to the customer's satisfaction, in order to win repeat sales;

(e) *Gathering information* about what the customer wants.

The selling tasks above are those of the travelling sales representative. Selling tasks of the sales department may include:

(a) product delivery (remember the milkman);

(b) order taking inside the seller's store;

(c) order taking 'outside' by a field sales force;

Notes

(d) order taking by telephone;

(e) building up goodwill (such as by merchandising work);

(f) the provision of technical or engineering advice to customers, perhaps in helping a customer to draft specifications for a product;

(g) 'creative' selling of tangible products (such as door to door brush salesmen);

(h) 'creative' selling of intangible products (for example people involved in the sale of services such as banking, or insurance).

Personal and non-personal selling

Since the work of the sales force is only one element in the sales mix, greater dependence on advertising and sales promotion will mean a lesser dependence on direct selling. At one extreme, direct mail firms do not need any sales force. It is unlikely, however, that sales staff - even shop assistants - could sell without some advertising or sales promotion back-up.

A *sales plan* or *budget* should attempt to co-ordinate personal and non-personal selling, so that:

(a) the sales staff have sufficient sales literature to show to prospective customers;
(b) their task is aided by a sales promotion activity;
(c) advertising campaigns are used to prepare the ground for sales effort.

Exercise 16

The number of buyers in a market, and the extent of their geographical dispersion, are influences on the optimum mix of personal and non-personal selling. State how, in your opinion, the mix will vary as a result of these factors.

Although the emphasis of the above is the co-ordination of elements in the *sales mix*, the marketing effort as a whole will call for a co-ordination of all the elements in the *marketing mix* - product, price and place as well as promotion. Indeed, one of the tasks of a manufacturer's sales force might be to extend the reseller network by obtaining new reseller customers, so that the selling effort would be directed towards improving the 'place' in the marketing mix. Another example of co-ordinating the mix is the need to ensure that the sales force has a product to sell, so that stocks must be available and delivery dates promised should be adhered to.

Size of the sales force

An important problem is to decide the optimum size of the sales force. Provided that an organisation has sufficient resources to increase its output and distribution, the sales force could be increased up to the point where the marginal costs of extra sales effort begins to exceed the marginal revenue from the incremental sales. Effectively, however, the overall size of the sales organisation is restricted by the resources available to the company and by company policy, and by the balance in the sales mix between personal and non-personal selling.

Differing views exist as to whether sales staff should be given an equal workload (which relates to the number of calls and the size of customer) or whether they should be given sales territories of equal sales potential (regardless of geographical area) in order to optimise their efficiency. There are practical considerations here: the sales rep asked to cover South-East London will have less travelling to do between calls than the rep asked to cover the North of Scotland. The fact that these areas may have the same sales potential is less relevant.

Every organisation will have some idea about what it can afford to spend on selling. In practice 'rules of thumb' are usually applied. If it is decided that selling expenses should not exceed, say, 10% of sales and if a sales representative, with selling expenses and commission, costs, say £30,000 per annum, turnover of £300,000 per annum would then be required to support each representative. So, if a company budgets annual turnover of, say, £6 million, then the total sales force could then not exceed 20 staff.

The figures above are hypothetical, but should indicate to you how a rule of thumb judgement can be made about the maximum economic size of a sales force, based on annual turnover and selling costs. Obviously, a complex sales force organisation would be inappropriate for a firm with only a relatively low sales turnover.

Exercise 17

The power of direct selling, and the qualities that make a good salesperson, seems to exert a fascination over businessmen, academics and even the general public. Next time you are in a station bookstall, or your local W H Smith, notice how many books there are with titles like *Getting to yes, Clinching the deal* and so on. Maybe you should buy one!

The selling organisation

The type of selling organisation will be influenced by various factors.

(a) Intensity of competition, and possibly the structure of a competitor's selling organisation, will affect a company's own sales organisation structure. If, for example, specialisation appears to give a marketing advantage to a rival product, a company might need to use specialised selling itself.

(b) If it is decided that personal selling by sales representatives is the most efficient way to sell, the quantity and quality of the sales force will reflect this decision (so low dependence on advertising may result in a greater reliance on personal selling).

Notes

(c) Whenever possible, specialisation of the sales force should be introduced (whether by function, product, type of customer, outlet or market).

(d) The extent to which dealers are used will affect the sales organisation. If a company sells only to a limited number of multiple stores and wholesalers, a small sales organisation will be sufficient.

(e) Generally, direct selling is appropriate for industrial goods but sales are often confined to a few customers, so that the number of orders is small but their value high, and consequently:

 (i) the number of orders/size of sales force ratio is low;
 (ii) the value of orders/size of sales force ratio is high.

The personal sales process

Many guides have been written on ways of improving the performance of personal selling. In this section, the main stages of the personal sales process are highlighted with some common guidelines for each stage.

Stage 1: prerequisites

Before a salesperson begins work, a number of prerequisites should have been met.

(a) The salesperson should have a *good knowledge* of the company and its products and service.

(b) The salesperson should know the *limits of negotiation* within which the deal can be made regarding price, delivery terms, volume and cash discounts, credit and other relevant items.

(c) The salesperson should feel that he has top *management support*.

(d) The salesperson should feel a *respected* member of the organisation in order to have self-respect.

Stage 2: gain the customer's attention

Here the aim is to define the customer's need by identifying the problem which the customer is buying the product or service to solve. A good salesperson should aim to follow these eight steps to attract and keep the customer's attention.

(a) Don't mention the product until the *need* is identified.
(b) Try to identify how the *decision* is to be made (such as by consideration of alternatives).
(c) *Gain attention* quickly before the client loses interest.
(d) Have a *good first sentence* (which is not 'Can I help you?').
(e) Show he can *solve the problem.*
(f) Ask *positive questions* (Have you? Can you? Are you?, not 'Haven't you?' etc).
(g) *Avoid external distractions* (TV, telephone, other people).
(h) Maintain *eye contact.*

Notes

Stage 3: create interest

This stage involves making the prospect interested in the product. At this stage, a good salesperson tries to match the product to the needs of the customer. The salesperson should:

(a) *demonstrate* the product or service to let the prospect see for himself how it works;
(b) get information from the prospect about his *needs*;
(c) involve him in *conversation*;
(d) not simply let the prospect look at brochures and so *lose his attention*, enabling the prospect to say 'I'll read it and come back later'.

Stage 4: stimulate the desire to buy

Here the salesperson should be seeking proof that the product does match the customer's needs. The customer accepting that it does so is the proof which is being sought. The salesperson should:

(a) sell the idea or problem solution, not the product itself;

(b) get the customer to decide on *principles* and sort out the *details* later;

(c) *involve the customer* in the process;

(d) remember that *repetition can reinforce*;

(e) try to satisfy the customer's *special requests;* this involves him more closely and makes him feel special;

(f) *anticipate events* - talk as though the sale is concluded and discuss after-sales issues (but do not write out the order until he agrees to buy);

(g) show that the purchase is seen as *inevitable*, because radiating conviction can induce the prospect to buy;

(h) invite the client to spell out remaining *objections* and then clear them up;

(i) if no decision is made, if appropriate *keep in touch* with the prospect and try to make a further appointment (which should always be kept).

Stage 5: conclude the sale

The final part of the process can be the most difficult: the client must make the final decision, the salesperson cannot do it for him. The salesperson should:

(a) ask questions that require *positive answers* whilst making sure that negative answers allow the sale to continue;

(b) know what to say *whatever the response* of the prospect;

(c) offer alternatives which are *positive* ('would you prefer this one or that one?');

(d) *invite the prospect to agree* several times, moving closer to the sale each time.

Notes

These sales stages are bound to be generalisations and tend to imply a *non-specialist buyer*. Selling to a *specialist buyer* (such as an organisational buyer) is a more sophisticated process although similar principles can be of some use.

Exercise 18

Can you think of some of the differences in attitude and approach between an organisational buyer on the one hand and an individual consumer on the other?

Sales force organisation

A sales force may be organised in several different ways, including:

(a) territorial design;

(b) a specialised structure of the sales force with salesmen specialising in:

   (i) types of product;
   (ii) types of outlet (which is a form of specialisation by customer).

Many companies use a combination of these different types of sales force organisation.

It has already been suggested that design of the sales territory will influence selling efficiency.

(a) A sales person needs an area of *adequate sales potential*. Semlov (1959) has suggested that if sales areas have unequal potential, the extra productivity of the salesman in an area with better area potential will be more than offset by the decline in productivity of the salesman with the worse area potential.

(b) A salesman should not be given a sales area which is beyond his *workload capabilities;* equally, there must be sufficient sales potential in the area to motivate the salesman.

(c) The lower costs of *territorial organisation* should be considered against the possible loss of custom which might result as a failure to *specialise*. A sales force structured by type of customer or by product may cost more than a simple territorially based sales force, but it could be capable of winning many more sales.

A further aspect of sales territory design is *sales call planning*. Given that a sales area must have adequate sales potential and workload, it should be possible to plan the number of calls a salesman should be able to make over a period of time. 'Standards' should exist for the average number of calls per day, or average miles travelled per day; and by planning the salesman's workload, it should be possible to prevent time lost through inefficient routing, or spending too long with difficult or reluctant customers.

Territorial design

Eventually, all large sales organisations involve a territorial breakdown. Where there is no specialisation, the sales organisation may be based entirely on *geographical* divisions.

(a) There may be a *pyramid organisation* structure with top management at head office, sales supervisors controlling the sales force in a region, and a salesman or sales force for each territory in a region.

(b) The span of control of a sales supervisor is influenced by:

  (i) the amount of work to be done;
  (ii) the physical conditions under which it is done (such as how much travelling is involved);

(c) The amount of supervision required depends on two factors.

  (i) The initiative which individual sales staff are allowed (if they can arrange delivery dates, price and production possibilities, they must have easy communication access back to their immediate superiors).

  (ii) The size of sales commission will determine how much salesmen are willing to work without the need to be supervised.

(d) The size of each sales territory should be such that the amount of time wasted by sales staff in travelling is not excessive; there should be a good 'frequency of call' rate.

It is most suited therefore, to the sale of products in a homogeneous range (because it is important for the salesman to know his products as well as his customers). If the range of products is wide, and technically complex, it is unlikely that an individual sales person will be able to learn enough about them to sell them effectively.

The size of the sales area will depend on the expected workload for each sales person, or the sales potential of any area. An organisation might need several sales areas in South East England whereas the whole of Scotland might be a single area.

Exercise 19

What might be the administrative and logistical benefits of a territorial structure?

Specialised structures

Specialisation may be introduced into a sales organisation, and may take any of the following forms (or combination of several).

(a) *Specialisation by function:* for example, advertising group, market research group, new production group, sales/production liaison group, sales training and personnel section. This type of specialisation is more relevant to the marketing and selling department as a whole rather than to the sales force itself.

Notes

(b) *Specialisation by the nature of goods:* the more complex the nature of the goods to be sold and the more knowledgeable the customer, the more it is necessary to employ sales staff with a skilled knowledge of the product.

(c) *Specialisation by the range of goods*

(i) If a company manufactures a range of goods, its sales staff may specialise in a section of the range; for example, in the sale of a range of office equipment some salesmen may specialise in calculators and others in document copiers.

(ii) It is also possible to employ *product managers* who specialise in a product or range of products and who advise the sales force who sell the entire range without specialising. This type of organisation has drawbacks because it may be difficult to decide to what extent product managers should simply be advisers and how much authority they should be allowed over sales executives.

(iii) Sales staff must know their products; therefore if the company's product range is broad and complex, product specialisation may be desirable. Several sales staff would be required to cover the same sales area.

Disadvantages of product specialisation are that:

(i) travelling time and expenses are higher than with a territorial sales organisation;

(ii) one customer buying two different products from the same company might have to deal with two different salesmen.

(d) *Specialisation by range of market:* by market segments. Examples of specialisation by market segment are:

(i) home and overseas sales;
(ii) industrial and non-industrial sales;
(iii) male and female markets (eg clothiers).

The *advantage* of market specialisation is that salesmen get to know the needs of a particular market segment.

The *disadvantages* of market specialisation are:

(i) travelling time and costs;

(ii) potential problems for product designers when different market segments begin to show differing requirements;

(iii) the potentially complex organisation structure, such as possible problems of identifying boundaries between one segment of the market and another, especially when new market segments are evolving.

(e) *Specialisation by range of customers:* in selling industrial goods, a specialised sales force should be organised so that each sales person deals with a small number of potential customers in order to foster a better understanding of the motivation of the customers. This could be vital for securing large or valuable industrial orders.

The *advantages* of specialisation by types of customer are as follows:

(i) the sales force will be more alert to the specific needs of each type of customer;

(ii) in selling industrial goods, knowledge about the customer's industry and needs might be crucial in winning sales over the bids of competitors.

(f) *Specialisation by range of outlets:* with changing patterns of consumer and wholesale buying, such as the growth of multiple stores and superstores, specialisation by sales staff in dealing with different types of outlet may improve a manufacturer's selling efficiency.

A combination of these different types of sales force designs can be used. For example, sales staff might specialise in a type of customer or type of product within a sales area or in a type of product for a restricted number of potential customers.

Evaluation of sales force performance

Evaluation should be made of the sales function as a whole and for individual sales personnel. Performance should be measured against objectives which may be *quantifiable* such as the number of new accounts, or more *qualitative* such as customer satisfaction.

After-sales service

After-sales service is especially important in industrial markets where technical service may be required long after purchase.

Exercise 20

Before reading on, try to list some of the purposes of good after-sales service. Some are fairly obvious, but others need a little thought.

Much of the work on after-sales service involves producing instruction manuals and the like. The overall product offering (including heavy industrial manufacturing equipment) has a service element included. This can be pre-sale (for example, design and installation services) or postsale (for example, maintenance and training services). After-sales service is one way in which organisations can build a competitive advantage and is increasingly valued by the customer. An increased awareness of developing service quality can lead to important benefits.

(a) *Greater customer retention rates and customer loyalty.* If customers are satisfied with the service the supplier provides, they are less likely to switch to another supplier.

(b) *Attraction of new customers from word of mouth recommendation.* Customers are more likely to recommend a high quality service to their friends, family and business colleagues than they are a poor quality service. If, in conversation, the topic of

Notes

quality of service arises, the opportunity for recommendation may be taken up if the customer is satisfied by the service. Such recommendations are much more potent than other forms of promotion because the customer is seen as an objective judge.

(c) *Greater market share.* This advantage flows from the first two. If maintained, higher levels of customer care can lead to greater market share. Higher levels of service quality are more difficult for competitors to copy; price competition can be matched by rivals quickly but a system of higher service quality takes much longer to embed into the rival's operating procedures and so increased market share is maintained for longer.

(d) *Improved employee morale.* Higher service quality means fewer customer complaints and higher levels of satisfaction with the service. Service personnel are more likely to gain job satisfaction if not faced by a constant stream of complaints and abuse. Employees are thus more likely to have positive attitudes to their jobs, to feel more professional and to be more committed to their organisation. As a result staff turnover is likely to be lower and fewer mistakes are likely to be made; both of these in turn lead to higher service quality and lower costs (in training, for example). As a group of staff work together over time, team spirit develops and the group cohesion further reduces staff turnover and associated costs.

(e) *Insulation from price competition.* If customers evaluate suppliers in terms of *value for money* rather than purely in cost terms then service quality is more difficult for competitors to copy. As noted above it is relatively easy for competitors to reduce their prices in the short term. It is not so easy to improve their service quality in the short term. Thus, higher service quality is likely to insulate the supplier from price competition.

(f) *Lower advertising and promotion costs.* As noted above, word of mouth recommendation is much more potent than paid for advertising in gaining new business; it is also cheaper. Thus the supplier may see gains in numbers of customers without the need to increase advertising and other promotion costs.

(g) *Lower operating costs.* Cost can be saved in a number of ways:

(i) from reduced staff turnover;
(ii) in training and retraining costs;
(iii) in rectifying transaction mistakes;
(iv) in administrative costs;
(v) from customer complaints being reduced.

(h) *Increased productivity* should flow from these advantages and should lead to increased financial performance and profitability.

Personal selling is still the most important element in the sales mix for the selling of industrial goods and for sales to government markets. Similarly, personal selling plays an influential role in sales to reseller markets. However, the rapid increase in labour costs (and travelling costs) especially during the 1970s inevitably turned management attention to the cost effectiveness of sales staff, with the following results.

(a) In many shops, there has been a switch to self-service displays and a reduction in the selling role of shop assistants.

(b) Advertising is used in advance of a sales campaign, so that salesmen do not have to start 'cold' with prospective customers.

(c) Selling by telephone (or at least, obtaining initial customer reactions by telephone, with a follow up personal visit if a sale might be in prospect) is a way of cutting down travelling time and selling costs. Salesmen can reach more prospective customers by telephone than by personal visits - even if they work in a very restricted geographical area.

(d) Sales managers pay more attention to sales call planning and sales territory design. Sales call planning should help to reduce the average cost per call, and efficient sales territory design should enable a higher average sales value per call to be achieved.

(e) The growth of large retail chains (notably supermarket chains) with a central buying department has meant that the manufacturer must now sell to a small group of purchasing managers instead of to a large number of individual stores. Although personal selling is an important feature of selling to these retail chains, the number of salesmen required to do the job is much less than in selling to individual shops.

Personal selling is probably one of the most expensive forms of promotion in terms of cost per person contacted. The extent to which sales staff are used varies with different products and different markets, but there are few occasions when some element of personal selling is not needed. The use of personal selling is probably most extensive in industrial markets where the number of buyers is small, the value of the account potentially large and there is often a demand for a specialised or customised product. A particular strength is that personal selling allows for feedback in communication process.

Chapter roundup

(a) We began by looking at a general model of the communication process which emphasised the importance of 'noise', perception and feedback.

(b) In the context of marketing, communication is a process embracing advertising, sales promotion, publicity and public relations, direct marketing and personal selling.

(c) We looked in detail at the planning of an advertising campaign, and examined a six-step procedure: identify the target audience, specify the message, select media, schedule media, set the budget, evaluate effectiveness. We also looked at the use of advertising agencies.

(d) We looked at the wide variety of sales promotion activities that may be undertaken. To aid your memory, it may be convenient to remember them under the categories of consumer promotions, retailer (or middleman) promotions, sales force promotions and industrial promotions.

(e) We defined 'publicity' in the context of marketing, and looked at the kinds of activities included in the term, especially sponsorship.

(f) We looked at the techniques of direct marketing and at the regulations which surround it.

(g) Personal selling remains a crucial aspect of marketing for many organisations and we looked at the techniques involved and at the means by which a sales force may be organised and controlled.

Notes

Quick quiz

1 Sketch a model of the communication process.

2 What is meant by 'push' and 'pull' effects in the context of the marketing communications mix?

3 Distinguish between advertising and sales promotions.

4 List five possible objectives of advertising.

5 Identify six steps in planning an advertising campaign.

6 Compare the merits of (a) national newspapers; (b) television; (c) cinema, as advertising media.

7 List five factors that advertisers may attempt to measure in evaluating the success of a campaign.

8 List six types of consumer promotions.

9 What is meant by merchandising?

10 What sort of price would you expect to pay for the use of a typical mailing list generated by someone else?

11 What factors influence the way in which a sales organisation is structured?

12 What benefits are produced by good after-sales service?

Solutions to exercises

1 No

(a) It may not be opened
(b) It may not be read by the intended recipient
(c) Even if read, it may not be understood

And of course even if communication *has* taken place (the letter has been read and understood by the intended recipient) there is no guarantee that he or she will accept its contents or take the necessary action.

2 Guinness is good for you. Nice one, Cyril. Heineken refreshes the parts other beers cannot reach. It's the real thing. No FT, no comment.

3 The list is almost endless. Detachable coupons ('Buy three packs of X, tear off the coupons, and you will receive...); 'two for the price of one' offers; introductory discounts; trading stamps; free air travel (the recent fiasco involving Hoover's offer of free transatlantic flights is a spectacular example of how *not* to pitch a sales promotion).

Notes

4 You may have seen the billboard advertisements for the Economist magazine - large, red, empty space. Or the ads for Silk Cut cigarettes, which do not name the product anywhere, but use a variety of images showing cuts in silk fabric. Some years ago, a billboard campaign consisted of nothing but various anagrams of the letters IFEL. Not until the evangelist Billy Graham eventually came to town was the 'product' revealed - nothing less than eternal 'life'.

5 Obviously there can be no definitive answers to this one, but two strands of thought can be identified fairly confidently.

(a) Gold Blend coffee drinkers have a glamorous life style - Gold Blend itself is glamorous.

(b) Viewers are interested enough in soap operas to positively look forward to the next instalment - they *want* to be exposed to the advertisement.

7 (a) He can try to induce fear ('Dental plaque will ruin your teeth unless you buy...').

(b) He can employ humour (from the gentle humour of a dog running off with the toilet roll, to the more bizarre humour of, say, the Heineken ads).

(c) He can try the soap opera effect (Gold Blend).

Obviously the list is not exhaustive.

8 (a) *National newspapers*. Newspapers have a short life (one day) but a high attention value. If the product advertised has peak periods of demand during the week or month (for example, entertainment at the weekend) newspaper advertising can be timed to coincide with greater customer interest in the product. Some positions in the newspaper are more attention-getting than others but the positioning decisions are made by the newspaper's own advertisement manager. Some firms now rely almost exclusively on newspaper advertisements to sell their products by post.

(b) *Regional newspapers*. Local newspapers reach a concentrated geographical area, and are suitable for advertising to a geographical market segment. Many advertisements in local newspapers are by local firms (for example car dealers, estate agents) but a national firm might also use regional newspaper advertising of its product or service (for example the local electricity or gas showrooms) or to test a proposed national campaign at a local level.

(c) *Magazines and trade press*. The advertiser can select a magazine for advertising according to the content of the magazine which identifies the interests of the audience. Magazines have a longer duration of interest than a newspaper and actual readership is many times in excess of the number of copies sold. Detailed marketing research information about specialist magazines is not usually available, because specialist magazines are not included in the coverage of the National Readership Survey.

Notes

(d) *Television.* Television is a mass medium which can be received in most homes in the UK. It is therefore used to advertise mass produced consumer goods. The country is divided into separate independent television regions, however, and a company will not usually advertise at the same time in all regions. The great advantage of television is that the advertising message can be communicated in a mixture of sound, vision and movement (which is unrivalled by any other medium except the cinema). Television reaches every socio-economic group, but the emphasis of the message may generally slant towards the lower groups (the greater numbers). Although television operates seven days a week and for many hours in the day, the prime 'slots' will depend on peak viewing time and the popularity of the programmes shown at any of those times (in comparison with the programmes offered by the rival BBC stations).

(e) *Commercial radio.* The first full year of commercial radio was in 1974. The audience for most stations is local (though there are exceptions: both Classic FM and Virgin 1215 have national coverage) and the target audiences are mainly housewives, younger listeners and commuting motorists.

(f) *Posters and transport advertising.* This medium is often used as a complement to television advertising on the grounds that it can provide a reminder at, or near, the point of sale. As an example, poster advertisements for car seat belts have been positioned on the back of buses so that drivers following the buses could be reminded at the time of driving that they should be wearing their seat belt.

The disadvantage of posters are that the 'copy' needs to be short; there are problems of maintenance (due to damage by weather and vandals) and the prime poster sites are often held by a few industries and firms on long-term contracts.

(g) *Cinema.* The Screen Advertisers Association claim that the cinema is an advertising medium for reaching young adults (single persons with high discretionary spending power, engaged couples or young married couples). Although television is cheaper in terms of cost per 1,000, cinema offers a more specific target market and cinema advertisements (unlike television) have a captive audience.

9 It implies that the advertising spend should be determined by sales revenue. In reality it is much more plausible (though not demonstrably true) that sales revenue is at least partly determined by the advertising spend.

10 (a) Advertising is only one part of a marketing mix. Other factors influencing sales might be price changes, whether retailers have stocked enough of the products to meet an increase in demand or whether competitors are also advertising rival products at the same time.

(b) Advertising might succeed in maintaining a firm's existing market share, without actually increasing sales. There are obvious practical difficulties in estimating accurately what the fall in sales would have been if an advertising campaign had not been undertaken.

Notes

11 (a) From the media owner's point of view:

(i) they reduce the number of organisations with whom they have to deal;

(ii) agencies are bound to conform to the British Code of Advertising Practice in order to obtain their commission.

(b) From the advertiser's point of view:

(i) an agency's specialised services are likely to be cheaper than an internal advertising department;

(ii) an agency will have broader contacts with ancillary services such as printers and photographers;

(iii) the advertiser receives expert advice (for example from the agency's account executive) free of charge;

(iv) agency employees have a broad experience in the field of advertising.

14 You may have attended fund-raising events, such as the local fete, at which a local sponsor's name was prominent. Or you may have bought a programme at a musical or theatrical performance and found it filled with advertisements for the sponsors of the event.

16 A small number of buyers, particularly if they are close geographically, can favour personal selling. With many buyers, scattered over a wide area, the importance of advertising increases.

18 The subject of buyer behaviour - both in individuals and in organisational buyers - has been covered in Chapter 5.

19 The benefits of a territorial sales force design are:

(a) to reduce travelling time and costs;
(b) to enable the sales staff to get to know their customers and sales areas;
(c) to motivate sales staff by giving them autonomy over their area;
(d) to give sales staff an equal workload or equal sales potential;
(e) to keep the organisation and administration simple.

10 MARKETING STRATEGY

> *Your objectives*
>
> After completing this chapter you should:
>
> (a) be aware of the possible marketing strategies an organisation may adopt, and of the ways in which a strategy is formulated;
>
> (b) understand how a marketing plan is formulated

1 Marketing strategy

Introduction

Marketing has traditionally been seen as a separate functional activity with a primarily *tactical* role to play in business development. However, this view is being replaced by the recognition that marketing has a key *strategic* role to play. *Strategic planning* sets or changes the *objectives* of an organisation. *Tactical planning* is concerned with decisions about the efficient and effective use of an organisation's resources to achieve these objectives and strategic targets.

In addition, consumers are becoming more sophisticated and quality conscious. To deal with such rapid change, it becomes important for an organisation to adopt a planned approach to its business to guide its development in an increasingly unknown and uncertain future. Effective planning will enable any organisation to adopt a *proactive* stance to its markets and to anticipate changes to ensure that it sustains a competitive position. Given the uncertainty which prevails, it is crucial that plans are flexible and adaptable.

The development of *corporate strategic plans* is intended to guide the overall development of an organisation. Within that framework specific plans regarding marketing strategies will be determined. These plans, to be effective, will inevitably be interlinked and interdependent with those for other functions of the organisation. This chapter focuses on the development of *marketing plans*, recognising that these will contain both strategic and operational components. The strategic component of marketing planning focuses on the direction which an organisation will take in relation to a specific market or set of markets in order to achieve a specified set of objectives. Marketing planning also requires an operational component which details specific tasks and activities to be undertaken in order to implement the desired strategy.

Developing such a planned, strategic approach ensures that the marketing efforts of any organisation are consistent with organisational goals, internally coherent and tailored to the needs of identified consumer markets. It should also ensure that the resources available within the organisation are allocated in a systematic manner consistent with specified objectives.

Strategies

Within any organisation, strategies develop at several levels. *Corporate strategy* deals with the overall development of an organisation's business activities, while *marketing strategy* focuses specifically on the organisation's activities in relation to the markets served. Strategy can take many forms; two commonly identified ones are deliberate and emergent strategies.

(a) *Deliberate strategies* exist as the result of conscious, planned activities.

(b) *Emergent strategies* are the outcome of activities and behaviour which develop unconsciously but which fall into some consistent pattern.

In practice, it is frequently the case that most strategies which are pursued by firms are part deliberate and part emergent. To the extent that they are deliberate, they are typically the outcome of some planning process which is concerned with guiding the development of the business.

In the context of developing a marketing plan, the notion of strategic marketing can be seen as having three key components:

(a) the designation of specific, desired objectives;
(b) commitment of resources to these objectives;
(c) evaluation of a range of environmental influences.

A key feature of strategy is that it does not just focus on organisational *efficiency;* arguably, its more important function is that of enabling the organisation to be *effective.*

Exercise 1

Do you understand the distinction between efficiency and effectiveness? If not, try to find definitions of both terms to bring out the difference between them.

However, an organisation can only be effective if it is aware and responsive to the environment in which it operates. In a sense, it can be argued that marketing is by definition 'strategic', since to be able to market a product successfully ultimately requires that the firm has the right type of product and is operating in the right markets.

It should also be emphasised that the concept of strategy has a dynamic component. We have stressed the importance of strategy in enabling an organisation to be effective, but to be truly effective that organisation should not only be 'doing the right things now', it should also be aware of and prepared to anticipate future changes to ensure that it will also be 'doing the right things in the future'. Planning and strategy do not give the organisation the ability to predict the future. Rather, planning enables managers to think through the possible range of future changes, and hence be better prepared to meet the changes that actually occur.

Notes

The planning cycle

The process of developing marketing strategies and marketing plans has already been described as being closely related to the development of overall corporate strategies and corporate plans. The nature of this link will be made clearer if we consider their relative positions in the planning cycle. The first stage of a typical planning cycle begins with the collection of information by planners from all areas of the organisation. This will include financial and production data, but arguably one of the most important sources of such data will be the marketing department. Much of the information collected will be factual but there will also often be information in the form of opinions and attitudes, since this is the opportunity for individual functional departments to make an input to the corporate planning process. This phase is often described as *'bottom up' planning* since the main information flow is from lower to higher levels of management.

The second phase of the planning cycle involves the organisation and analysis of the information which has been collected in order to formulate an overall *corporate plan*. This will specify the objectives which the organisation wishes to achieve in the short, medium and long term, as well as specifying the way in which it intends to achieve them. The plan at this level will focus on broad aspects of overall corporate development and thus provides a framework within which specific functions such as marketing can develop their own plans. This phase is typically referred to as *'top down' planning* since the flow of information is now from senior to junior levels.

This combination of 'bottom-up' and 'top-down' planning enables senior levels of management - specifically, corporate planners - to provide a coherent structure for the organisation's development. The benefits of this structure are as follows.

(a) A framework is provided to enable managers to think ahead and anticipate change.

(b) Patterns of resource allocation within the organisation are clearly identified, which should minimise the extent of inter-departmental conflict. At the same time, because there is an important input to the planning process from functional managers, the plan will benefit from the specific experience of these managers who are closest to markets or functions within the organisation.

Finally, we should remember that although the planning cycle has been presented as having two discrete phases, in practice it is a continual process. Annual plans will be developed to guide short-term developments, but these will be generated within the framework of medium and long-term plans which will themselves be updated as the operating environment changes.

Marketing planning and strategy

The key requirement from any format for a marketing plan is that it should follow a logical structure, from historical and current analyses of the organisation and its market, on to a statement of objectives, then to the development of a strategy to approach that market, both in general terms and in terms of developing an appropriate marketing mix, and finally to an outline of the appropriate methods for plan implementation. The issues of implementation often appear briefly at the end of any discussion of marketing plans; and yet, arguably, the process of monitoring and controlling marketing activities is the most crucial factor in determining whether a plan is successful or not. The main function of the plan is to offer management a coherent set of clearly defined guidelines, but at the same time it must remain flexible enough to adapt to changing conditions within the organisation or its markets. The stages in strategic planning are as follows.

Development of the organisation's mission statement

↓

Statement of objectives

↓

Situational analysis

↓

Strategy development

↓

Specific plans

↓

Implementation

Company mission statement

The company mission statement is simply a statement of what an organisation is aiming to achieve through the conduct of its business; it can even be thought of as a statement of the organisation's reason for existence. The purpose of the mission statement is to provide the organisation with focus and direction. The precise nature of the corporate mission depends on a variety of factors. Corporate history will often influence the markets and customer groups served - thus, in the banking sector Credit Agricole retains strong links with its farming depositors, while Coutts concentrates primarily on high income consumers in its retail banking activities.

Corporate culture and organisational structures may also influence the approaches to markets and customers. The commonest approach to determining the corporate mission is to rely on the product/market scope. The mission statement is then essentially based on customer groups, needs served and technology employed. This approach may be of particular use from the perspective of marketing since it forces managers to think of the customer groups and the particular set of needs/wants which the firm is looking to satisfy.

It is not sufficient, for example, for a bank to identify its mission as being 'banking' - it would be more appropriate to identify that mission as being, for example, 'meeting consumer needs for financial transactions.' A mission statement of this nature can offer guidelines to management when considering how the business should develop and in which directions. With the benefits of a clear mission statement, future growth strategies can rely on what are regarded as distinctive competences and aim for synergies by dealing with similar customer groups, similar customer needs or similar service technologies.

Statement of objectives

Objectives enter into the planning process both at the corporate level and at the market level. Corporate objectives define specific goals for the organisation as a whole and may be expressed in terms of profitability, returns on investment, growth of asset base, earnings per share etc. These will feed down through the planning process and will be reflected in the stated objectives for marketing, branch and other functional plans. Clearly, the objectives specified for marketing will not be identical to those specified at the corporate level and an important component of the marketing planning process is the translation of corporate (often financial) objectives into market specific marketing objectives. These may take the form of targets for the size of the customer base, growth

Notes

in the usage of certain facilities, gains in market share for a particular product type etc. Whatever the status of a set of objectives, they must conform to three criteria; they must be achievable, they must be consistent and they must be stated clearly and preferably quantitatively.

Once a clear statement of the corporate mission has been achieved and corporate objectives have been determined, this information, in conjunction with further detailed analysis of the environment, provides the input for the next stage in the planning process.

Exercise 2

Look at the statement below, which the National Westminster Bank used to publish (untitled) every year on the first page of its annual report and accounts. Is it a mission statement or a statement of objectives? What do you think was NatWest's aim in publishing it?

The NatWest Way is to bring:

QUALITY TO OUR CUSTOMERS

We value our customers as the foundation of our business. Our relationships with customers and suppliers are based on principles of respect and mutual benefit.

We aim to develop profitable and lasting relationships. We want to build on what we do well and to innovate to meet changing customer needs.

QUALITY TO OUR INVESTORS

We have a long term responsibility to everybody who has a stake in the Group to operate with care, efficiency and at a profit.

Our objective is to earn the profits needed to provide a consistent increase in the value of our shareholders' investment, obtain the highest credit ratings and finance the development of our business.

QUALITY TO OUR PEOPLE

We respect each other's experience and skills and value the contribution each of us makes to the NatWest team. We recognise that pride and enjoyment in the job come from commitment, leadership by example and accomplishment.

Our goal is to work together to reward, train and develop people in ways that acknowledge performance and individual abilities.

QUALITY TO THE COMMUNITY

We recognise that our actions must acknowledge our responsibilities for the well-being and stability of the community.

We aim to support the community through the involvement of our people and the contribution of 1% of our Group profits.

Notes

Situation analysis

Although environmental factors will have affected the mission statement and the identification of objectives, a much more comprehensive analysis is required for the development of overall and market specific strategies. Situation analysis requires a thorough study of the broad trends within the economy and society, as well as a detailed analysis of markets, consumers and competitors. In particular, it may involve some consideration of the nature and extent of *market segmentation*. It also requires an understanding of the organisation's internal environment and its particular strengths and weaknesses. Market research and external databases provide the main source of such information relating to the external environment while an audit of the organisation's marketing activities provides information on the internal environment. The use of a *marketing information system* provides the ideal system for processing and analysing this type of data, while techniques such as SWOT analysis (see below) are of use in organising and presenting the results of such analysis.

Strategy development

The process of strategy development is a key link between corporate level plans and market level plans. In developing strategy, most large organisations will have important *resource allocation* decisions to make. With a variety of products and divisions financial and human resources must be allocated in a manner consistent with the achievement of corporate objectives. Some areas will be designated for expansion, others perhaps for contraction. This process of resource allocation is a key component of corporate strategy and it indicates the direction in which specific markets or products are expected to develop. It therefore provides direction for the development of *market level plans*.

Market specific plans indicate the organisation's intentions with respect to particular markets, or in some cases, particular products. They are closely tied to the corporate plan through the statement of objectives and the resource allocation component in strategy development. Situation analysis must continue at the market level to supply further information on patterns of competition, consumer behaviour and market segmentation. This will provide input to the development of marketing objectives and market specific strategies.

The market specific variables which are typically under the control of the marketing department are, as we have already seen, product, price, promotion and place. The development of the marketing mix is guided by the need to ensure that the product is appropriate to the market in terms of its features, its image, its perceived value and its availability.

The level of marketing expenditure will be determined largely by resource allocation decisions at corporate levels, but nevertheless a statement of the budget required and the way it is to be spent will be an important component of any marketing plan.

Implementation

This requires an identification of the specific tasks which need to be performed, the allocation of those tasks to individuals and the establishment of a system for monitoring their implementation - identifying the nature of any short-term marketing research which needs to be undertaken to determine how appropriate the product is, the nature of customer reactions etc. The implementation procedure may also include some elements of contingency planning. However well thought out the marketing plan may be, the market is always

Notes

changing. Consequently, certain planned activities may turn out to be inappropriate or ineffective; it is important to be aware of these and be in a position to respond - to modify the strategy as new information becomes available.

We will now take a more detailed look at how strategies can be formulated.

2 Strategy formulation

In developing a marketing strategy, the company is seeking to find the most appropriate position in its operating environment. This may involve adjusting the nature of the company's strategy to fit into the existing market environment, although in some cases it may involve attempting to change the environment to fit with the company's strategy. The resulting strategy must enable the company to meet the specific needs of its consumers and to do so more effectively than its competitors.

SWOT analysis

This simple technique provides a method of organising information in identifying possible strategic direction. The basic principle of SWOT analysis is that any statement about an organisation or its environment can be classified as a Strength, Weakness, Opportunity or Threat. An *opportunity* is simply any feature of the external environment which creates conditions which are advantageous to the firm in relation to a particular objective or set of objectives. By contrast, a *threat* is any environmental development which will present problems and may hinder the achievement of organisational objectives. What constitutes an opportunity to some firms will almost invariably constitute a threat to others.

A *strength* can be thought of as a particular skill or distinctive competence which the organisation possesses and which will aid it in achieving its stated objectives. These may relate to experience in specific types of markets or specific skills possessed by employees. A strength may also refer to factors such as a firm's reputation for quality or customer service. A *weakness* is simply any aspect of the company which may hinder the achievement of specific objectives such as limited experience of certain markets/technologies, extent of financial resources available.

This information would typically be presented as a matrix of strengths, weaknesses, opportunities and threats. There are several points to note about presentation and interpretation. First, it should be remembered that effective SWOT analysis does not simply require a categorisation of information, it also requires some evaluation of the relative importance of the various factors under consideration. In addition, it should be noted that these features are only of relevance if they are perceived to exist by the consumers. Listing corporate features that internal personnel regard as strengths/ weaknesses is of little relevance if they are not perceived as such by the organisation's consumers. In the same vein, threats and opportunities are conditions presented by the external environment and they should be independent of the firm.

Notes

SWOT Analysis

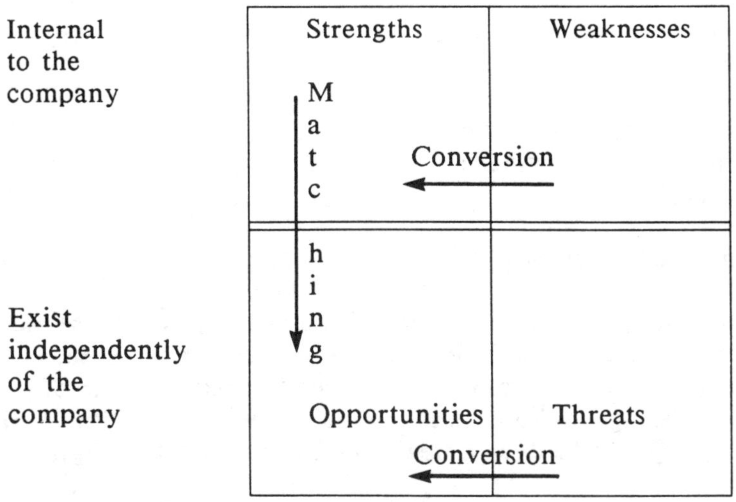

Having constructed a matrix of strengths, weaknesses, opportunities and threats with some evaluation attached to them, it then becomes feasible to make use of that matrix in guiding strategy formulation. The two major strategic options are as follows.

(a) *Matching*
This entails finding, where possible, a match between the strengths of the organisation and the opportunities presented by the market. Strengths which do not match any available opportunity are of limited use while opportunities which do not have any matching strengths are of little immediate value from a strategic perspective.

(b) *Conversion*
This requires the development of strategies which will convert weaknesses into strengths in order to take advantage of some particular opportunity, or converting threats into opportunities which can then be matched by existing strengths.

Although SWOT provides some guidance on developing a match between the organisation's environment and its strategic direction, it is also necessary to consider more specific aspects of strategies such as how best to compete, how to grow within the target markets etc. To aid this process there are a number of analytical techniques which can be used; the role of these techniques is not to offer definitive statements on the final form that a strategy should take, but rather to provide a framework for the organisation and analysis of ideas and information. No one technique can always provide the most appropriate framework and those discussed below can and should be regarded as complementary rather than competitive.

Competitive strategies

Initially, a key factor is that management must identify the way in which it will compete with other organisations and what it perceives as the basis of its competitive advantage. The American strategist Michael Porter argues that the strategy adopted by a firm is essentially a method for creating and sustaining a profitable position in a particular market environment. The profit made by the firm depends first on the nature of its strategy and second on the inherent profitability of the industry in which it operates. An

Notes

organisation in a basically profitable industry can perform badly with an unsuitable strategy while an organisation in an unprofitable industry may perform well with a more suitable strategy.

The profitability of an industry depends on the structure of the industry and specifically on five key features:

(a) bargaining power of suppliers;
(b) bargaining power of consumers;
(c) threat of entry;
(d) competition from substitutes;
(e) competition between firms.

Developing a competitive strategy requires a thorough analysis of these factors and from this analysis the organisation must decide whether to compete across the entire market or only in certain segments *(competitive scope)* and whether to compete through low costs and prices or through offering a differentiated product range *(competitive advantage)*. This decision can lead to four possible strategies as outlined in the diagram below.

Competitive strategies

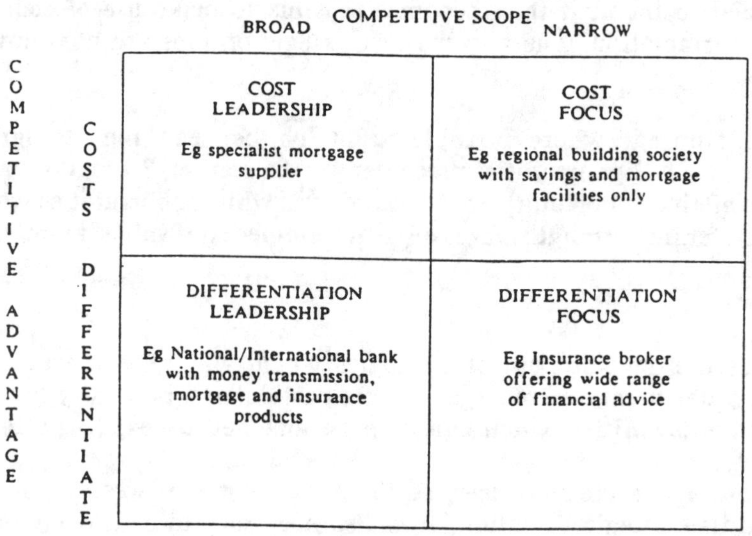

Source: Ennew C T, Watkins T and Wright M (1990) *Marketing Financial Services*, Heinemann

(a) *Cost leadership*
The strategy is to attempt to control the market through being the low cost producer. Typically, the product is undifferentiated, although differentiation cannot be ignored, since the cost savings for the consumer must compensate for the loss of product features, while the discount offered by the firm should not be so high as to offset cost advantages.

(b) *Differentiation*
The strategy is to offer products which can be regarded as unique in areas which are highly valued by the consumer. It is the products' uniqueness and the associated customer loyalty that protects the firm from competition. However, the price premium received must outweigh the costs of supplying the differentiated product for this strategy to be successful; at the same time, the customer must feel that the extra features more than compensate for the price premium.

(c) *Focus/nicheing*
This strategy uses either costs or differentiation but rather than serving the entire market, the organisation looks to operate only in particularly attractive or suitable segments or niches. Differentiation focus is the most common form of focus strategy and implies producing highly customised products for very specific consumer groups.

An important feature of any approach is the need to avoid being 'stuck in the middle' - trying to be all things to all consumers. The firm trying to perform well on costs and on differentiation is likely to lose out to firms concentrating on either one strategy or the other.

Growth strategies

A common framework for the analysis and determination of growth strategies is Ansoff's Product/Market matrix which suggests that the strategy decision rests on whether to use new or existing products in new or existing markets. This produces four possible options.

Exercise 3

Can you remember the four options identified by Ansoff? If not, refer back to Chapter 6.

A market is not a mass, homogeneous group of customers, each wanting an identical product. Market segmentation is based on the recognition that every market consists of potential buyers with different needs, and different buying behaviour. These different customer attitudes may be grouped into segments and a different marketing approach will be taken by an organisation for each market segment.

Market segmentation may therefore be defined as 'the subdividing of a market into distinct and increasingly homogeneous subgroups of customers, where any subgroup can conceivably be selected as a target to be met with a distinct marketing mix'. 'The danger of thinking in terms of single, mass homogeneous markets has been recognised. Market segmentation, as an approach, emerged from the recognition of this danger.' (Tom Cannon *Basic Marketing: Principles and Practice*).

The important elements in this definition of market segmentation are as follows.

(a) Although the total market consists of widely different groups of consumers, each group consists of people (or organisations) with common needs and preferences, who perhaps react to 'market stimuli' in much the same way. For example, the market for umbrellas might be segmented according to the sex of the consumers. Women might seem to prefer umbrellas of different size and weight. The men's market might further be subdivided into age (with some age groups buying few umbrellas and others buying much more) or occupation (eg professional classes, commuters, golfers). Each subdivision of the market (each subsegment) will show increasingly common traits. Golfers, for example, appear to buy large multi-coloured umbrellas.

Notes

(b) Each market segment can become a target market for a firm, and would require a unique marketing mix if the firm is to exploit it successfully. In other words, recognition of segmentation will enable a company to adopt the proper approach to selling to a given group of potential customers, which will be more successful than an undifferentiating market approach to all customers.

A total market may occasionally be homogeneous but this is likely to occur only rarely. At one time, for example, the Coca Cola Company successfully sold one type of drink in one bottle size to a mass market (although it has since recognised market segments in the soft drinks market). Sometimes consumer differences may exist, but it may be difficult to analyse them into segments. A segmentation approach to marketing succeeds when there are identifiable 'clusters' of consumer wants in the market.

3 The marketing plan

The marketing plan in detail consists of several inter-related decisions.

(a) *Sales targets* must be set for each product and each sales division (with sub-targets also set for sales regions, sales areas and individual salesmen). Sales targets may be referred to as sales quotas.

(b) The *total marketing budget* must be set.

(c) Given an overall marketing budget, resources (cash) must be allocated between:

(i) salaries and other staff costs;
(ii) above the line expenditure (advertising);
(iii) below the line expenditure (sales promotion items, price reduction allowances etc).

(d) The overall sales target set by top management will incorporate *sales price decisions;* but within the formulation of the marketing plan there is likely to be some room for manoeuvre and an element of choice in the pricing decision. In other words, top management will decide on a 'rough pricing zone' and a specific price within this zone will be fixed later within the marketing plan.

(e) Expenditure on marketing will also be allocated to different products or services within the organisation's product or service range. Some products might justify additional marketing expenditure; whereas others, nearing the end of their life cycle, may lose a part of their previous allocation.

Market plan decisions - about sales targets, total marketing expenditure budget, the marketing mix and the allocation of expenditure to products - are the main elements of *marketing programming*. They are very much inter-related, and a marketing plan should not be set without proper consideration of alternative choices.

None of this can take place without detailed forecasts of future outcomes, particularly sales forecasts.

Sales forecasting

Sales forecasting is a key element in budgeting and in long-term strategic planning, both essential disciplines in running a business of any size. Without an accurate idea of a business's future sales it becomes difficult to make any meaningful plans for the short term, let alone the longer term.

Exercise 4

How do you think a manager sets about making a sales forecast? To keep it simple, assume we are talking about a smallish company (say £5m turnover) with computerised accounting systems and a limited range of products.

Companies must be aware of factors both inside and outside their control so they can plan effectively for the future. Sales figures do not simply depend on how well the sales force is performing or even how well the product fits customer requirements. In the long run performance will depend on the general economic climate, the level of technology and rate of technological change, to name just a few factors. Forecasting is a tool which, when used correctly, enables management to make informed decisions about the future.

There is a vast array of forecasting techniques that can be applied to sale forecasting but here we will only deal with a small number. Some forecasting methods are very basic, for instance using last month's sales figures to predict this month's. Others are very complex such as some econometric models. The use of computers has aided the development of forecasting techniques.

Managers should be aware of the different types of product that exist to serve a particular market before attempting to forecast demand. For example, a coffee producer must decide which forecast suits his objectives: a forecast for the total coffee market, the decaffeinated coffee market or the instant coffee market. The manager must also make a decision about the geographical area the forecast should cover. Companies can estimate sales at different levels of marketing effort and expenditure.

Assumptions will have to be made about the marketing environment, which are the external uncontrollable factors such as the economic, technological and political environment. Companies can attempt to make forecasts for these factors. Sales forecasting should not simply take into account competitor sales so market shares can be established. Government statistics in industry sectors can be used to evaluate past sales and base forecasts on future sales. Specialist research companies issue market reports (eg Mintel) that can be used to assess present positions.

Companies often arrive at sales forecasts in three stages:

(a) environmental forecast;
(b) industry forecast;
(c) company sales forecast.

There are three basic ways forecasts can be made. The first surveys the opinions of consumers, sales people or experts within the field. For example, an economist's opinion may be sought to give an assessment of future interest rate levels. The second method looks at what people do if the product is made available. For example, a supermarket may make a new flavoured yoghurt available in a small number of stores and analyse the sales

Notes

to test whether to distribute the yoghurt throughout its stores. The third method looks into the past to evaluate what was purchased and when. The method which is used to estimate sales will depend upon product characteristics. The *product life cycle* which was discussed in Chapter 6 can be a useful tool in sales estimates. The shape and length of the PLC will depend upon the frequency of purchase. Companies should estimate first time and replacement/repeat sales.

The diagram below shows some examples of forecasting requirements of a company, illustrating how many different forecasts are needed in addition to sales forecasts.

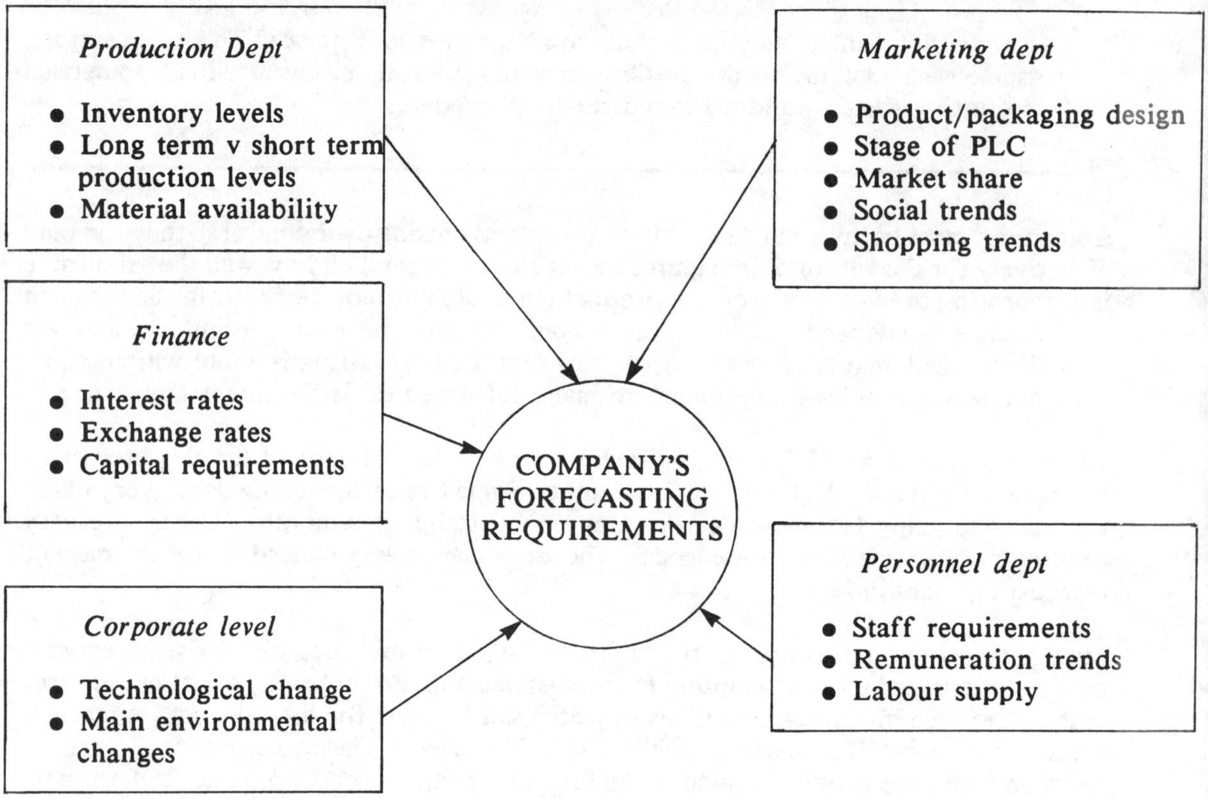

Forecasts should take the following into account.

(a) *Accuracy*. Although this seems obvious the level of desired accuracy can differ. The longer the time span involved generally the less accuracy is possible.

(b) *Time period*. Short-term forecasts can be made to allow for the smooth production and delivery of products. Longer-term forecasts are usually used to help managers make strategic decisions.

(c) *Detail*. The level of detail required by a forecast will differ amongst functional departments. Production will want a very detailed assessment of the future demand for the product to enable them to make necessary adjustments.

Forecasting techniques

There are many different forecasting techniques available at different levels of complexity. Here we shall be evaluating the three broad categories of forecasting methods: time series, causal and qualitative techniques.

Notes

Time series forecasts

Historical (past) data is analysed and trends or patterns are projected into the future. This type of analysis is, of course, more useful in stable industries that have been in existence for some amount of time. This means that data is available and is relatively reliable. In essence it is a short-term technique rather than a long-term one.

Statistical techniques are available that take into account seasonal variations, such as occur, for example, in the sales of fireworks. In the long term, fireworks may be used in more displays and entertainments throughout the year rather than the traditional Guy Fawkes night. Where the seasonal sales pattern is not expected to continue unchanged for the foreseeable future, in the longer term time series analysis may be less useful. Statistical methods that are used to make projections into the future include moving averages or weighted moving averages and exponential smoothing. More complex approaches are Chow's and the Box Jenkins methods.

Causal models

Causal models use equations to explain the relationship between a dependent variable (the one being forecast) and a number of independent variables. Past data can be used in the model and with the use of computers complex models can be evaluated. Causal models are linked to probability so a forecast may be that there is a 95% chance that sales will achieve a certain target. They are useful for longer term forecasting as independent variables can be altered and their impact noted. An example of a causal model can be seen below, where demand for electricity may depend upon a number of independent variables.

Demand for electricity = aPE + bPA + cEA + dPD

Where PE = price of electricity
PA = price of alternative energies
EA = electricity appliances already in operation (so locked into supply)
PD = past demand of electricity

a, b, c and d are weights attached to each independent variable according to their importance.

The mathematical technique of regression analysis is used to analyse causal models. Macroeconomic forecasting uses causal models to predict economic growth rates, for example. Demand for goods can also be forecast using causal models, and these can take into account many diverse aspects such as advertising and demand for complementary or substitute goods.

Qualitative forecasting

Qualitative forecasting techniques do not depend on historical data as the quantitative methods (time series and causal) do. Qualitative techniques are used either where quantitative data is unavailable or for long-term forecasts. They are used mainly in technological forecasting, corporate planning and monitoring changes in consumer tastes and culture. There are two types of qualitative forecasting: *explorative* and *normative*. *Explorative techniques* start with the current state of affairs and attempt to predict changes. *Normative techniques* start with a desired state of affairs in the future and work

Notes

back to consider ways in which to get there. So, for example, qualitative techniques can attempt to forecast new product adoption, technological change and innovations. Examples of individual techniques are Delphi, Morphological analysis and relevance trees.

The marketing budget

Strategic marketing decisions are an integral part of the corporate plan. Top management must set an overall sales strategy and a series of sales objectives; only then should a more detailed marketing plan be prepared.

There are three types of annual budget planning for a marketing budget:

(a) top down planning involves the setting of goals for lower management by higher management;

(b) bottom up planning exists where employees set their own goals and submit them to higher management for approval;

(c) 'goals down - plans up' planning is a mixture of the two styles, whereby top management sets overall goals and employees lower in the organisation hierarchy then set plans for achieving those goals. This type of planning is well suited to the formulation of sales budgets.

Budgeting for sales revenue and selling costs is plagued with uncertainty. The variables are so many and so difficult to estimate, even within a wide tolerance (largely because of competitive action and changing customer habits and tastes) that both setting budgets and budgetary control on the marketing side are different from the more 'mechanical' approach which can be adopted with other budgets.

However, it is plainly unsatisfactory to engage in minute cost control systems in production, and then hope that all other costs (eg research, distribution, sales) will look after themselves. A sales and marketing budget is necessary because:

(a) it is an element of the overall strategic plan of the business (the master budget) which brings together all the activities of the business;

(b) where sales and other non-production costs are a large part of total costs, it is financially prudent to forecast, plan and control them;

(c) the very uncertain nature of factors which influence selling makes the need for good forecasts and plans greater, and it can be argued that if budgets are to be used for control, the more uncertain the budget estimates are, the more budgetary control is necessary.

Matching forecast demand with estimated available capacity

One of the problems in setting budgets is matching the forecast demand from customers with the estimated available capacity. There are three aspects to this problem.

(a) It is difficult to make an accurate forecast of demand.

Notes

(b) It is difficult to predict available capacity accurately too, given uncertainties about:

   (i) efficiency and productivity levels;
   (ii) the availability of staff, or cash;
   (iii) the likely down-time or time lost through industrial disputes;
   (iv) whether overtime or double shift working will be available;
   (v) the likelihood that changes in equipment (eg introduction of new equipment and replacement equipment) will take place in the budget period.

(c) There are often practical difficulties in matching demand with capacity. Demand might be seasonal, and if services or non-standard products are required, it will not be possible to build up inventories in periods of slack demand in anticipation of periods of high demand.

In order to match demand with capacity, management must be flexible, and be prepared to take action:

(a) to suppress demand if it exceeds capacity, by raising prices, for example;

(b) to stimulate demand if there is excess capacity, such as by advertising or price reductions;

(c) to reduce excess capacity by selling off surplus assets;

(d) to supplement production when there is undercapacity by subcontracting work to other organisations, and perhaps to take steps to increase capacity (by acquiring new premises, equipment and labour, or by negotiating for more overtime from existing employees).

The advertising budget decision

This is an important feature of the marketing budget. The theory behind setting an advertising budget is the theory of *diminishing returns*. For every extra £1 of advertising spent, the company should earn an extra £x of profit. Further expenditure on advertising is justified until the marginal return £x diminishes to the point where £x < £1.

Unfortunately, the marginal return from additional advertising cannot be measured easily in practice because:

(a) advertising is only one aspect of the overall marketing mix;

(b) advertising has some long-term effect, which goes beyond the limits of a measurable accounting period;

(c) where the advertising budget is fixed as a percentage of sales, advertising costs tend to follow sales levels and not vice versa.

Research has shown that in the UK, most advertising budgets are fixed by some rule of thumb, non-scientific method, such as:

(a) a percentage of the previous year's sales;
(b) a percentage of the budgeted annual sales;
(c) a percentage of the previous year's profit.

Notes

There is no reason, however, why advertising costs should relate directly to either total turnover or profits. Given that large amounts of expenditure may be incurred on advertising, these arbitrary guesswork systems reveal an alarming lack of proper financial control.

Other methods of setting the advertising budget include the following.

(a) Fixing advertising expenditure in relation to the expenditure incurred by *competitors*. This is unsatisfactory because it presupposes that the competitor's decision must be a good one.

(b) *The task method*. The marketing task for the organisation is set and an advertising budget is prepared which will help to ensure that this objective is achieved. A problem occurs if the objective is achieved only by paying out more on advertising than the extra profits obtained would justify.

(c) *Communication stage models*. These are based on the idea that the link between advertising and sales cannot be measured directly, but can be measured by means of intermediate stages (increase in awareness, comprehension, and then intention to buy). An example of such a model is Colley's *DAGMAR* model (Defining Advertising Goals for Measured Advertising Results). A major problem with the use of such models is that it is not yet clear how the use of indices of customer opinion will enable management to set an effective advertising budget.

Recommended practice for fixing advertising cost budgets would be the use of:

(a) *empirical testing* (for example, in a mail order business or in retail operations, since it may be possible to measure the effect of advertising on sales by direct observation);

(b) *mathematical models* using data about media and consumer characteristics, desired market share, and using records of past results. Regression analysis can be conducted to find out the likely cost of advertising (through several media) to achieve a given target.

Control

Once the plan has been implemented, the task of management is to control the use of resources. Aspects of control include:

(a) a comparison of actual sales against the budget;

(b) a comparison of actual marketing costs against the budgeted expenditure levels and against actual sales;

(c) analysis of the profitability of individual products, and distribution outlets;

(d) strategic control, ie checking whether the company's objectives, products and resources are being directed towards the correct markets.

Allocation of costs

The allocation of *direct selling costs* to products, type of outlet and so on is fairly straightforward, but *indirect costs* such as administration overheads must be allocated on an arbitrary basis (such as to products by value of sales). This aspect of cost allocation should be carefully considered when deciding whether to eliminate an unprofitable expenditure from selling or distribution.

(a) The cost of distributing goods to a distant area may seem to be relatively unprofitable; but if, by not selling the goods in this area, there will be unused production capacity, the products which are produced and sold will have to bear a higher proportion of fixed costs which will still be incurred.

(b) The allocation of fixed selling costs to products may make a product seem unprofitable, but the product may still be making a *contribution* to those fixed costs.

Example: allocation of costs

A business incurs £100,000 fixed costs per annum. It produces and sells two products, A and B.

	A	*B*
	£	£
Per unit of product		
Sales price	10	8
Direct costs of production and sale	5	5
Contribution	5	3
Fixed (indirect) cost allocation	3	3
Profit	2	0

It may seem not to be worthwhile to produce product B at all. However, if sales of product A are insufficient to make £100,000 in contribution (in other words, if sales of product A are less than 20,000 per annum), then the business will make a loss overall. So, for example:

	£
Contribution from product A (assume sales of 18,000 units per annum) @ £5 per unit	90,000
Fixed costs	100,000
Loss	(10,000)

If at least 3,333 units of product B could be sold, then the loss would be wiped out because another £10,000 of contribution would be earned. In accountants' terms, the business would *break even:* cover its costs but make no profit.

Eliminating unprofitable selling and distribution expenditure is sound commercial practice, but the concept of avoidable and unavoidable costs should be used in deciding what is unprofitable. If the removal of one part of selling costs relieves a company of a cost which is higher than the contribution towards profit gained from it, then this part of selling activity can and should be eliminated. The unavoidable fixed costs of production as well as selling and distribution should be taken into account in any such decision.

Notes

Exercise 5

A company trades from head office premises and from two other (geographically separated) sites, North and South.

You are given the following forecasts for 1994.

	North	*South*
	£'000	£'000
Sales revenue	7,500	12,300
Direct costs of production and sales	2,800	4,100
Contribution	4,700	8,200
Fixed costs directly attributable to North	2,900	
Fixed costs directly attributable to South		4,200
Head office costs allocation	2,100	3,100
Forecast (loss)/profit	(300)	900

How much better off or worse off would the company be in 1994 if the decision were taken to close down North at the end of 1993?

Marketing audits

Top management is responsible for ensuring that the company is pursuing optimal policies with regard to its products, markets and distribution channels. Carrying out this responsibility is known as strategic control of marketing, and the means to apply strategic control is the marketing audit.

A marketing audit does not exist in the compulsory formal sense that an external financial audit does. For proper strategic control, however, a marketing audit should:

(a) be conducted regularly;

(b) take a comprehensive look at every product, market, distribution channel, ingredient in the marketing mix and so on and should not be restricted to areas of apparent ineffectiveness such as an unprofitable product, a troublesome distribution channel, or low efficiency on direct selling;

(c) be carried out according to a set of predetermined, specified procedures: it should be systematic.

The 'auditors' should, where possible, be independent, so that their findings and suggestions for remedial action are not coloured by their own particular job interests.

Notes

The audit procedure

A marketing audit should consider the following areas.

(a) *The marketing environment*

   (i) What are the organisation's major markets, and what is the segmentation of these markets; what are the future prospects of each market segment?

   (ii) Who are the customers, what is known about customer needs, intentions and behaviour?

   (iii) Who are the competitors, and what is their standing in the market?

   (iv) Have there been any significant developments in the broader environment (eg economic or political changes, population or social changes).

(b) *Marketing objectives and plans*

   (i) What are the organisation's marketing objectives and how do they relate to overall objectives? Are they reasonable?

   (ii) Are enough (or too many) resources being committed to marketing to enable the objectives to be achieved; is the division of costs between products, areas etc satisfactory?

   (iii) Is the share of expenditure between direct selling, advertising, distribution etc an optimal one?

   (iv) What are the procedures for formulating marketing plans and management control of these plans; are they satisfactory?

   (v) Is the marketing organisation (and its personnel) operating efficiently?

(c) *Marketing activities*

   (i) A review of sales price levels should be made (looking at, for example, supply demand, customer attitudes or the use of temporary price reductions).

   (ii) A review of the state of each individual product (its market 'health') and of the product mix as a whole should be made.

   (iii) A critical analysis of the distribution system should be made, with a view to finding improvements.

   (iv) The size and organisation of the personal sales force should be studied, with a view to deciding whether efficiency should be improved (and how this could be done).

   (v) A review of the effectiveness of advertising and sales promotion activities should be carried out.

Notes

Chapter roundup

(a) The formulation of marketing strategy takes place within the context of strategic planning for the organisation as a whole. SWOT analysis is sometimes used to give focus to the process of formulating strategy.

(b) Possible marketing strategies have been identified by a number of researchers, most notably: Porter; Ennew, Watkins and Wright; and Ansoff.

(c) A marketing plan is devised in order to implement the marketing strategy. It will incorporate forecast sales revenue as well as forecast marketing expenditure.

Quick quiz

1 Distinguish between deliberate strategies and emergent strategies.

2 Distinguish between efficiency and effectiveness.

3 What is meant by bottom-up planning?

4 What is a mission statement?

5 Porter identified five key factors determining the profitability of an industry. List as many of them as you can.

6 What are the four strategic marketing options identified in Ansoff's product/market maxtrix?

7 Describe how, in theory, the determination of a marketing budget depends on a law of diminishing returns. Why does practice differ from theory?

8 What is meant by a marketing audit?

Solutions to exercises

1 The distinction is that efficiency relates to doing a given task well, making the best use of the resources available to do it; whereas effectiveness means working in a way best calculated to achieve a given objective. If your objective is to get from London to Bristol quickly, and your resources are a bicycle, then careful route planning and staged rests will get you there as efficiently as possible; but a more effective approach might be to sell the bicycle and buy a rail ticket.

2 If you re-read the sections in the text on mission statements and statements of objectives, you will see that the NatWest statement has elements of both. As for their aim in publishing it, the aims of most businesses is usually profit maximisation. If profits come from teamwork, there are reassuring messages here for all members of the team: the customers, the providers of capital and the providers of labour.

4 In practice, the starting point is often the historical sales record, product by product. Trend analysis - which in this case may be less sophisticated than it sounds - might give a pointer to how sales are developing. Market information will help - the activities of competitors, the plans of intermediaries such as distributors and so on. Then internal plans must be taken into account: changes in the product mix, changes in the level of advertising, and so on.

In a larger company, as we shall see, it all becomes more complicated.

5 The company would be worse off by £1,800,000. This is the amount of profit forecast to be made by North *before* the allocation of head office costs. Closing down North will not eliminate those head office costs; it will eliminate North's contribution to covering them.

REVIEW FORM

Name:

College:

We would be grateful to receive any comments you may have on this book. You may like to use the headings below as guidelines. Tear out this page and send it to our Freepost address:
BPP Publishing Ltd, FREEPOST, London W12 8BR

Topic coverage

Objectives, exercises, chapter roundups and quizzes

Student-friendliness

Errors (please specify and give a page number)

Other